Culture-Centered Counseling Interventions

DATE DUE

JAN 2 6 1998	
MAR 2 0 1998	
NOV - 6 1998	
DEC 2 1 1998	
NOV - 4 1999	
NOV - 3 1999	
NOV 2 3 2001	

BRODART   Cat. No. 23-221

In loving memory of my wife, Anne Bennett Pedersen.
August 16, 1940 – June 10, 1996

Anne B. Pedersen, December 6, 1987
(for my mother)

I was thinking.
If my mind is my thoughts,
when I am not thinking,
which is quite a bit,
where is my mind?
Is it in chaos?

Must I "gather the little pebbles of my thoughts"
to think or think well?
What guides my thoughts?

During thought gaps,
is thinking being strengthened?
Or being weakened
by no thought?

I think that in thought gaps
my thought is nestling with your thought
and all your thoughts that have gone before.

A spirit stirs our thinking
apart from one another.
My mind is my memory.
My thoughts are my dreams

Come dream with me.

Culture-Centered Counseling Interventions
Striving for Accuracy

Paul B. Pedersen

SAGE Publications
International Educational and Professional Publisher
Thousand Oaks   London   New Delhi

For information:

SAGE Publications, Inc.
2455 Teller Road
Thousand Oaks, California 91320
E-mail: order@sagepub.com

SAGE Publications Ltd.
6 Bonhill Street
London EC2A 4PU
United Kingdom

SAGE Publications India Pvt. Ltd.
M-32 Market
Greater Kailash I
New Delhi 110 048 India

Printed in the United States of America

Library of Congress Cataloging-in-Publication Data

Pedersen, Paul B., 1936-
    Culture-centered counseling interventions : striving for accuracy
/ author, Paul B. Pedersen.
        p.   cm.
    "This book is an expansion of a presentation in the Master lecture
series at the American Psychological Association meetings in Los
Angeles, California, in 1994."
    Includes bibliographical references and index.
    ISBN 0-7619-0249-X (cloth). — ISBN 0-7619-0250-3 (pbk.)
    1. Cross-cultural counseling. 2. Psychotherapy. I. Title.
BF637.C6P36 1997
158'.3'08—dc20   96-35663

This book is printed on acid-free paper.

97 98 99 00 01 02 03 10 9 8 7 6 5 4 3 2 1

Acquiring Editor:	Jim Nageotte
Editorial Assistant:	Kathleen Derby
Production Editor:	Sherrise Purdum
Production Assistant:	Denise Santoyo
Copy Editor:	Joyce Kuhn
Typesetter/Designer:	Danielle Dillahunt
Indexer:	Teri Greenberg
Cover Designer:	Lesa Valdez

Contents

Acknowledgment

This book is an expansion of a presentation in the Master Lecture Series at the 1994 American Psychological Association meeting held in Los Angeles, California. The opportunity to make that presentation stimulated a number of new ideas about the cultural context of counseling, many of which are included in this book.

Introduction

We frequently hear about how multiculturalism or cultural differences present problems to counselors and counseling—usually in the form of quotas or measures of imposed equity. Culture has frequently been seen as a barrier to counseling rather than as a tool for helping counselors be more accurate and as a means of facilitating good counseling. As long as our understanding of cultures is limited to labels for narrowly defined perspectives, the generic relevance of multicultural counseling is not likely to be appreciated. The culture-centered perspective complements rather than competes with traditional theories of behavioral, psychodynamic, or humanistic counseling because counseling from whatever theoretical perspective is interpreted from the counselor's own cultural viewpoint and is then applied to the client's cultural context.

Many counselors believe that multiculturalism is a trivial topic and that those writing about culture should focus on issues more "central" to counseling. When challenged, I then ask them whether they believe accurate assessment, meaningful understanding, and appropriate intervention are important to them. Almost without exception they agree that accuracy is a central issue, to which I respond that it seems we are in agreement. The reason why I hope to make culture a "central" issue in the counseling process is to increase accurate assessments, meaningful understandings, and appropriate interventions by counselors working with culturally different clients.

Culture is the context in which all behaviors are learned. Imagine yourself surrounded by thousands of people whom you have met, learned from, and come to appreciate in your lifetime. Each of these "culture teachers" has taught you something that you have incorporated into your identity. You do not have just one cultural identity; rather, thousands of different "potential" identities are defined by ethnographic, demographic, status, and affiliation categories, to mention a few, as they take turns whispering advice into your ear.

As you read this book, keep in mind the image of yourself surrounded by a thousand "culture teachers." The next time your client enters your office and closes the door, do not assume there are only two of you in that room. There are thousands of people waiting to hear what you will say. If you hope to be accurate in your assessment, meaningful in your understanding, and appropriate in your intervention, you must become mindful of the culture teachers surrounding your client who define the context in which counseling is provided.

The search for accuracy is the search for the client's identity within a cultural context. That context is complicated, drawing aspects from many past and present experiences the client has had. Simple solutions have betrayed us into cultural encapsulation. That context is dynamic, with the salient identity changing from time to time and place to place. Each of us is constantly changing in response to the many changes going on around us.

Spengler, Strohmer, Dixon, and Shivy (1995) define accuracy as multidimensional: "We recognize that multiple worldviews of reality lead to multiple sources of evidence and ways of explaining and predicting human behavior" (p. 508). Accuracy means observing how one observes, finding patterns in complex data, the ability to self-correct faulty inference, and being guided by the context itself. Unfortunately, clinical judgment has tended to make fundamental attribution errors—blaming the individual more and the context less for pathology. Sleek (1996) describes how "practitioners tend to judge lower-class patients as more seriously disturbed than higher-class clients. They detect schizophrenia in black people more than in whites. And they often judge women patients as more disturbed than male patients presenting identical problems" (p. 30). Conversely, practitioners who have more cognitive complexity, integrating greater amounts and types of information, make more accurate judgments by taking a more multidimensional view of each client in context (Spengler & Strohmer, 1994).

EXERCISE

THE CULTURAL CONTEXT

Objective: To provide a framework for you to see the basic outline of a client's cultural context

Instructions: In your first session, fill in the cells of the following grid. On one dimension, you will see the personal roles of the counselor, the client, and significant others. On the other dimension, you will see the social categories of nationality, ethnicity, place of residence, age, gender, status (social, educational, and economic), lifestyle, job or professional role, formal affiliations (family, career, religion), and informal affiliations, such as an "idea" or "value" in which you believe.

		A. *Counselor*	*B.* *Client*	*C.* *Significant Others*
1.	Nationality			
2.	Ethnicity			
3.	Gender			
4.	Place of Residence			
5.	Status			
6.	Age			
7.	Lifestyle			
8.	Job Role			
9.	Affiliations			
10.	Informal Affiliations			

Note the cells where there is a cultural or value orientation difference in the counseling relationship.

Debriefing: By matching 10 social systems on the left-hand column with the role of the counselor, client, and significant others it will be apparent that many cultures are interacting in the counseling interview. You may want to discuss the following questions to identify the implications of the complicated cultural context:

- What are the similarities among the counselor, client, and others?
- What are the differences between the counselor, client, and others?
- Which culture is most likely to be salient for the counselor, client, and others?
- When the culture of the client is different from the culture of the counselor, what are the likely consequences for counseling?
- Who has more power: the client, counselor, or significant others?
- To what extent are these cultural affiliations explicit in the counseling interview, and to what extent are they unstated/implicit?
- How can a counselor best prepare for a culture-centered interview with the client?
- How can a counselor maintain a balance in the cultural context defined by the counselor, client, and significant others?

PART

The Culture-Centered Context

In this section, culture is defined as the context in which all learning occurs (Chapter 1). Culture controls behavior through assumptions learned in a cultural context (Chapter 2). Managing the cultural context requires a high level of self-awareness and awareness of the client's cultural context (Chapter 3).

Defining Culture in Context

- **Primary Objective** Describe multiculturalism as a generic theoretical perspective of counseling in any and all contexts or situations

- **Secondary Objectives** (1) Present the argument for a broad rather than narrow definition of culture and (2) Describe a balanced perspective of counseling sensitive to a client's cultural context

---

Psychology in the near future promises to become a culture-inclusive science, that is, a science that routinely takes cultural variables into account. In contrast, today's mainstream psychology routinely neglects and underestimates the power of cultural variables. Soon, there will appear in connection with many psychological theories and methods a series of questions:

> Under what circumstances and in which culturally circumscribed situations does a given psychological theory or methodology provide valid explanations for the origins and maintenance of behavior? What are the cultural boundary conditions potentially limiting the generalizability of psychologi-

cal theories and methodologies? Which psychological phenomena are culturally robust in character, and which phenomena appear only under specified cultural conditions? (Gielen, 1994, p. 38)

This multileveled theory of cultural relationships accommodates both a cultural relativist and a universalistic perspective. The universalistic explanation of human behavior more frequently associated with the discipline of psychology is based on the nomothetic truth in the aggregate and lends itself to quantitative data analysis but is not always helpful in a particular cultural context or situation. The relativist perspective more frequently associated with the field of anthropology describes the ideographic truth of the particular instance but does not lend itself to generalizations across instances.

A multicultural counseling theory (Sue, Ivey, & Pedersen, 1996) seeks to provide a conceptual framework that recognizes the complex diversity of a plural society while at the same time suggesting bridges of shared concern that bind culturally different persons to one another. The ultimate outcome of a multicultural theory, as Segall, Dasan, Berry, and Poortinga (1990) suggest, is a contextual understanding:

There may well come a time when we will no longer speak of cross cultural psychology as such. The basic premise of this field—that to understand human behavior, we must study it in its sociocultural context—may become so widely accepted that all psychology will be inherently cultural. (p. 352)

During the past 20 years, multiculturalism has become recognized as a powerful force not just for understanding "specific" groups but for understanding ourselves and those with whom we work.

CULTURE NOTE

Select a meeting you attended in the past week or two. Ask yourself why you attended the meeting and what you "expected" to occur as a result of attending it—perhaps to learn something, to have fun, or to fulfill a professional obligation. Then ask yourself what "value" was important to that expectation, such as learning, pleasure, or duty. Finally, ask yourself where you learned that value or those values. You learned them from many "culture teachers" in your cultural context.

Multiculturalism has more often been regarded as a method than as a theory. To the extent that multiculturalism refers exclusively to narrowly defined culture-specific categories such as nationality, race, or ethnicity, then it might indeed best be considered a method of analysis. The multicultural method is usually applied to understanding the encounter of specific cultural groups with one another while emphasizing the culture-specific characteristics of each group.

To the extent that multiculturalism refers to broadly defined social system variables in addition to ethnographic categories such as status and formal or informal affiliation, then it might better be considered a theory. In that case, the underlying principle of multicultural theory would be to emphasize *both* the culture-specific characteristics that differentiate *and* the culture-general characteristics that unite. The accommodation of both within-group and between-group differences is required for a comprehensive understanding of complicated cultural contexts.

THE BROAD DEFINITION
OF CULTURE

By defining culture broadly—to include demographic (age, gender, place of residence, etc.), status (social, educational, economic, etc.), and affiliation (formal and informal) variables along with ethnographic variables (nationality, ethnicity, language, religion, etc.)—the construct "multicultural" becomes generic to all counseling relationships. The narrow definition of culture has limited multiculturalism to what might more appropriately be called "multiethnic" or "multinational" relationships between groups with a shared sociocultural heritage that includes religion, history, and ancestry. Ethnicity and nationality are *important* to individual and familial identity as one aspect of culture. But the culture context—broadly defined—goes beyond national and/or ethnic boundaries. Persons from the same ethnic or nation group may still experience cultural differences. Not all Blacks have the same experience, nor do all Asians, American Indians, or Hispanics, nor all women, nor all old people, nor all those handicapped. No *particular* group is rigidly unified in its perspective. Therefore, the broad definition of culture is particularly important in preparing counselors to deal with the *complex* differences among clients from every cultural group.

CULTURE NOTE

A young man in a wheelchair presents for counseling. Having just been trained in multicultural counseling I want to be sensitive to the young man's culture. After an hour of counseling, he leaves, frustrated because his problems regarding age, gender, socioeconomic status, and affiliation had been ignored. In my myopic zeal, I had focused my counseling on his disability, which he did not consider culturally defining/salient for himself.

Just as differentiation and integration are complementary processes, so are the emic (culture-specific) and etic (culture-general) perspectives necessarily interrelated. The terms *emic* and *etic* were borrowed from "phonemic" and "phonetic" analysis in linguistics describing the rules of language used to imply a separation of general from specific aspects. Even Pike (1966) in his original conceptualization of this dichotomy suggested that the two elements be treated not as a rigid dichotomy but as a way of presenting the same data from two complementary viewpoints. All people experience loneliness (etic), but each specific group has learned to deal with loneliness in a particular and unique way (emic). Although research on the usefulness of emic and etic categories has been extensive, the notion of a "culture-free" (universal) etic has been just as elusive as the notion of a "culture-pure" (totally isolated) emic. Combining the specific and general viewpoints provides a culture-centered perspective. The more inclusive perspective is an essential starting point for mental health professionals seeking to be more accurate and to avoid cultural encapsulation by their own culture-specific assumptions (Sartorius, Pedersen, & Marsella, 1984).

There is also an argument against the broad definition of culture. Triandis, Bontempo, Leung, and Hui (1990) distinguish between cultural, demographic, and personal constructs. Cultural constructs are those shared by persons speaking a particular dialect, living in the same geographical location during the same time, and sharing norms, roles, values, associations, and ways of categorizing experience described as a "subjective culture" (Triandis, 1972). This view contends that demographic constructs deal with these same topics but are shared only by *particular* demographic groups within a culture, such as men and women or old and young. Personal-level constructs then belong to categories of individual differences and cannot be meaningfully interpreted with reference to demographic or cultural membership.

The problem with this narrow perspective is that it tends to be arbitrary in defining the point at which shared constructs constitute cultural similarity. As Triandis et al. (1990) point out,

> We cannot expect that 100% of a sample agrees with a position. We decided arbitrarily, that if 85% of a sample shares the construct, it is cultural. Similarly, if 85% of the men share it, we consider it gender linked. If less than 85% share the construct we might examine if it is shared by the majority of a sample but if less than 50% of a sample share the construct, we definitely do not consider it shared. (p. 304)

Lee (1991) likewise makes a persuasive argument against the broad definition of culture. He argues that the term *multicultural* is in imminent danger of becoming so inclusive as to be almost meaningless. The broad definition includes ever expanding constituent groups who perceive themselves as being disenfranchised in some fashion. This has resulted in diffusing the coherent and focused conceptual framework of multiculturalism in training, teaching, and research. Locke (1990) responds that the broad view of multiculturalism at best serves as a prologue for a narrow or "focused" perspective: "As the term has been increasingly stretched to include virtually any group of people who consider themselves 'different' the intent of multicultural counseling theory and practice has become unclear. . . . Such a system views cultural differences as no more than individual differences" (p. 24).

The distinction between individual differences and cultural differences is real and important. We learn our individual identity in a cultural context. The cultural identities to which we belong are no more or less important than our individual identity. Although culture has traditionally been defined as a multigenerational geographic phenomenon, the broad definition of culture suggests that cultural identities and culturally significant shared beliefs may develop in a contemporary time frame independent of geography and still be distinguished from individual differences.

CULTURE NOTE

Your skin color at birth is an individual difference. What that skin color has come to *mean* is culturally learned.

Miles (1989) points out that it is a mistake to limit the parameters of multiculturalism by reference to skin color. The extensive evidence of racism and related exclusionary practices requires that we include other categories such as sexism, ageism, and nationalism. Miles rejects Katz's (1978) definition of racism as a White person's problem as simplistic in its disregard for the differential access to different kinds of power across all populations. At the same time he supports Katz's contention that Whites have been socialized into a perspective that presumes white superiority. Every attempt to simplify culture and cultural differences according to skin color alone has resulted in simplistic, stereotyped, or polarized alternatives that disregard the necessary complexity of multiculturalism. The cultural context is complex and dynamic.

APPLICATIONS OF THE BROAD
DEFINITION OF CULTURE

Poortinga (1990) defines culture as "shared constraints that limit the behavior repertoire available to members of a certain sociocultural group in a way different from individuals belonging to some other group" (p. 6). Segall et al. (1990) affirm that ecological forces are the prime movers and shapers of cultural forms that in turn shape behaviors: "Given these characteristics of culture, it becomes possible to define it simply as the totality of whatever all persons learn from all other persons" (p. 26). Culture is part of the environment, and all behavior is shaped by culture, so that it is rare (perhaps even impossible) for any human being ever to behave without responding to some aspect of culture.

Another contemporary application of the broad definition of culture is "cultural psychology," which presumes that every sociocultural environment depends on the way human beings give each cultural context meaning and are in turn changed in response to that sociocultural environment. Shweder (1990) defines cultural psychology as "the study of the ways subject and object, self and other, psyche and culture, person and context, figure and ground, practitioner and practice live together, require each other, and dynamically, dialectically and jointly make each other up" (p. 1).

CULTURE NOTE

Two persons can disagree without one being right and the other wrong—when their arguments are based on culturally different assumptions.

It becomes possible for a counselor to identify "common ground" between two apparently culturally different people whose positive expectations and ultimate goals are the same even though their behaviors may be very different. Even the same individuals may change their cultural referent group during the course of the interview—from emphasizing gender, to age, to socioeconomic status, to nationality or ethnicity, to one or another affiliation. Unless the counselor is skilled enough to understand that each of these changing *salient* cultures requires a different understanding and interpretation of that person's behavior, the counselor is not likely to be accurate in assessing the person's changing behavior. The same culturally learned behavior may have very different meanings across people and even for the same person across times and situations (Pedersen, 1994).

Behavior is not meaningful data until and unless the behavior is understood in the context of the person's culturally learned expectations. If you believed your life was in danger right now as you read this, you might behave in ways that others around you would misinterpret as paranoid. Similar behaviors may have different meanings, and different behaviors may have the same meaning. It is important to interpret behaviors accurately in terms of the expectation. If two people share the same positive expectation—for success, accuracy, fairness, or safety—they do not have to display the same behaviors to find common ground. In this paradigm, "cross-cultural" is defined as an interaction where two persons have the *same* positive expectation but *different* behaviors.

CULTURE NOTE

You are interviewing two people for the same job. One person agrees with everything you say, but you do not trust him. The other person argues with everything you say, but you do trust him. Will you make your selection based on behavior (agree vs. argue) or on expectation (trust vs. distrust)?

Smiling is an ambiguous behavior. For example, it may imply trust and friendliness, or it may not. The smile may be interpreted accurately, or it may not be. Outside its culturally learned context the smile has no fixed meaning. Two persons may both expect trust and friendliness even though one is smiling and the other is not. If these similar positive expectations such as trust or respect are undiscovered or disregarded, then differences of behavior will be *presumed* to indicate negative expectation, resulting in conflict. If, however, the two culturally different persons understand how they perhaps really have the same positive expectations even though their behaviors may be very different, they may agree to disagree or recognize that they are both approaching the same goal from different directions in complementary ways.

THE CULTURALLY
ENCAPSULATED COUNSELOR

Just as there is a danger in defining culture too narrowly and too broadly, there is also a danger in polarizing the particularistic and universalistic perspectives of multiculturalism as the only two alternatives from which one must choose. Multicultural counseling need not proceed from the assumption of radical cultural relativism that each culture is totally unique and different and that each culture defines truth and justice independently. Just as cultural relativism understands each culture in its own terms, customs, symbols, norms, and beliefs, cultural absolutism assumes universal identity of psychological functions and the ways those functions relate to behavior.

The universalist position assumes that the same psychological processes are operating in all humans independent of their cultural context. Patterson (1978, 1986) takes a universalist position in criticizing counselors for modifying counseling to fit different cultures. Although counseling needs to be modified for clients of different ages, genders, experiences, and social backgrounds to fit the different expectations of clients, Patterson disputes the need for different sets of skills, emphases, and insights for use in each culture. While this position disregards the need for culturally intentional counseling, it constructively raises questions about the limits of cultural accommodation and the appropriate role of universal versus the particular components of counseling (Draguns, 1989).

The rhetoric in support of cultural differences and multicultural counseling has been in professional documents of accreditation, certification, and licensure for many years. From the narrow definition of culture, these statements have been perceived as political—favoring the special interests of one group or another. From the broad definition of culture, however, multiculturalism goes beyond the self-interests of any particular group to redefine the cultural context of identity for both the counselor and the client, regardless of their skin color, age, gender, socioeconomic status, or affiliations.

There is a bottom-up, consumer-driven movement in counseling favoring the multiplicity of special interest groups. The revolution of culturally different consumers has been most pronounced in educational settings. The schools were battlegrounds for civil rights, textbook censorship, and social change, and now the pressure is on to deal with cultural diversity among the students and the community: "This movement for diversity has been dubbed multiculturalism and has become a major force in American education, from city to suburban elementary schools, from high schools to universities" (Cohen, 1990, p. 75).

The multicultural revolution has also led to a phenomenon of "politically correct," or PC, behavior. Philosophically, PC means the subordination of the right to free speech to the right guaranteeing equal protection under the law. The PC position contends that an absolutist position on the First Amendment (you may slur anyone you choose) imposes a hostile environment and therefore a perceived threat on minorities and other oppressed groups or individuals perceived as different. Promotion of diversity is one of the central tenets of PC. The content of PC is in some ways not controversial. For example, who would defend racism? What *is* distressing is that in the schools tolerance is having to be imposed rather than taught, thus substituting one repressive orthodoxy with another:

> Yes, of course conflict is inevitable, as the university makes the transition—somewhat ahead of the rest of society—toward its multiethnic future. There are in fact some who recognize the tyranny of PC but see it only as a transitional phase, which will no longer be necessary once the virtues of tolerance are internalized. (Adler et al., 1990, p. 54)

There is a still greater danger in the "PC perspective," and that is the simplistic polarization of alternatives. Both the advocates and the opponents of PC are in danger of oversimplifying multiculturalism by presuming a single "correct" orthodoxy.

CULTURE NOTE

Multicultural training that limits itself to a list of politically correct rules across situations is in danger of training "clever racists" who learn how to not get caught by following the "rules" while at the same time maintaining their underlying racism.

Recognizing that the particularist and the universalist views of culture are in conflict with each other, Ravitch (1990) describes two polarized futures:

> Two versions presently compete for dominance in the teaching of American culture. One approach reflects cultural pluralism and accepts diversity as a fact: the other represents particularism and demands loyalty to a particular group. The two coexist uncomfortably, because they are not different by degree. In fact, they are opposite in spirit and in purpose. (p. A44)

There is a potential for error by both the particularist and the universalist perspectives. Whereas the particularist perspective may indeed define culture too narrowly and result in the ethnocentric domination by culturally defined special interest groups, the universalistic perspective may result in the continued domination by the more powerful majority culture at the expense of minority cultures. Polarized thinking suggests the possibility of easy answers or obvious wrongdoing while ignoring the complexity of changes required by multiculturalism. Although the "right" way to accommodate multiculturalism remains unclear and the "wrong" ways have not worked, we will never be able to return to an "earlier age," as the more conservative perspective of D'Souza (1991) seems to advocate. Polarized thinking has resulted in racism. We need a third alternative.

There is already an extensive literature in counseling in support of a complex and dynamic perspective. Disregard for cultural complexity has resulted in bias (Lopez, 1989), racism (Ridley, 1989), and social injustice (Casas, 1984). Counseling as a process has nonetheless continued to ignore complexity because of the difficulties it presents to research, teaching, and administrative orderliness. Broadening the categories provides an alternative to oversimplification and to the disregard of culture in counseling.

Wrightsman (1992) describes how the perspectives of behaviorism, psychoanalysis, and humanism are supplemented by a "fourth alternative" based on George Kelly's personal construct theory. Wrightsman describes this new movement as more collectivistic, resembling non-Western indigenous psychologies:

> We are living in a time when the conventional wisdom about human nature and the nature of society is under attack. Technology has run amok; many now question our ability to bring technology under manageable control. Bureaucracy—a social structure originally established to provide for person growth—now stifles human development and generates a philosophy that human nature is lazy, irresponsible and extrinsically motivated. The communal movement has challenged a pessimistic drift in our society. Through study of the movement's assumptions, aims, procedures and outcomes, we may gain an understanding of the future of philosophies or human nature. (p. 293)

Stoltenberg and Delworth (1987) talk about broadening the complex categories of culture in the developmental counseling literature, and Abramson (1988) applies a broad perspective to social cognition. Counselors develop through stages toward progressively more complex and adaptive facility in making decisions and processing information.

Ivey (1988) describes intentionality as an essential core concept of complexity for counseling. Intentional interviewing does not judge a single response as correct for all situations. Intentionality involves increasing the counselor's response repertoire to match a culturally appropriate response in each culturally different context. If, indeed, our perceptions of the world around us are culturally learned and culturally mediated, if persons from different cultural backgrounds perceive the world around them differently, and if counseling requires an accurate and profound understanding of the world around each client, then it would seem extremely important for all counselors to take a broad multicultural perspective.

THE CONSEQUENCES OF A
BROAD PERSPECTIVE OF CULTURE

The broad definition seeks to avoid exclusionary bias. Multiculturalism and the importance of cultural awareness has been widely recognized for a long time, especially among authors from a minority background such as W. E. B. Du Bois (1908/1990). There is a history of moral exclusion, when individuals or groups are perceived as outside the rules that define fairness and as nonentities, expendable, or undeserving (Opotow, 1990). This exclusionary perspective has been described as a form of encapsulation (Wrenn, 1962, 1985). It assumes five basic identifying features. First, we define reality according to one set of cultural assumptions and stereotypes that become more important than the real world. Second, we become insensitive to cultural variations among individuals and assume that our view is the only real or legitimate one. Third, each of us has unreasoned assumptions that we accept without proof and protect without regard to rationality. Fourth, a technique-oriented job definition further contributes toward and preserves the encapsulation. Fifth, when there is no evaluation of other viewpoints, then there is no responsibility to accommodate or interpret the behavior of others except from the viewpoint of a self-reference.

CULTURE NOTE

Just as genetic diversity is essential for a healthy biological ecosystem, cultural diversity contributes to a more accurate and meaningful psychological perspective.

This tendency to depend on one authority, one theory, and one truth has been demonstrated to be extremely dangerous in the sociopolitical setting. It is no less dangerous in a counseling context. The encapsulated counselor is trapped in one way of thinking that resists adaptation and rejects alternatives. By contrast, a broader definition leads counselors toward a more comprehensive understanding of alternatives and a more complete perspective of one's own beliefs. All aspects of a client's cultural context are included in the broad perspective.

Although counseling has traditionally emphasized the importance of freedom, rational thought, tolerance, equality, and justice, it has also been used as an oppressive instrument by those in power to maintain the status quo (Sue & Sue, 1990). Whenever counselors restrict rather than enhance the well-being and development of culturally different persons, they are voicing overt or covert forms of prejudice and discrimination. The culturally different client approaches counseling with a majority counselor cautiously, asking, "What makes you, a counselor/therapist, any different from all the others out there who have oppressed and discriminated against me?" (Sue & Sue, 1990, p. 6).

The politics of minority versus majority culture is part of the cultural context of multicultural counseling. Ponterotto and Casas (1991) document the perception that "the majority of traditionally trained counselors operate from a culturally biased and encapsulated framework which results in the provision of culturally conflicting and even oppressive counseling treatments" (pp. 7-8). Counselor training programs are often presumed to be proponents of the status quo, stimulating considerable criticism regarding counseling research about racial/ethnic minority groups. Weaknesses in research on the cultural context of counseling have also contributed to a cultural bias.

There are some functional benefits in defining each complicated cultural context broadly rather than narrowly. First, it allows and forces counselors to be more accurate in matching a client's culturally learned expectation with the client's behavior. Second, it helps counselors become more aware of how their own culturally learned perspective predisposes them toward a particular decision outcome. Third, it helps the counselor become more aware of the complexity in cultural identity patterns that may or may not include the obvious indicators of ethnicity and nationality. Fourth, it encourages counselors to track the ever changing salience of a client's different, interchangeable cultural identities within a counseling interview.

It is no longer possible for counselors to ignore their own cultural context or the cultural contexts of their clients. However, until the multicultural perspective is recognized as making the counselor's job easier instead of harder and for increasing rather than decreasing the quality of a counselor's life, little real change is likely to happen.

DEFINING BALANCE IN THE CLIENT'S CULTURAL CONTEXT

The construct of balance was defined by Heider (1958), Newcomb (1953), and McGuire (1966) in consistency theory as the search for an enduring consistency in an otherwise volatile situation. Cognitive balance was achieved by changing, ignoring, differentiating, or transcending inconsistencies to avoid dissonance (Triandis, 1977). As defined in this chapter, however, balance can also be described as a tolerance for inconsistency and dissonance (Pedersen, 1990). Rather than resolve differences, it thrives on differences in which *both* one side *and* the other side of a perspective make valuable contributions to our understanding. Garrett and Meyers (1996) describe a "rule of opposites" based on the Native American Indian "circle of life" worldview: "For many Native American clients the understanding and reconciliation of discordant opposites is an essential therapeutic goal in achieving a unity of greater harmony and balance among the four directions—mind, body, spirit and natural environment" (p. 102).

CULTURE NOTE

Too often, counselors define success in "one-directional" terms of simply and merely reducing pain and increasing pleasure. The task of culture-centered counseling may be to find meaning in the necessary and complementary balance of both pleasures and pain rather than merely to resolve conflict in favor of increased pleasure.

Social change in this context is perceived as a continuous and not an episodic process. Balance as a construct seeks to reflect the metaphors of organismic systems in holistic health. The dying patient may not seek pleasure as much as meaning from counseling. The alcoholic would find much more pleasure from drinking than from counseling. Problems, pain, and otherwise negative aspects of our experience may also provide necessary resources for the dark side of healthy functioning in an ecological analysis of the psychological process (Berry, 1980).

Balance as a construct for multicultural counseling involves the identification of different or even conflicting culturally learned perspectives without necessarily resolving the differences. Healthy functioning in a multicultural or pluralistic context may require a person to maintain multiple conflicting and culturally learned roles without the opportunity to resolve the resulting dissonance. The following 10 examples of observable and potentially measurable counseling abilities, while rooted in traditional theories of counseling, demonstrate skills that are valuable for culture-centered counseling.

1. *The ability to see positive implications in an otherwise negative experience from the client's cultural viewpoint*

Ivey (1988) emphasizes the importance of a "positive asset search" in counseling. It would be simplistic of a provider to assume that the negative experiences of culturally different clients are not also related to positive outcomes and consequences. Adjusting to an unfamiliar culture may be painful but necessary for the sojourner.

2. *The ability to anticipate potential negative implications from an otherwise positive experience*

Leaving home may be painful even if it is necessary for a client's long-term success. Each solution that a counselor brings to a culturally different client will almost certainly also have potential negative effects that must also be considered from the client's viewpoint.

3. *The ability to articulate statements of meaning helps to interpret or integrate positive and negative events in a constructive way*

Tolerance for ambiguity is emerging as an important characteristic of multiculturally skilled persons (Kealey, 1988; Ruben & Kealey, 1979). The meaning of each event is usually ambiguous and not simple. Both positive and negative events must be understood in the client's cultural context. Ivey's (1988) microskill "reflection of meaning" directs counselors to explore basic and often conflicting concepts in their multiple cultural identities.

4. *The ability to resist the temptation of simple solutions to complex problems and acknowledge the intricacies and constraints of a client's cultural context*

Ivey (1988) describes the "premature solution" as the most frequent mistake made by beginning counselors. This mistake occurs even more frequently in a multicultural setting. In many cultures, the problem is anthropomorphized as a demon possessing the client (Pedersen, 1988).

5. *Sensitivity to how collective forces influence an individual's behavior*

Ivey (1988) frequently points out how traditional counseling is biased toward an individualistic perspective. In a more collectivist culture, the welfare of the unit or collective forces may be more important than the individual. Good multicultural counseling may require balancing the welfare of the individual client against the welfare of those collective forces in a way that satisfies both the individual and the collective.

6. *Sensitivity to the changing power of the person being interviewed over time*

Strong (1978) describes social influence theory's contribution to understanding the importance of power in counseling. Power is culturally defined, and good multicultural counseling is sensitive to whether treatment/therapy is enhancing or diminishing a client's power.

7. *Sensitivity to the changing power of the person being interviewed across different topics*

For counselors to differentiate among clients and among contexts for a given client, they must note changes in social influence and power across topics as well as across time. A good multicultural counselor is able to identify areas of both expertise and deficiency in a culturally different client. The importance of self-esteem and the destructive effects of perceived helplessness apply especially to a client attempting to cope in a culturally unfamiliar context (Pedersen, Fukuyama, & Heath, 1989).

8. *Sensitivity to the changing power of the person being interviewed in culturally different social roles*

Clients who function very well in some roles may not function adequately in others. Lopez (1989) points out how biased counselors frequently disregard differences in clients' role-functioning ability across cultures.

9. *The ability to adjust the amount of culturally defined influence by the interviewer*

To help the client develop a balanced perspective, the counselor needs to provide enough but not too much control, influence, or power as defined by the cultural context. If the counselor exerts too much control on a strong client, the client may rebel and reject the counselor as more troublesome than the problem. If the counselor exerts too little control on a weak client, the client may abandon the counselor as inadequate and unable to provide the necessary protection (Pedersen, 1981, 1984, 1986b).

10. *The ability to maintain harmony within the interview*

Lambert (1981) points out that good rapport consistently emerges in the research as a necessary but not sufficient condition of good counseling across all settings. Ivey (1988) also comments on the importance of measuring counseling techniques by their contribution to a harmonious rapport between client and counselor, even though they may be from different cultural backgrounds.

These 10 examples of observable counselor abilities describe some of the essential aspects of how culture-centered counseling depends on a balanced perspective where the process and relationship are more important than the solution of a problem. These abilities are in the traditional counseling research literature and are not, by themselves, controversial. Because these examples are familiar, they may provide a bridge for counselors to develop culture-centered counseling skills with culturally different clients.

Wittkower and Warnes (1974) suggest that cross-cultural preferences in therapy depend on etiological views and ideological differences, which is why they claim psychoanalysis gained ground in the United States cultural context emphasizing individualism, work therapy in the Soviet Union because of Marxist ideology, and Morita therapy in Japan because of culturally imposed rigid self-discipline. Highly controlled and overregulated cultures might encourage therapies that provide a safety valve for feeling and emotions through individual freedom while underregulated cultural contexts with less rigid norms might encourage therapies with externalized social control like a clear and well-structured plan at the expense of self-expression.

CULTURE NOTE

Watts (1961) described counseling as a social game based on conventional rules that define boundaries between the individual and the cultural context. The duty of a therapist is to involve participants in a "countergame," which restores a unifying perspective of ego and environment so that the person can be liberated and a balanced context restored.

Draguns (1981) suggests several guidelines for adjusting balance through therapy. The more complex the social and cognitive structure, the more a society will prefer hierarchy and ritual characterized by elaborate techniques for countering psychological distress. The stronger a society believes in the changeability of human nature and plasticity of social roles, the more they will favor therapy techniques as vehicles of change. The more a society's attitudes toward psychological disturbance reflect deep-seated prejudices about human nature, the less tolerant and accepting they will be of the mentally ill. The counselor acts much as a social engineer compensating for a lack of harmony in the cultural context through counseling and therapy.

In some cases, a counselor restores the balance through therapy by bringing in a third party, the "mediator." There are many examples of the counselor becoming a mediator to achieve harmony and restore balance. Bolman advocates the approach of using two professionals, one from each culture, collaborating in cross-cultural counseling with traditional healers as co-counselors. Weidman (1975) introduced the notion of a "culture broker" as an intermediary for working with culturally different clients. Slack and Slack (1976) suggest bringing in a co-client who has already effectively solved similar problems working with chemically dependent clients. Satir (1969) has introduced mediators in family therapy for problems of pathogenic coalitions, with the therapist mediating to change pathogenic relating styles. Counseling itself is a "mediating" process, whereby the therapist is the catalyst for resolving conflict. Trimble (1981) suggests that a third person as mediator might work better in some cultures (such as American Indian) than in others. For example, a poorly chosen mediator may seriously distress Hispanic clients through embarrassment, misinterpretations, inaccuracies, invasions of privacy, or a variety of other reasons (LeVine & Padilla, 1980).

THE BALANCED INFLUENCES
IN A CULTURAL CONTEXT

There are several implications of considering balance as a criterion for good counseling:

- Concepts of knowledge must be enlarged to go beyond the boundaries of rational process. Knowledge in other cultures has many forms, such as that accumulated through experience. Logical inconsistency and paradox become valuable approximations of truth in many societies. Logic is only one form of validation, dependent on a scientific, objective, rational, and abstract principle to describe human behavior. In some cultures, subjective evidence can also be used to validate truth.

- The importance of relationships must be recognized when working with clients from cultures that do not emphasize individualism. In many societies, individual development is considered a lower stage of growth toward "fulfillment." Appropriate spiritual alternatives describe the self as participating in a unity with all things and not limited by the changing illusions of self and nonself. In the non-Western perspective, an individual's unity with the universe goes beyond the self to being part of a larger context in the cosmos.

■ Westernized perspectives, which have dominated the field of mental health, must not become the criteria of "modernized" accomplishment. Although non-Western cultures have had a profound impact on the West in recent years, many less-industrialized non-Western cultures seem more determined than ever to emulate the West as a social model. There is also evidence that the more modernized a society, the more their problems and solutions resemble those of a Westernized society. While industrialized society is fearful of technological domination that might deteriorate social values and destroy the meaning of traditional culture, less industrialized societies are frequently more concerned that the technology will not be available to them. The task is one of differentiating among modernized alternatives outside the Western model.

■ Change is not inevitably a positive and good outcome of social services. A balanced perspective between changing and unchanging values requires that we recognize that many cultures do not accept change and development as desirable. A frequently heard English-language proverb is "if you don't know what to do, at least do something!" In rapidly changing industrialized and modernized cultures there is a strong predisposition toward valuing change itself as intrinsically good, moving toward a solution, reconciling ambiguity, and promising better things for the future. A contrasting perspective suggests that change may be bad. Both perspectives are necessary to a balanced worldview. To understand this change process, we need to identify those values that do not change but, rather, become the "hinges" on which the door of change swings.

■ We do not control our environment, but neither does our environment control us. In the range of value orientations there is a clear division between those who believe it is our right and even responsibility to control the environment and those who believe just as firmly that we are controlled by our environment. A third group holds that we interact with our environment and thus the question of control is irrelevant. Whichever basic assumption is made will profoundly affect the criteria for intercultural training in any situation. An increased awareness of ecological balance has helped us understand the interaction with persons and environment as a complex phenomenon.

■ Ability to recover from mistakes is more important than perfection as a criterion for good counseling. The skilled professional will make as many errors as the novice. The difference is that the skilled professional will be able to recover. In learning about intercultural criteria it is important to break out of a "success/fail" dichotomy because ultimately the outcomes of social interaction are seldom defined clearly as a success or as a failure. The emphasis in identifying intercultural criteria needs to go beyond dichotomies to develop the potentially positive effects of each problem, as an analogue or a range of possibilities.

■ Very few institutions offer specializations in cross-cultural counseling, although increasingly departments of counseling and therapy are offering courses in cross-cultural or multicultural issues. There is a need for a network across disciplines and institutions to coordinate the efforts of multicultural social services. There is furthermore a need to involve the "real world" of the community in counselor education and reduce the artificiality of classroom training.

■ The literature on intercultural counseling is diffuse, varies a great deal in quality, and is published in journals of limited circulation. There is a need for a series of review publications that establish the threshold for quality control in these journals. The need also exists for more attention to multicultural issues in national meetings of professional associations, which presently devote less than 2% of their time on cross-cultural or multicultural presentations. There is a need for developing criteria from research on the range of non-Western alternatives to "talk therapy."

■ Finally, research has failed to develop multicultural theory for social services. There are a number of reasons why this is true. First, the emphasis of multicultural research has been on abnormal rather than normal behavior across cultures. Second, only in the 1970s did research identify universal aspects across cultures and then only for the more serious categories of disturbance, such as schizophrenia and affective psychoses. Third, the complexity of multicultural variables in research is difficult to quantify. Fourth, multicultural research generally has lacked an applied emphasis and remained largely theoretical or abstract. Fifth, there has not been sufficient interdisciplinary collaboration among mental-health-related disciplines on multicultural research. Sixth, the emphasis of multicultural research has been on the symptom rather than on the interaction of person, profession, institution, and community.

We are at the starting point in developing culture-centeredness as the criteria for effective counseling. Only those who escape the web of their own assumptions and maintain a balanced perspective will be able to communicate effectively with other cultures. The dangers of cultural encapsulation (Wrenn, 1962, 1985) and the dogma of increasingly technique-oriented definitions of social services have been frequently mentioned in the rhetoric of professional associations in the social services as criteria for accreditation. To escape from cultural encapsulation, social service providers need to challenge the cultural bias of their own untested assumptions about counseling. To leave our assumptions untested or, worse yet, to be unaware of our culturally learned assumptions is not consistent with the standards of good and appropriate social service.

CONCLUSION

The underlying assumptions of culture-centered counseling are (a) that all behaviors are learned and displayed in a cultural context and (b) that each culture is complicated and dynamic. Our cultural identity has grown from what we learned and continue to learn from each cultural context. The search for accuracy is directed toward assessing and understanding each client in his or her own complicated and dynamic cultural context. The culture-centered approach described in this chapter makes several fundamental assumptions:

- If all behavior is learned in a cultural context, culture controls one's life and defines reality for each of us with or without our permission. The "rules" for success are different in each context, and what works "on the job" might not work "at home."
- Counseling is interpreted differently by the culture teachers surrounding each client. By acknowledging the central role these culture teachers have for the client, the counseling is more likely to be interpreted accurately.
- Values and worldviews are not themselves the culture but have been constructed as ways to find meaning in each cultural context. At the same time, they influence the context in which they were learned or being applied. Religious literature of the Bible, Koran, Talmud, and other sacred writings give meaning to one's life experiences while at the same time influencing how one responds.
- All behavior is displayed in a cultural context. Attempts to assess, understand, or change a behavior that disregards the cultural context are not likely to be successful. Empathy involves our ability to take the client's culturally learned perspective rather than impose our own self-reference criterion on the client.
- The same apparent cultural context is experienced differently by each individual at different times and places. Attempts to impose a single, unimodal, and unchanging cultural identity defined by nationality, ethnicity, gender, or other affiliation disregard how each individual changes over time in response to changing circumstances.
- Groups develop patterns, rules, and stories that give meaning to their cultural context. We can understand the cultural context of others by studying their patterns, rules, and stories through their literature, proverbs, or sayings and their habits, customs, or rules of life.

- Group similarities are generalized from how group members experience their cultural context in a more or less similar way. Within-group differences reflect the many complicated affiliations such as gender, age, and socioeconomic status as they influence group members. It is dangerous to make judgments about individuals based on aggregate data because doing so can easily lead to stereotyping.

- As the cultural context changes, the behavior of individuals within that context will also change. If a group attempts to maintain outdated patterns or rules that are inappropriate to the "new" culture, those attempts will not succeed. Rapid increases in urbanization around the world have caused many changes in village and family habits, patterns, or rules.

- Only when the cultural context has been changed will individuals in that context change accordingly. Imposing the rules of an outside culture can only be successfully done at the cost of destroying the original cultural context. The examples of modernization and colonization provide evidence of how destructive the new rules can be to old ways.

- The more we depend on abstractions and generalizations based on aggregate data, the less utility those guidelines will have for individuals seeking to construct meaning in their own cultural context. Conversely, the more we limit our analysis to each individual's unique and subjective perspective, the less useful those data are to understanding the group.

In their review of cultural theories, Thompson, Ellis, and Wildavsky (1990) divide definitions of culture into (a) the "mental products" (e.g., values, beliefs, norms, rationalizations, symbols, or ideologies) and (b) the "total way of life" of a people in a holistic context. The cultural context, as they describe it, requires a more inclusive perspective:

> What matters most to people is how they would like to relate to other people and how they would like others to relate to them. Whereas most theories in the social sciences tell us how individuals or groups go about getting what they want from government or markets, cultural theory seeks to explain why they want what they want as well as how they go about getting it. (p. 97)

The culture-centered approach to counseling is focused on the context where all behaviors are learned and displayed. These underlying assumptions are expanded in the following chapters to demonstrate the ways a culture-centered perspective can be helpful to the accurate practice of counseling.

EXERCISE

DESCRIBING CULTURAL IDENTITY

Objective

To identify the complex culturally learned roles and perspectives that contribute to an individual's identity

Instructions

In the blanks below, please write answers in a word or phrase to the simple question "Who are you?" Give as many answers as you can think of but try to identify at least 20 descriptors. Write the answers in the order that they occur to you. You will have 7 minutes to complete the list.

I AM _____

I AM _____

I AM _____

I AM _____

I AM _____

I AM _____

I AM _____

I AM _____

I AM _____

I AM _____

I AM _____

I AM _____

I AM _____

I AM _____

I AM _____

I AM _____

I AM _____

I AM _____

I AM _____

I AM _____

Debriefing

Ask volunteers to read their list out loud and count the numbers of others in the class who also used approximately the same label. Keep count of the labels on a flipchart, blackboard, overhead, or whiteboard given by all, by many, by some, by few, or by only one to demonstrate the extent of similarity and difference in the group. If students would prefer to keep their identity labels confidential, their lists can be turned in anonymously and coded by the instructor for feedback to the class later. The instructor may use these data to discuss the importance of between-group and within-group differences.

2

Managing Culturally Learned Assumptions

■ **Primary Objective** Increase awareness of culturally learned assumptions relevant to counseling interventions

■ **Secondary Objectives** (1) Describe the importance of cultural assumptions in understanding the complex cultural context and (2) Identify alternative assumptions for use in culture-centered counseling interventions

---

Cultural patterns of thinking and acting were being prepared for us even before we were born, to guide our behavior, shape our decisions, and put our lives in order. We inherited these culturally learned assumptions from our parents and teachers who taught us the "rules" of life. As we learned more about ourselves and others, we learned that our own way of thinking was one of many different ways. By that time, however, we had come to believe that our way was the best of all possible ways, and even when we found new or better ways it was not always possible to change. We are more likely to see the world through our own eyes and to assume that others see the same world in the same way using a "self-reference" criterion.

CULTURE NOTE

We have learned to use the self-reference criterion our whole lives. The Golden Rule says "Do unto others as you would have them do unto you." What if they don't *want* done unto them like you want done unto you? Should you do it to them anyway?

There are several ways to protect yourself against the error of the self-reference criterion. These are examined in terms of underlying assumptions about culture and about counseling.

PEOPLE ARE *BOTH* SIMILAR
AND DIFFERENT AT THE SAME TIME

No matter how different another person is from you, there is *always* some degree of similarity. No matter how similar the other person is, there is *always* some degree of difference. Avoid overemphasizing similarities or differences. If you overemphasize diversity and differences between people you end up with stereotyped, disconnected categories that tend to be hostile toward one another. If you overemphasize similarities, you rob persons and groups of their individual identities, which then get dissolved in the "melting pot," and typically the strongest group in that pot defines *their* way as best. There is a third way, which is to emphasize both similarities and differences at the same time.

An accurate culture-centered perspective requires us to be "cross-eyed," with one eye always clearly focused on differences and the other eye focused clearly on similarities. In this way, we honor the important cultural differences that give individuals and groups their identity while at the same time celebrating the "common ground" we share.

CULTURE NOTE

Many countries such as the United States (*E pluribus unum*) and Indonesia have national mottos emphasizing that both plurality and unity are needed to achieve national strength.

CULTURE IS COMPLEX

Complexity is a positive force that keeps you from accepting easy answers to difficult questions. It is tempting to create simple models that can be explained and understood, but they do not reflect the complexity of a real-world cultural context. The "just say no" approach to drug addiction among youths is an example of a simplistic solution. The problems of drug addiction require continuous support and presents a complicated problem. It is dangerous to confuse these simple explanations and labels with the more complex reality because it creates failure and makes it much more difficult to try again with a more realistic approach.

Psychological interventions that ignore the cultural context are dangerous because they give the illusion of having "done something." You cannot consider the cultural aspects of a situation without including the client's complicated cultural context. People who learn to accept complexity see many more alternative answers to each question, see connections and relationships between trends, and identify more choices open to them when confronted with a problem. Yet the overwhelming complexity of culture has led many teachers, researchers, administrators, and direct service providers to disregard cultural similarities and/or differences. Culture is complex, but it is *not* chaotic. There are *patterns* that make it possible to manage complexity.

Multiculturalism has frequently been viewed as a method for helping persons from one cultural group communicate with members of other groups. If we define culture inclusively to include ethnographic (nationality, ethnicity, religion, language), demographic (age, gender, place of residence), status (social, educational, economic), and affiliation (formal and informal) variables, then *every* relationship and context becomes multicultural.

If multiculturalism refers *exclusively* to nationality and ethnicity, then it might best be described more narrowly as a method of analysis. However, if culture is defined *inclusively*, according to the thousand or more complex and dynamic culturally defined roles taking their turn at being salient, then multiculturalism becomes a generic theory for explaining failures and predicting successes in all relationships.

CULTURE NOTE

Imagine that your thinking is a rocket set to follow a straight trajectory of flight and your assumptions the adjustments that decide which direction the rocket will fly. Imagine that someone else's "rocket" is adjusted to fly straight and true to course but the assumptions adjusting the direction of flight are different. Both viewpoints may be rational and consistent, but each will reflect differences in the underlying assumptions each of you make.

BEHAVIORS ARE NOT MEANINGFUL DATA

Behavior is not meaningful until and unless it is understood in the context of a person's culturally learned expectations. Behaviors can be accurately interpreted only in their cultural context. Similar behaviors might have different meanings, and different behaviors might have the same meaning. Not everyone who smiles at you is your friend, and not everyone who frowns at you is your enemy. If two persons share the same expectation for trust and respect they do not have to display the same behaviors to get along with one another. For example, if two culturally different persons understand that they share the same positive expectation of "respect," for example, even though their behaviors are very different they may agree to disagree or recognize that they are both approaching the same goal from different directions in complementary ways. The natural tendency, however, is to judge behaviors out of context. It is dangerous to define counseling as merely changing behaviors without regard to their cultural context.

CULTURE NOTE

Think of your best friend and ask yourself first whether that friend behaves exactly like yourself (almost certainly not) and second whether a total stranger could behave toward you *like* your friend with the same consequences (almost certainly not). You have found "common ground" through your friendship in spite of differences.

NOT ALL RACISM
IS INTENTIONAL

Counselors who presume they are free of racism underestimate the power of modern advertising. In most cases, racism emerges as an unintentional action by well-meaning, good-hearted, caring professionals who are probably no more or less free from cultural bias than the general public. Racism is defined as a pattern of systematic behaviors resulting in the denial of opportunities or privileges to one social group by another. Racism can refer therefore to aversive behavior of individuals or of institutionalized social groups. Overt racism is intentional, where a particular group is judged inferior or undeserving. Covert racism is unintentional, where misinformation or wrong assumptions lead to inaccurate assessments or inappropriate treatments. Covert, unintentional racism is less likely to be challenged or changed because there is no awareness of doing wrong. The key to changing unintentional racism lies in self-awareness and examining basic assumptions.

A number of factors predispose counselors to racist practices (see Ridley, 1995, pp. 10-13):

- Counselors often assume that their good intentions automatically make them helpful.
- Some counselors assume they are prepared to counsel clients from any background.
- Many counselors are ineffective with minority clients because they overlook societal factors that influence the behavior and adjustment of these clients.
- Either/or thinking that lends itself to racism is the predominant mode of thinking in the Western worldview.

Ridley (1989, 1995) also identified several examples of unintentional racism. First, the counselor might claim to treat all persons equally regardless of color. Color-blindness can be a rationalization for someone who is uncomfortable dealing with the controversies of racial differences and compensates by homogenizing all racial differences in a "one size fits all" abstract category. Second, a counselor might assume that all of a person's problems derive from that person's culture in an inevitably racist "deficit hypothesis" about other "underprivileged" or "deprived" cultures. Third, the client might transfer good or bad feelings to the counselor from his or her previous contact. The counselor might not recognize this transference of feelings in their cultural context and so misunderstand the client. Fourth, the counselor might transfer good or bad feelings to the client from previous interactions with people resembling this client. This countertransference distorts the counselor's view of the client. Fifth, the sympathetic counselor might overcompensate for culturally different clients whose cultural group has been exploited. A more dependent counselor with guilt feelings might easily be manipulated, focusing on the counselor's own unmet needs rather than the client's educational progress. Sixth, the client might respond to elements of racism in the counselor that the counselor is unaware of and interpret them as hostility. Seventh, the counselor might interpret a client's nondisclosure as unfriendly without recognizing that different cultures teach different levels of privacy. Unintentional racism is a primary contributor to the problems of cultural encapsulation.

WE ARE VULNERABLE
TO "CULTURAL ENCAPSULATION"

Wrenn (1962) first introduced the concept of cultural encapsulation, of which he identified five basic features described in Chapter 1. Cultural encapsulation refers to the protective "capsule" or "cocoon" that some counselors construct around themselves to protect them from meaningful contact with persons from other cultures. First, reality is defined according to one's own set of cultural assumptions. Second, one becomes insensitive to cultural variations among individuals and assumes one's own view is the only right one. Third, one's cultural assumptions are not dependent on reasonable proof or rational consistency but are believed true regardless of evidence to the contrary. Fourth, one seeks solutions through technique-oriented job definitions and quick or simple remedies. Fifth, one judges everyone from the viewpoint of one's self-reference criterion without regard for the other person's separate cultural context.

We are captured by cultural encapsulation when we (a) measure all persons according to a hypothetical "normal" standard, (b) assume that individualism is equally important in all societies, (c) define our professional boundaries narrowly and exclude other disciplines, (d) depend on abstract jargon and fail to put our concepts in a cultural context, (e) disregard the importance of dependency for collectivist cultures, (f) disregard the social fabric of support systems, (g) presume that all thinking is linear and based on cause-effect relationships, (h) insist on always changing the individual to fit the system, (i) disregard the historical roots of relationships, and (j) presume ourselves to be free of racism and cultural bias.

INCLUSION IS
PREFERRED TO EXCLUSION

A broad and inclusive definition of counseling interventions includes both the educational and the medical model to accommodate the diversity of culturally different consumer populations. "Even our definitions of health and pathology can be culture-bound, especially in the area of mental health. Thus what constitutes healthy human development may also vary according to the sociocultural context" (Kagitcibasi, 1988, p. 25). The task is to match aspects of each cultural context with significant and salient antecedents to achieve appropriate outcomes. It is essential to recognize the importance of an inclusive perspective for accurately understanding each cultural context.

The educational model of counseling lends itself to a more inclusive interpretation than the medical model does. According to the educational model the client is typically regarded as an essentially healthy, normal person with a serious problem. The provider's task is to "teach" the client ways of dealing with the problem, and the client's task is to "learn" new strategies. Just as all counseling interventions are to some extent educative, so too educational change has a therapeutic dimension to it. The inclusive perspective of the educational model provides the counselor and the client a wider range of choices and alternative explanations.

The inclusive perspective recognizes and accommodates differences between Western and non-Western perspectives. In many non-Western cultures, the "teacher" is expected to guide persons toward appropriate personal growth goals. Seeking help from a mental health specialist for a "mental" problem in these cultures almost certainly reduces that person's status in the community. However, a teacher can provide the same functions of counseling guidance and learning in ways that enhance one's status. Those who carry out the *educational functions* of counseling interventions in non-Western cultures would be surprised or even insulted to be labeled mental health service providers.

MANAGING THE CLIENT'S
INTERNAL RESOURCES

In many non-Western cultures where professional counselors are unavailable, the clients seek help by going inside themselves (discussed in Chapter 5). This process might involve remembering advice given previously by family or trusted friends, recalling a memorized saying or parable, or listening to the imagined voices of those "culture teachers" they have accumulated over their lifetime. These endogenous or inside-the-person resources are frequently overlooked as a treatment mode.

The internal resources might be as simple as sitting silently and thinking about a problem, running it through your mind, and seeking an appropriate solution quietly by yourself. In other cultures, conditions of stress lead to mobilizing these self-healing modes, which occasionally result in altered states of consciousness—as in dreams—dissociated states, religious experiences, or even psychotic reactions. Torrey (1986) cites numerous examples in which "self-righting" approaches have been mobilized by healers and through spirits.

At best, counselors are likely to neglect the valuable resources of the client's internal dialogue, which can prove a potent force in bringing about change. Some of the literature on visualization or holistic health advises paying attention to the client's positive attitude, which facilitates good health generally, but this approach usually appears only as a footnote in the more traditional counseling literature. At worst, counselors are likely to pathologize a client's tendency to "escape" from reality by internalizing (Beardsley & Pedersen, 1997).

There are few psychological studies of altered states of consciousness because researchers have typically avoided internal, intangible, inaccessible mental states as too complicated for experimental research (Ward, 1989). Among the scientific studies of how clients mobilize these internal resources, Prince (Valla & Prince, 1989) has been among the most prominent in his study of endorphins as a physiologically endogenous resource that influences body chemistry. The absolute authority of a "dualistic-materialistic paradigm" associated with Western medicine is being challenged by an increased interest in "holistic health" perspectives typically associated with non-Western cultures:

Western medicine has tended to look upon the body as a sort of machine that can be treated in total isolation from the mind, but even before the major paradigm shifts, it was becoming clear that this mechanical approach was simply not working. This was especially apparent in areas where psychosomatic linkages were showing that the mind does have a major impact upon bodily functions. (Shiekh & Shiekh, 1989, p. v)

As later chapters discuss in more detail, counselors working with culturally different clients will want to consider mobilizing the positive resources of religious experiences and other self-healing mechanisms as an underdeveloped resource in counseling across cultures. By defining counseling interventions according to both externalized and internalized functions of the client, the counselor develops a more inclusive framework (Katz, 1993).

CONCLUSION

Culturally learned assumptions become the building blocks of a meaningful life. Persons operating from different assumptions are not likely to understand one another as each individual has learned his or her own assumptions in different cultural contexts. It is possible for a culture-centered counselor to work within a client's assumptions without necessarily agreeing to those assumptions. Taking such a perspective becomes an important feature of culture-centered counseling and is more likely to result in accurate empathy.

Culture-centered counselors faces two problems: first, to identify their own culturally learned assumptions, which are often so taken for granted they are difficult to identify; and second, to identify the culturally learned assumptions of a client. This is best achieved through a meaningful dialogue with persons whose assumptions are different from one's own. The following chapters discuss the implications and consequences of those assumptions identified in this chapter as they apply to culture-centered counseling.

EXERCISE

THE "CROSS-CULTURAL TRADE-OFF" GAME

Objective

To provide the structure for a programmed series of interactions between a visitor and a host culture resident for exchanging feedback on their alternative perspectives

Instructions

"Cross-Cultural Trade-Off" is different from other games because both participants can win. It is like other games in depending on the mutual consent and cooperation of players. The object is to improve the relationship between participants who come from different cultural backgrounds. The system works best with two persons from different cultures who know one another, but it can be modified for three or more. The game has eight steps. For each, the participants should set aside about an hour free from outside distraction. It is best to take no more than two steps in any one day, but at minimum one step a week should be taken. Sometimes, the situation will warrant ignoring the game and focusing on cross-cultural interactions the game has stimulated.

There is a significant body of research evidence that increased interethnic contact is more likely to occur under unfavorable conditions with negative results than under favorable conditions. Unfavorable conditions apply when the contact situation produces competition between groups, when contact is unpleasant and involuntary, when contact lowers the status of either group, when members of either group are frustrated by failure, when the two groups have conflicting moral standards, or when the minority group is of lower status. The immediate and urgent task facing contemporary society is to match the demographic redistribution of culturally defined groups both nationally and internationally with an appropriate educational response. "Cross-Cultural Trade-Off" is an attempt to bring two persons from different cultures together in a structured interaction under favorable conditions.

What one of you hears may not be what the other is saying. Misinterpretation is particularly likely when the communication is across cultures, when we may easily confuse cultural differences with interpersonal differences. Our culture teaches us about a role we are expected to follow and about the roles we can expect others around us to follow. The problem is that different cultures teach different roles. Think about the culturally defined role you have to play in interacting with your partner and how that role makes you feel good or bad. Then think about the culturally defined role your partner is expected to play and how that makes you feel good or bad. Because each of you is talking about *your own* feelings about yourself and one another, it doesn't matter whether those feelings are justified. Save your criticism and evaluation until later when you both better understand each other's expectations.

STEP 1

Make a list, being as specific as possible, of

1. Things about my cultural role that make me feel good.
2. Things about my cultural role that make me feel bad.
3. Things about my partner's cultural role that make me feel good.
4. Things about my partner's cultural role that make me feel bad.

After you have made the lists, exchange papers, read what each of you has written, and discuss your feelings with one another until each of you can restate the other person's role to the other's satisfaction.

STEP 2

You have to know one another before you can really trust each other. You also have to know yourself. You may think you know yourself and one another, but you may be wrong. This step helps each of you discover how you see each other by checking adjectives that are both positive and negative in four columns:

- Those adjectives that describe you as you see yourself.
- Those adjectives that describe you as your culture would like you to be.
- Those adjectives that describe your partner as you see him or her.
- Those adjectives that describe your partner as his or her culture would like that person to be.

Go through the list of adjectives and make a check mark beside each *most* appropriate adjective in each of the four columns. About 10 checks should be made in each column. Also make an "x" beside those adjectives that are *least* appropriate. Write in any specific comments or explanations that would help your partner understand your choice.

Try not to confuse the picture of you or your partner as you are with the picture of you or your partner as you would like that person to be. Feel free to add as many new adjectives as you want.

	Me As I See Myself	Me As My Culture Wants Me to Be	You As I See You	You As Your Culture Wants You to Be
1. adventurous				
2. false				
3. affectionate				
4. ambitious				
5. anxious for approval				
6. appreciative				
7. argumentative				
8. big-hearted				
9. neat				
10. competitive				
11. complaining				
12. critical of others				
13. demanding				
14. distant				
15. dogmatic				
16. dominating				
17. easily angered				
18. easily discouraged				
19. easily influenced				
20. efficient				
21. encouraging				
22. enthusiastic				
23. forgiving				
24. frank, forthright				
25. fun-loving				
26. give praise readily				
27. good listener				
28. helpful				
29. indifferent to other				
30. impulsive				
31. intolerant				
32. jealous				
33. kind				
34. optimistic				
35. loud				
36. independent				
37. orderly				

	Me As I See Myself	Me As My Culture Wants Me to Be	You As I See You	You As Your Culture Wants You to Be
38. need much praise				
39. obedient				
40. rebellious				
41. resentful				
42. responsible				
43. sarcastic				
44. discourteous				
45. self-centered				
46. self-respecting				
47. self-satisfied				
48. sentimental				
49. show love				
50. shrewd, devious				
51. shy				
52. sociable				
53. stern				
54. submissive				
55. successful				
56. sympathetic				
57. tactful				
58. talkative				
59. teasing				
60. thorough				
61. thoughtful				
62. touchy, can't be kidded				
63. trusting				
64. uncommunicative				
65. understanding				
66. varied interests				
67. very dependent on other				
68. well-mannered				
69. willing worker				

STEP 3

Go back over the adjectives checked by yourself and those checked by your partner. Look for similarities and differences. Instead of the two of you, there are really four people. There is your self image, you as your partner sees you, your partner's self image, and your partner as you see him/her. Look for surprises in comparing the adjectives you checked with those your partner checked. Whether you decide to change your views or not is still up to you, but knowing what others think should help you decide.

Place your and your partner's paper side by side and compare the following:

- Your view of yourself and your partner's view of you
- Your ideal for yourself and your partner's self-ideal
- Your real view of yourself and your ideal for yourself

Discuss the way you view yourself and the aspirations or goals you have with your partner. Are you being fair to yourself? Are you being fair to your partner?

STEP 4

Conflict-producing elements of a culture are evident where incompatible values coexist, as in valuing ambition and humility, competitive success and sympathy for the loser, and frankness and tact all at the same time. These dilemmas can be confusing in our home culture and even more disturbing when we seek to understand someone else's culture. The confusion is particularly likely to result in conflict when an individual or minority group is being acculturated to a dominant majority value system foreign to them. Cultures vary in how they deal with these areas of potential conflict. Surrounded by a cocoon of pretended reality, culturally encapsulated individuals are able to evade reality either through saying their way is always the best way or by saying that all individuals should be allowed to do whatever they want. Neither alternative is likely to produce a satisfactory partnership. This step tries to help your partner and yourself work out a better compromise in your relationship.

Take a look at the difference between your partner and yourself to see if you really want to change or not. If you allow these differences to control you, they may lead you to (a) get mad at the other person over some small detail; (b) give in to the other person even when you believe you are right; (c) deliberately embarrass the other person in some way; (d) not speak to the other person; (e) pretend that you really don't care, although you really do; or (f) run away from the other person. Discuss the differences and come to an agreement that either the differences are too small to bother about or that each of you can compromise your expectations in some way to accommodate the other.

Which is the best way to handle differences? There are a number of cues to help find the best way: Can you still work with the other person? Does the way you both handle differences strengthen your relationship with one another? Can both of you accept this way of handling your differences? Does this way of handling differences solve the problem permanently? Does this way of handling differences hurt you or the other person? Can you think of a better way than you have been using?

STEP 5

Up to now you and your partner have been sharing information. This step help you take action. Step 5 has two moves:

- The first move builds on the positive shared feelings and on things you and your partner have in common. This may set guidelines for conduct you both want to continue and a basis for the future.
- The second move focuses on differences, disagreement, and conflict between you and your partner. In this move, you can seek to clarify the difficulty and find ways to work together.

Fill in the blanks below:

Differences and disagreements between you and I are _____

_____

The source of our disagreement seems to be _____

_____

I handle these disagreements by _____

_____

You handle these disagreements by _____

_____

I might try _____

_____

You might try_____

_____

I think this way might work because _____

_____

Debriefing

You bring together all the information you have collected about yourself and your partner from previous steps and work out a plan for the future. From Step 2 you might want to do more things that make your partner feel good and avoid things that make your partner feel bad. From Steps 3 and 4 you might formulate new goals for yourself or revise your expectations about your partner. From Step 5 you might find new ways to prevent misunderstandings.

It is not easy to change what you are used to doing. You might "try out" several new approaches to see if they make any difference, leaving you and your partner free to change your minds again later. You will need each other's help to make the decision a success.

Besides seeking help on problems or difficulties in the relationship with your partner, you might find that he or she can help you on some of your own personal problems as well.

Situation, problem, or difference:_____

_____

What I intend to do about it: _____

_____

What I might do in spite of myself: _____

_____

How I would like you to help me: _____

_____

Now review your relationship with your partner. By now you have had a chance to try out the approaches you decided on and you might want to make additional changes. You might want to review what both of you said in earlier steps or add new ideas to what you wrote.

The whole idea of "Cross-Cultural Trade-Off" is to help both of you learn from each other and share your feelings and reactions, views and ideals, and areas of agreement and disagreement. You should be able to work together better now than before you started. Trade ideas with your partner about how the approaches you "tried out" worked or didn't work. Be willing to change your approach if you find something that might be better.

You have now completed "Cross-Cultural Trade-Off," although you may want to return to one or more of the steps later. You may find that the trust you have together now would make it a completely new game when played again. You may want to apply approaches from "Cross-Cultural Trade-Off" to your day-to-day relationship.

Today, we spend years of formal study analyzing the history of people and nations, language structure, laws of nature, and the mechanics of operating tools and machines. But one of the most important subjects has not been studied. Each of us depends on many intercultural relationships, which we allow to develop haphazardly and spend little time analyzing. We can help ourselves and others by taking a look at these cross-cultural relationships. "Cross-Cultural Trade-Off" provides an opportunity to do just that.

3

Managing the Cultural Context

- **Primary Objective** Describe ways a counselor can change a client's cultural context

- **Secondary Objectives** (1) Understand culture in its historical context and (2) Understand how cultural change affects individual clients

Culture without history is an abstraction. History is the aggregate of stories about how different individuals managed their own cultural contexts in successful and/or unsuccessful ways. Managing the cultural context in counseling means having correct and sufficient information about one's own culture as well as the client's culture. This information is available through lectures, group discussions, written materials, and media presentations. Historical facts relate to economic, political and social reality, physical and social climate, decision-making styles, habits, and underlying values. The first two chapters on defining culture in context and managing one's own assumptions about culture depend on knowing the historical background of the cultural context.

Knowledge provides the tools for managing the cultural context, and yet effective management goes beyond the collection of facts about other cultures. In a contextual approach culture becomes a source of meaning to understand behaviors and the expectations behind those behaviors much as suggested by the social constructionist view. By understanding the cultural context a counselor is better able to understand how people describe, explain, or account for their behavior. History helps us understand significant trends as the cultural context changes over time and in response to new situations. Culture serves to organize experience in patterns that have meaning for the client. Managing the multicultural context requires knowledge of those patterns.

THE HISTORICAL CONTEXT OF CULTURE

Multicultural relations have been characterized by political controversy and socioeconomic inequity. Given that cultures have been dealing with their similarities and differences as long as people and groups have been able to communicate with one another, multiculturalism has a long history. The term *multiculturalism* is, however, relatively new, having evolved from academic disciplines in Europe and areas colonized by Euro-Anglo powers. In many cases, the study of cultural similarities and/or differences was motivated as a defense of and rationale for social, economic, and political colonization of other countries and cultures.

In 18th-century Europe, there was much concern with social development and the study of "civilization" in contrast to "savage" and "primitive" people. European colonial powers sent scholars, philosophers, naturalists, and physicians on scientific expeditions to study the cultural and physiological differences among people. By the 20th century, German scholars had taken the lead in studying the "mentality of primitive people" and "folk psychology" (Segall et al., 1990). The disciplines of psychology, anthropology, and sociology began to emerge from this European cultural context.

The psychological study of cultures assumed that there was a fixed state of mind whose observation was obscured by cultural distortions and that related cultural behaviors to some universal definition of normative behavior. The anthropological position, however, assumed that cultural differences were clues to divergent attitudes, values, or perspectives that differentiated one culture from another, based on a culture-specific viewpoint. Anthropologists have thus tended to take a relativist position when classifying and interpreting behavior across cultures, whereas psychologists have linked social characteristics and psychological phenomena without much regard for different multicultural viewpoints.

Counseling represents the application of psychological, sociological, and anthropological knowledge in managing clients in their cultural contexts, drawing clear boundaries between self and nonself. Kagitcibasi (1996) describes how this separated self has become the universally accepted healthy prototype:

> American (and Western) psychology, both reflecting and reinforcing the individualistic Western cultural ethos, has drawn the line narrowly and sharply, constituting a clear boundary between self and non-self. Other cultural conceptions differ from this construal of the self in varying degrees. However, American psychology enjoys a dominant position and is self contained so the knowledge it creates (based on its own empirical reality) is often assumed to be universal. (p. 56)

The rise of cross-cultural psychology and counseling and the increased importance of contextual interpretation have highlighted a growing recognition of the cultural context as providing meaning to behaviors by social constructionists, interpretive anthropologists, cultural psychologists, person-environmentalists, ecological theorists, ecocultural theorists, and dozens of other theoretical perspectives (Kagitcibasi, 1996). As all psychology is the product of a cultural context and because human behavior is both learned and displayed in a cultural context, all psychology and all counseling, properly understood, are culture centered.

Berry, Poortinga, Segall, and Dasen (1992) point out the importance of an interdisciplinary contemporary study of psychological phenomena from multiple perspectives to get a clear view of the cultural context:

> Thus, in our frame of reference we need to avoid reducing culture to the level of psychological explanations, of psychological phenomena to biological explanations, biological to chemical, and so on. That is, we must recognize that there are, for example, cultural phenomena that exist and can be studied at their own level. (p. 6)

There is an ethnocentric bias in counseling partly due to its historical roots and development based on Euro-American scholarship, but there is also an increased awareness of this limitation as counseling becomes more international and explicitly culture centered.

CULTURE NOTE

Beginning in the 1990s, more psychological research is being generated outside than inside the United States. The field of psychology may thus be gradually shifting its power base to international cultures and countries (Gielen, 1994).

The recent popularity of culture and multiculturalism for understanding human behavior in context has been the result of global changes (Sloan, 1990). Counselors who ignore this trend risk the danger of being left behind by their colleagues for the following 10 reasons:

1. There is a growing awareness of development—with negative and positive consequences—in "Third World" countries due to increased international communication and transportation opportunities. There is thus an increased probability of counselors working with clients from these rapidly changing countries.

2. The 18th-century rationale is no longer functional to define international relationships in the postcolonial future. Changes in the socio-political-economic power balance have changed how "foreigners" are perceived.

3. The social sciences have been necessarily internationalized at the practical and theoretical levels. Development has now become a primary goal.

4. National liberation movements have radicalized special interest groups internationally. Plans for gradual and eventual development have lost credibility.

5. Cross-cultural psychology has introduced a paradigm shift in methodology at the practical level. The centrality of culture for accurate assessment is being recognized.

6. Leading psychologists of this generation were trained during the activist 1960s in a cultural context emphasizing idealistic goals. The contemporary emphasis on human rights, international cooperation, and peace research reflect those idealistic priorities.

7. Interdisciplinary cooperation has become more popular and necessary for solving practical problems. Science and technology have been challenged to become more relevant to all people by enlisting the cooperation of colleagues working on the same problem in related fields.

8. New forms of cultural diversity have emerged with increased numbers of immigrants, refugees, migrant workers, students, tourists, and other migrating sojourners. The problems of voluntary and involuntary migration have imposed a global context on counseling.

9. Educational exchange and collaboration of social scientists through professional organizations and internet technology has presented a global opportunity to counselors. Social scientists from around the world spend more time than ever in direct contact.

10. There is a growing interest in "indigenous psychology," where a people are studied from within their own historical-cultural context. Solutions to social problems developed indigenously might provide new solutions to social problems elsewhere.

MULTICULTURALISM IN A RACIAL CONTEXT

Counseling has tended to confuse the cultural categories with racial categories rather than recognizing racial identity as one aspect of each cultural context. Although racial identity is a powerful and important social and political perspective, it is important for counselors to understand the historical background of race as a social construct rather than a scientific classification. The tendency to differentiate races according to inherited characteristics and to rank them hierarchically according to ability and potential dates back to European imperialism of the 16th century and before. The biological concept of race has become more and more controversial as evidence discrediting race as a scientific construct but emphasizing the political importance of racial identities has increased (Yee, Fairchild, Weizmann, & Wyatt, 1993).

Statements by the United Nations Educational, Scientific, and Cultural Organization (UNESCO; see Yee et al., 1993) on race and prejudice relate directly to the psychological relevance of race as a construct. The statements, drafted by distinguished scholars in psychology, anthropology, economics, sociology, anatomy, medicine, genetics, and biology, "portray race as a misleading and dangerous concept. Mindful of World War II, UNESCO worked to debunk the idea of race as a biological fact so that it could never again be used to support aggression and genocide" (Yee et al., 1993, p. 1132).

Two centuries ago, Carl Linnaeus classified *homo sapiens* into 4 races based on phenotypic traits. Since then, other taxonomists have argued for as few as 3 and as many as 37 races (Molnar, 1992). Physical anthropologists define race on the basis of population gene frequencies, but the problems of identifying genetically discrete populations are so complicated they cause disagreement on how many races there are or even if the concept is useful (Yee et al., 1993). A statement by the American Association of Physical Anthropologists objects to the use of 19th-century notions of race:

> Hereditary potentials for overall intelligence and cultural development do not appear to differ among modern human populations, and there is no hereditary justification for considering one population superior to another. Racist political doctrines find no foundation in scientific knowledge concerning modern or past human populations. (Yee et al., 1993, p. 1133)

The popular literature about race ignores heterogeneity, assumes unproven race-behavior causal relationships, and disregards cultural factors of bias, ethnicity, and socioeconomic differences. Use of the term *race* oversimplifies the differentiation of cultural groups resulting in controversies of law, human rights, values, sociopolitical policy, methodology, and statistics that are frequently less than helpful. Discussions about race, its meanings, and the usefulness of this construct have resulted in confusion, controversy, and partisanship. Such discussions have suffered from a "scholarship versus advocacy" dilemma driven by outside pressure to include or exclude racial classifications. This tendency is evident in a number of social scientists' research:

- J. Philippe Rushton (1988) argues for a three-way racial division of Asian, Blacks, and Whites, based more on folk beliefs than on genetics. Variations within these three groups are interpreted as "error," and Rushton contends that aggregating data from different samples of racial subgroups will result in reliable mean race scores as an "obvious" fact not requiring proof.
- Arthur Jensen's (1992) research has generated more controversy regarding sociopolitical policy, human values, morality, radicalism, and free speech than about scientific genetic theories with regard to Black-White differences: "By stressing Black-White racial differences so assiduously, Jensen lost control of scholarly goals while fueling racist and sociopolitical forces" (Yee et al., 1993, p. 1136). The research defending race as a scientific biological term is flawed, even though race and racism continue to be important categories of sociopolitical analysis.
- Hernstein (1994) claims that high and low levels of intelligence are based on permanent genetic differences, suggesting that remedial programs of affirmative action are a waste of money because they can never overcome the genetic gap between racial groups. Instead, these programs are devel-

oping a "cognitive elite" of high-IQ individuals who attend the same schools and rise to the same levels of power and wealth, whereas those genetically condemned to lower IQ levels are the victims. The irony is that the Hernstein book itself contributes to that unjust polarization by disregarding (a) how intelligence is measured and (b) how racial affiliation is measured in culturally different contexts. Although the implications of this very popular book have a racist "feel," authors and supporters of this viewpoint are likely not unintentionally racist but, rather, are swept along by commonly accepted and unchallenged assumptions about race and intelligence.

■ If one defines racism as prejudice plus the power to enforce that prejudice on others, Ponterotto and Pedersen (1993) suggest that racism is increasing rather than decreasing in domestic and international sociocultural-political contexts. This increase is explained by the definition of power as an essential variable in understanding racism.

■ Pinderhughes (1984) examined the feelings and behaviors related to power differences across ethnic and racial groups. The "more powerful" tend to feel or experience comfort, gratification, good luck, safety, security, pleasure, happiness, superiority, masterfulness, entitlement, hopefulness, high esteem, anger toward noncompliant people, fear of anger by less powerful groups, guilt about injustices, and fear of losing power. The "less powerful" people in her sample felt or experienced less comfort and gratification, anxiety, frustration, vulnerability, pain, depression, deprivation, incompetence, inferiority, exhaustion, being trapped, hopelessness, helplessness, low self-esteem, fear of abandonment, and loneliness. In terms of behavior, the "more powerful" acted to impact the system, create opportunity, take responsibility, exert leadership, blame the less powerful, devalue pain and suffering, distrust others, maintain control, justify power, display paranoia, isolate the less powerful, dominate others, display rigidity, blame the victim, and justify aggression. The "less powerful" acted to ignore opportunities or abilities to change the system, lacked access to leadership, attributed positive attributes to people in power, distrusted and guarded against powerful groups, denied powerlessness, displayed paranoia through passive dependency, were isolated from and avoided by the more powerful groups, became passive-aggressive, became rigid to control the effects of powerlessness, struck out aggressively, and identified with the aggressor. The conditions of social contact greatly influence the presence or absence of racism.

THE CONTACT HYPOTHESIS

This hypothesis predicts the favorable conditions necessary for harmonious consequences when different groups or individuals come in contact. Amir

(1969, 1992), Miller and Brewer (1984), and others reviewed literature from social psychology on the contact hypothesis and drew three conclusions: First, when groups come together under favorable conditions, the intergroup contact results in more positive relationships; second, when groups come together under unfavorable conditions, the intergroup contact results in an increase of negative relationships and disharmony; and third, spontaneous intergroup contact is more likely to occur under unfavorable conditions, resulting in more negative relationships and disharmony.

Favorable conditions that tend to reduce intergroup conflict exist when (a) there is equal-status contact between members, (b) the contact is between members of a majority group and the higher-status members of a minority, (c) the social climate promotes favorable contact, (d) the contact is intimate rather than casual, (e) the contact is pleasant or rewarding, and (f) the members of both groups interact in functionally important activities while developing shared goals.

Unfavorable conditions that increase the likelihood of intergroup conflict occur when (a) contact produces competition, (b) contact is unpleasant and involuntary, (c) one group's prestige is lowered as a result of the contact, (d) frustrations lead to scapegoating, and (e) moral or ethical standards are violated.

In applying his contact hypothesis to multiculturalism in the interpersonal context, Amir (1992, p. 23) identified the following factors as affecting a society's preferences:

- The presence or absence of a cultural, traditional religious, or ideological commitment is essential for the unification and blending of different subcultures into one cultural or national entity is important.
- Language use may become a divergent as well as a convergent factor, depending on whether the different subgroups do or do not use one common language.
- Status similarity or difference may produce effects in one or the other direction.
- Survival factors that include an outside military force or outside economic pressures may threaten the very existence of a society comprising different ethnic subgroups.
- The strength of tendencies to preserve or not preserve the cultural heritage of each ethnic subgroup must be considered. When contact results in an adjustment of personal priority, the result is culture shock.

Counselors attempting to create favorable conditions for positive change of a client need to consider the role and importance of context in that client's cultural perspective. Hall (1983) demonstrated that some cultures put a "high" emphasis on context, whereas others' emphasis is "low." By separating high-context (HC) from low-context (LC) messages on a continuum, Hall was able to differentiate cultural groups:

> High or low context refers to the amount of information that is in a given communication as a function of the context in which it occurs. A highly contexted communication is one in which most of the meaning is in the context while very little is in the transmitted message. A low context communication is similar to interacting with a computer—if the information is not explicitly stated, and the program followed religiously, the meaning is distorted. In the Western world, the law is low context, in comparison with daily transactions of an informal nature. People who know each other over a long period of years will tend to use high context communication. (p. 229)

The contexting process involves two simultaneous processes. First, the brain constructs a context based on past experiences as interpreted by the senses. This is primarily an internalized process. Second, there is the outside environment, situation, or setting in which events occur independently of their being perceived or interpreted. This is an externalized process. According to Hall (1994),

> The screens that one imposes between oneself and reality constitute one of the ways in which reality is structured. Awareness of that structure is necessary if one is to control behavior with any semblance of rationality. Such awareness is associated with the low context end of the scale. Yet, there is a price that must be paid for awareness—instability, obsolescence, and change at a rate that may become impossible to handle and result in information overload. Therefore, as things become more complex, as they inevitably must with fast-evolving, low context systems, it eventually becomes necessary to turn life and the institutions around and move toward the greater stability of the high-context part of the scale as a way of dealing with information overload. (p. 68)

An HC message is one where most of the information is either in the physical context or internalized in the person and very little is in the more explicit codes transmitted as part of the message. An LC communication is just the opposite, with most of the information described by the abstract codes themselves.

LC cultures are more likely characterized by individualism, overt communication, and heterogeneity, such as the United States, Canada, and Central or Northern Europe, where LC thinking is more evident. HC cultures emphasize collective identities, covert communication, and homogeneity, such as Japan, China, Korea, and many Latin American countries, where HC thinking is dominant.

CULTURE NOTE

Hall (1976) contrasts the American (low context) with the Japanese (high context) perspective regarding justice. In contrast with the protagonist/antagonist conflict in an American court, the Japanese trial puts the accused, the court, the public, and the injured parties together to work toward settling the dispute. The function of the trial is to locate the crime in context so that both the criminal and society see the consequences.

Gudykunst and Ting-Toomey (1988) contrast LC and HC cultures as they approach negotiation:

	LC Cultures	*HC Cultures*
Identity	Individual—autonomy and dissociation	Group—inclusion and association
Mode of communication	Direct	Indirect
Style	Control and confrontation	Accommodation and avoidance
Strategy	Competition	Collaboration
Explanations	Linear logic, analysis, instrument oriented	Nonlinear logic, synthesis, expression oriented
Conflict	Against the individual	Against the group
Exposure of a problem	Direct, confrontational	Indirect, nonconfrontational
Orientation	Action and solution oriented, with explicit communication codes and rational/factual rhetoric in open strategies	More relationship oriented, with implicit communication codes and intuitive/affective rhetoric in ambiguous or indirect strategies

Jandt and Pedersen (1996) demonstrate the importance of high and low emphasis on context for constructive conflict management in 25 case examples from the Asia-Pacific region. They demonstrate that cultural values, age, and gender as well as nationality or ethnicity have a profound impact on constructive conflict management. Ethnic conflict, in which two alternative cultural contexts each struggle for survival, is understandably much more volatile than conflict in which ethnicity is not an issue. Jandt and Pedersen offer 17 hypotheses that test the importance of high and low context in mediating conflict.

MULTICULTURALISM IN THE INTRAPERSONAL CONTEXT

Culture shock focuses the contact hypothesis on profoundly personal encounters (Pedersen, 1995b). Oberg (1958) introduced the concept "culture shock" to describe anxiety resulting from losing one's sense of when and how to do the right thing. This adjustment process involves a nonspecific state of uncertainty, where these persons do not know what others expect of them or what they can expect of the others with emotional, psychological, behavioral, cognitive, and physiological consequences.

Among the most frequently cited indicators of culture shock are the absence of familiar cues about how to behave, the reinterpretation of familiar values about what is good, an emotional disorientation ranging from anxiety to uncontrollable rage, a nostalgic idealization of how things used to be, a sense of helplessness in the new setting, and a feeling that the discomfort will never go away. Any radically new situation such as a new job, divorce, graduation, being fired, being arrested, having cancer, or other sudden changes involves an adjustment of role and identity resulting in culture shock. The cultural context is changed in unexpected ways.

The culture shock experience has been classified into five stages or categories (Adler, 1975):

- Initial contact, often called the "tourist" or "honeymoon" period because the visitor's experiences are exciting and fantasylike, detached from reality
- Disintegration of the familiar, in which the full impact of differences intrude in ways that cannot be ignored, resulting in the person experiencing loneliness, depression, self-blame, and withdrawal
- Reintegration of new cues, which begins with anger and fighting back against the host culture and then self-blame turns into hostility toward,

rejection of, and attacks against the new setting—considered the most volatile stage where violence is most likely to occur because things are getting better but not fast enough

- Developing a new identity, in which both similarities and differences are acknowledged and the person becomes more self-assured; both strengths and weaknesses of the old and new are accepted
- Biculturalism or multiculturalism, in which one's identity includes competence in both the old and the new settings

These stages are plotted on a U-curve, where they move from a higher to a lower and back to a higher level of effectiveness (Pedersen, 1995b).

Church (1982) discusses 11 empirical studies in support of the U-curve hypothesis. These data support the general hypothesis through the first three stages of an inverted J-curve, but other research suggests that the U-curve hypothesis is at best heuristic and not clearly supported by empirical data. Furnham and Bochner (1986) discuss some problems with the U-curve hypothesis. First, there are many dependent variables to consider such as depression, loneliness, and homesickness. Second, the definition of a U shape is uneven because different persons start out at different levels of original adjustment adequacy and then change at different rates. Third, research on interpersonal aspects of culture shock seems more promising than the intrapsychic aspects.

Recent research on culture shock has applied the educational growth model rather than the medical disease model. Berry et al. (1992) prefer the term *acculturative stress* and demonstrate that culture shock may be a painful but not necessarily negative experience, resulting in positive growth and insight. Kealey (1988) found that many persons who were successful abroad had experienced intense culture shock as a necessary but not sufficient condition for their success. Coffman (1978) points out how the culture shock model also applies to elderly mental patients moved from one ward to another and to persons going through career changes, divorce, widowhood, retirement, or disability. The greater the perceived differences between the old and the new environment, the greater the culture shock.

Coffman and Harris (1984) also suggest strategies for dealing with culture shock:

1. Recognize that transition problems are usually painful and that this is normal.
2. Maintain personal integrity and self-esteem as a primary goal.
3. Allow as much time as necessary to go through culture shock.

4. Recognize the patterns of adjustment as culture shock and develop appropriate new skills and insights.
5. Label the symptoms of culture shock to reduce the ambiguity.
6. Recognize that being well adjusted in one setting does not necessarily mean being well adjusted in other settings and may in fact increase feelings of homesickness.
7. Although culture shock cannot be prevented, it is possible to prepare for the experience.

MULTICULTURALISM IN AN IDEOLOGICAL CONTEXT

When intergroup contact fails, it often results in exclusionary behavior, specifically moral exclusion, which results from severe conflict or from feelings of unconnectedness and antipathy. Opotow (1990) lists rationalizations and justifications for the moral exclusion of minorities that help identify otherwise hidden examples of this exclusion through psychological distancing, displacing responsibility, defining group loyalty, and normalizing or glorifying violence.

Some examples of moral exclusion and consequent behaviors are the following:

- *Biased evaluation:* making unflattering comparisons
- *Derogation:* disparaging and denigrating others
- *Dehumanization:* repudiating others' dignity and humanity
- *Fear of contamination:* perceiving contact as threatening
- *Expanding the target:* redefining legitimate victims
- *Accelerating harm doing:* Engaging in destructive acts
- *Approving destructive behavior:* Condoning harm doing
- *Reducing moral standards:* defining harmful as proper
- *Blaming the victim:* displacing the blame for actions
- *Self-righteous comparisons:* justifying retaliation
- *Desecration:* harming others to demonstrate contempt

Other more subtle, hidden, and covert processes of moral exclusion and their consequences are these:

- *Groupthink:* striving for group unanimity

- *Transcendent ideologies:* exalting the group experience
- *Deindividuation:* feeling anonymous in the group
- *Moral engulfment:* replacing ethical standards
- *Psychological distancing:* not feeling another's presence
- *Technical orientation:* focusing on efficient means
- *Double standards:* having different sets of moral rules
- *Unflattering comparisons:* emphasizing one's superiority
- *Euphemisms:* conferring respectability on hurtful behavior
- *Displacing responsibility:* appealing to higher authority
- *Diffusing responsibility:* doing harm collectively
- *Concealing the effects:* minimizing injurious outcomes
- *Glorifying violence:* making violence legitimate
- *Normalizing violence:* accepting violent behavior
- *Temporal containment:* allowing a necessary exception

CULTURE NOTE

Extreme forms of moral exclusion are evident in "ethnic cleansing" by one group of another in the ethnic conflicts of Eastern Europe and Africa.

Moral exclusion is the obvious consequence of cultural encapsulation and can occur in degrees from overt and malicious evil to passive unconcern when intergroup contact fails. It is possible to be exclusionary by what you do not do as well as by what you do. Moral exclusion is pervasive and not isolated. Psychological and social supports may condone otherwise unacceptable attitudes, intentionally or unintentionally: "As severity of conflict and threat escalates, harm and sanctioned aggression become more likely. As harm doing escalates, societal structures change, the scope of justice shrinks, and the boundaries of harm doing expand" (Opotow, 1990, p. 13).

Others move in a similarly inclusive direction. Rather than define the self as self-contained, self-reliant, independent, standing out, egocentric, and selfish, Hermans, Kemper, and Van Loon (1992) promote a dialogical view of self beyond rationalism and individualism based on the stories or dialogues by which people understand themselves and construct their notion of reality: "The embodied nature of the self contrasts with conceptions of the self found in mainstream psychology, which are based on the assumption of a disembodied or rationalistic mind" (p. 23). If the world is objective, then people's different perceptions of the world are more or less inaccurate, their beliefs and perceptions are not relevant, context is not important, and all experiences are judged by rational rules. By disregarding context, this alternative presents a very rigid, narrow perspective for counseling.

Reality, according to this newly emerging contextual and constructivist view, is based not on absolute truth but an understanding of complex and dynamic relationships in a cultural context. Life is a narrative of stories and rules that locate the self in its cultural context (Bruner, 1986; Sarbin, 1986). Life is understood not abstractly but through relationships in a developmental alternative to linear, stage-based, convergent hierarchies (Steenbarger, 1991). As the sociocultural context changes, the self changes to accommodate and adapt as each person constructs and reconstructs meaningful reality.

Howard (1991) also documents how culture is made up of the stories we live by and have learned over our lifetime:

A life becomes meaningful when one sees himself or herself as an actor within the context of a story—be it a cultural tale, a religious narrative, a family saga, the march of science, a political movement, and so forth. Early in life we are free to choose what life story we will inhabit—and later we find we are lived by that story. (p. 196)

CULTURE NOTE

Bateson (1979), in his book *Mind and Nature,* tells about the man who invented the world's largest computer and typed in the most difficult question he could think of to test the computer's ability: "Will machines ever think like people?" The screen lit up with the words "That reminds me of a story."

MULTICULTURALISM IN
A FUTURE CONTEXT

Berry et al. (1992) believe that multicultural psychology plays an important role in dealing with the major problems facing the world:

To live up to such a promise will require three major changes to the field: the development of persistent and collaborative work in particular topics;

the incorporation of psychologists from all societies into this enterprise; and the convincing of our students and colleagues to accept the view that culture is indeed one of the most important determinants of human behavior. (p. 392)

This will be difficult. As Maruyama (1992) points out, the problem with contextual understanding is not just the complexity of complicated problems but our inadequate cognitive structure for thinking about those problems. "We need epistemological reorientation and reorganization before any further economic or technological restructuring" (p. 32).

CULTURE NOTE

We are moving toward a future that is so different it is beyond imagination. Those who are not prepared for this unimaginable future will not survive. The way to develop the adaptive facilities for survival is to interact with people who think, dress, act, and feel differently.

Sampson (1993) suggests that psychology and counseling have at best accommodated add-on eclectic strategies in response to culturally different movements and special interest groups without fundamentally transforming conventional frameworks for understanding the future: "Psychology is accused of using a framework of understanding that implicitly represents a particular point of view, that of currently dominant social groups, all the while acting as though its own voice were neutral, reflecting reason, rationality, and with its ever expanding collection of empirical data, perhaps truth itself" (p. 1221). The future of counseling psychology as a science requires more than additional data or even more inclusive samples in a defense of objective positivism; it requires the inclusion of more subjective constructivist and contextual perspectives based on the sociocultural context of culturally different people.

One promising movement in counseling is based on the concepts of chaos, nonlinear dynamics, and self-organization, as expressed by Barton (1994): "In recent years, a new paradigm for understanding systems has been gaining the attention of psychologists from a wide variety of specialty areas. This paradigm has no single name but has been described in terms of chaos, nonlinear dynamics (sometimes called nonlinear dynamical systems theory) and self-organization" (p. 5). These concepts can be considered a metaphor for the qualitative functions of counseling and therapy reflecting the inherent complexity of individuals and systems outside the laboratory. When chaos theory was originally conceived to describe weather forecasting (Geleick, 1987), it described chaotic systems as unpredictable locally, although when viewed globally they were essentially stable. Butz (1992a, 1993) applies this metaphor to the experience of anxiety in psychotherapy and systems theories of family therapy. The convergence of hard and soft sciences toward complexity rather than simplicity, toward subjectivity rather than objectivity, toward constructivist rather than "discovered" reality, and toward a contextual rather than abstract description of human behavior demands a new paradigm for counseling and therapy.

Applications of nonlinear dynamics have been applied to Jungian therapy (Abraham, Abraham, & Shaw, 1990; Butz, 1992a, 1992b; Eenwyk, 1991), psychoanalysis (Langs, 1992), posttraumatic stress (Glover, 1992), psychic development and individual psychopathology (Guidano, 1991), family systems (Elkaim, 1981), multiple personality disorders (Putnam, 1988, 1989), schizophrenia (Schmid, 1991), and psychiatric disorders (Sabelli, Carlson-Sabelli, & Javaid, 1990). These applications of nonlinear dynamics and self-organizing systems are beginning to prove productive in the physical sciences and hold promise as a new paradigm in counseling that can facilitate change to guide clients through the apparent chaos of their cultural context.

CONCLUSION

Managing the cultural context depends on defining culture in context and on managing one's own culturally learned assumptions. By valuing the historical path from which each cultural context has emerged, the counselor is in a much better position to influence the future direction of that cultural context for each client. As the social sciences have struggled with the role of culture and become more culture centered themselves, the focus has been less motivated by protocol than by accurate assessment, meaningful understanding, and appropriate intervention.

Fundamental cultural concepts such as race need to be understood both in terms of their scientific basis and in terms of their sociopolitical impact on identity formation. Absent this understanding, counselors are likely to misinform and be misinformed. The role of power or powerlessness in achieving equity can be applied for effectively managing the cultural context.

The practical implications for creating favorable conditions in cultural contact and for overcoming the internalized pressures of culture shock were also discussed. As the social sciences become more culture centered they will become more sensitive to the moral and ideological context within each culture, thus requiring counselors to balance volatile and complicated variables. New approaches in chaos theory and complexity theory are being developed to help counselors manage the cultural context more effectively in the future.

EXERCISE

CULTURE-CENTERED INTERVIEW GUIDE

Objective

The following categories demonstrate the complexity of a client's cultural context. This list can be used as (a) a self-assessment "test" to see how well you know your client's cultural context by being able to respond accurately to any or all the items, (b) an interview guide by selecting those categories most relevant to a client's presenting problem as a systematic framework for understanding that part of a client's cultural context, or (c) a study guide to help the counselor become more comprehensively aware of a client's cultural context by seeking out answers to the questions that follow. This list can be used by counselors to increase their cultural self-awareness of the implicit and explicit rules of their own cultural context, identifying areas of contrast with the cultural context of their clients.

Instructions

Identify a resource person from the target culture you wish to study. The resource person should be articulate—able to interpret his or her own cultural context—and authentic—well known and accepted by others who share the same cultural context.

Develop an agreement or contract with that resource person to go through the list of topics and help you understand the indicated behaviors in their cultural context from the target culture's viewpoint.

Establish a regular time to meet and discuss the items on this list of behaviors, recognizing that a meaningful discussion of these items will take many hours. You may want to focus on selected items or behaviors to reduce the time involved.

In many cases, explanations of behaviors in their cultural context are done through stories or examples. Remembering these stories will prove useful if you encounter the same behaviors later in counseling.

SOCIAL CUSTOMS

- Are the people overtly friendly, reserved and formal, or hostile to strangers?
- What are formal and informal greeting forms? Which may be used appropriately by a guest? By a child?
- What are appropriate manners for entering a house? (Do you remove your shoes or any other items of clothing before entering? Do you wait to be welcomed in by the owner or await the owner inside the door? Do you send a calling card in advance? Do you ring a bell, clap hands, or bang with your fist on the door?)

- What are appropriate manners when shopping? In a bazaar? In a haute couture salon? (Do you queue, call for a salesperson, or wait until a clerk approaches you? Do you bargain? Are you expected to carry your purchases? Do you provide your own containers for food purchases?)
- What are appropriate manners at the theater? (Do you clap hands, shout "bravo," or hiss or whistle to show approval? Do you seat yourself or await an usher? Do you tip the usher? How do you get a program?)
- What are appropriate manners in a beauty shop? (Do you make an appointment in advance or walk in? Do you bring your own beauty supplies? To whom do you give tips?)
- What are appropriate manners for entering a room? (Do you bow, nod, or shake hands with others there? Do you shake hands with everyone, only males, no one, or only the first person to greet you?)
- What is the appropriate moment in a new relationship to give one's name, ask the other's name, and inquire about occupation or family? How are names used for introductions? (When compound names are customary, which elements do you use? How do you present Sra. Maria Josefina Melina de Diez de Medina or Senorita Consuelo Vazquez Gutierrez del Arroyo?)
- Is it proper for a wife to show affection for her husband in public by a term of endearment, holding his hand, or greeting him with a kiss?
- What is the expected gesture of appreciation for an invitation to a home? (Do you bring a gift? What kind? Do you send flowers in advance or afterward? Do you send a thank-you note?)
- When gifts are exchanged, is it impolite to open the gift in the presence of the donor? Are gifts presented or received in a special manner? Is it proper to express appreciation for a gift? Are any gift items taboo?
- Are there any customs affecting the way one sits or where one sits? (Is it impolite to sit with feet pointed toward another person? Is the seat to the right of the host a position of special honor?)
- What are the ways of showing respect (hat off or on, sitting or standing, bowing, lowering head, etc.)?
- Are there special observances a guest should be familiar with before attending a wedding, funeral, baptism, birthday, or official ceremony?
- Is it offensive to put your hand on the arm of someone with whom you are talking?
- Do you offer your arm when escorting someone across the street?
- What are the reactions to laughing, crying, fainting, or blushing in a group situation?
- Are any particular facial expressions or gestures considered rude?
- Do people tend to stand more closely when talking? What is the concept of proper personal space?
- What constitutes "personal" questions?

- What is the attitude toward punctuality for social and business appointments?
- How do you politely attract the attention of a waiter in a restaurant?
- How can invitations be refused without causing offense? Is a previous engagement an acceptable excuse? What happens if the excuse of illness is used?
- How does one express condolence when death occurs in the family of an acquaintance or friend? What is the appropriate expression of concern when a prominent member of the host government dies?
- What is the appropriate response when an unknown person in apparent need comes to your home and asks for help, food, used clothing, or money?

FAMILY LIFE

- What is the basic unit of social organization—the individual, the basic family, the extended family, the tribe, the village, the region, the linguistic group, or the national state?
- What family members of which generations live together? If you are invited to a home, whom in the family would you expect to meet?
- Are the elderly treated with special respect? Are they greeted differently from other adults? Does a young person look forward to or dread old age?
- Is homemaking considered the preferred role for women? How do women figure in the labor force, the professions, officialdom?
- What are the duties in the family of women and of men? Who controls the family money? Who makes the decisions about the upbringing of children?
- How do the inheritance laws work? Can female offspring inherit land? Does the last born have a different legacy from the first born? What arrangements are usual for widows?
- What do girls aspire to become? What careers are preferred for boys? Do toys and games ascribe special roles to either sex?
- How are children taught (by role, by precept, by conceptual learning)? Who are their teachers in and out of school? What techniques are used at home and at school to reinforce desirable behavior and to correct disapproved behavior?
- What are the important events in family life, and how are they celebrated?
- When does a child become an adult, and is there a ceremony to mark passage from one stage to the next (debutante ball, circumcision rites, bar mitzvah, etc.)?
- Are marriages planned or by individual choice? What do people look for or want from marriage? Who pays for the wedding ceremony? Is a dowry necessary?
- At what age do most marry? What encounters between the sexes are approved prior to marriage? Is chastity a virtue? Is polygamy or concubinage approved? Is homosexuality accepted?

- Is divorce permitted?
- What are the symbols used in the marriage ceremony, and what do they signify?

HOUSING, CLOTHING, AND FOOD

- What functions are served by the average dwelling? Is there a separate structure for bathing, cooking, toileting, shelter of animals, or storage of foodstuffs?
- Are there differences in the kind of housing used by different social groups (location, type of building or furnishings, etc.)?
- Which textiles, colors, or decorations are identified with specific social or occupational groups and not considered appropriate for others (special colors for royalty, for mourning, etc.)?
- What occasions require special dress (weddings, funerals, holidays, religious events, etc.)?
- Are there some types of clothing considered taboo for one or the other sex?
- What parts of the body must always be covered by clothing?
- How many meals a day are customary?
- With what implements is food eaten? Is there a common bowl or individual servings? Is there an age or sex separation at meal times? Is there a special role for hosts and guests in regard to who eats where, what, and when? Are there any customary expectations about the amount of food guests must be offered or must eat? Any special rituals for drinking?
- Are there any foods unique to the country not eaten elsewhere?
- Which foods are of importance for ceremonies and festivals?
- Which are prestige foods (champagne and caviar equivalents, etc.)?
- What types of eating place, food and drink are indicative of appropriate hospitality for (a) relatives, (b) close friends, (c) official acquaintances, and (d) strangers?
- Is "setting a good table" important for social recognition?
- When dining, where is the seat of honor?

CLASS STRUCTURE

- Into what classes is society organized—royalty, aristocracy, large land-owners, industrialists, military, artists, professionals, merchants, artisans, industrial workers, small farm owners, farm laborers, or other?
- Are there racial, religious, or economic factors that determine social status? Are there any minority groups, and what is their social standing? Is wealth a prerequisite for public office?
- Does birth predetermine status?
- Is class structure in rural areas different from that of urban areas?

- Is there a group of individuals or families who occupy a predominant social position? Can they easily be identified? Is their status attributable to heredity, money, land, or political influence?
- Are there any particular roles or activities appropriate (or inappropriate) to the status in which Americans are classified? (Does high status imply facility for generous contributions to charitable causes? Does a man lose face by helping his wife with dishes or changing diapers?)

POLITICAL PATTERNS

- Are there immediate outside threats to the political survival of the country? What protection does the country have against any such threats? What defensive alliances? What technological advantages in weaponry? What traditional enmities color policy options?
- How is political power manifested (through traditional institutions of government, through control of military power, through economic strength)?
- What channels are open for the expression of popular opinion?
- What media of information are important? Who controls them? Whom do they reach? What are the sources of information available to the average citizen?
- What are the political structures for the cities (mayors, councils, etc.) and for the countryside (village chiefs, town councils, etc.)?
- How is international representation handled? What is the process for formulating foreign policy? Who receives visiting heads of state? Who negotiates treaties?
- If a profile of the power structure should be drawn, which individuals or groups, visible or "behind the scenes," would figure as key elements?
- In social situations, who talks politics? Is it a subject in which a guest may show interest?
- What channels, if any, are available to opposition groups to express dissent?

RELIGION AND FOLK BELIEFS

- To which religious groups do people belong? Is one predominant?
- How can the fundamental religious beliefs be described? About the origin of man, life after death, the source of evil, the nature of the deity(ies)?
- Are there any religious beliefs that influence daily activities (noon prayers, begging bowls, etc.)?
- Is religion institutionalized? What is the hierarchy of religious functionaries, and in what ways do they interact with the people?
- Which places have sacred value? Which objects? Which events and festivals? Which writings?

- Is there tolerance for minority religions? (Is proselytizing or educational activities of minority religions permitted?)
- What is said or done to exorcize evil spirits (knocking on wood, making the sign of the cross, etc.)?
- What is done with a new child or the commencement of a building project to ensure good fortune?
- What objects or actions portend good luck and which bad luck?
- What myths are taught to children as part of their cultural heritage (sandman, Jack Frost, Pere Noel, fairy godmother, etc.)?

ECONOMIC INSTITUTIONS

- How do geographic location and climate affect the ways food, clothing, and shelter are provided? (Has extensive irrigation or hydroelectric development been necessary? Has the terrain facilitated or obstructed development of air transport?)
- How adequate are the available natural resources? Which must be imported? Which are in sufficient supply to be exported?
- What foodstuffs, if any, must the country import?
- What are the principal products? Major exports? Imports? What is the gross national product?
- In the marketplaces, what items basic to a minimum standard of living do you find missing? Are luxury items available?
- What kinds of technological training are offered?
- Are industrial workers organized in unions, confederations, political parties, or none of these? What about rural workers?
- Are cooperatives important in the economy?
- Are businesses generally operated by families, large public corporations, or the government? Is the multinational corporation significant?
- What percentage of the population is engaged in agriculture, in industry, in service trades?
- What protections have been developed against natural disasters (floating construction to minimize earthquake damage, advanced warning systems for typhoons, extensive crop insurance backed by the government, private disaster relief, etc.)?

ARTS

- Which media for artistic expression are most esteemed?
- Are there professional artists? Art schools?
- Which materials are most used (stone, ivory, bone, shell, wood, clay, metal, reed, textile, glass)?

- What art objects would you find in a typical home, in a museum?
- What kinds of music and musical instruments are unique to the country?
- What forms of drama and dance are popular?
- Are there special songs for special occasions?

VALUE SYSTEMS

- Is life to be enjoyed or viewed as a source of suffering?
- Is competitiveness or cooperativeness most prized?
- Is thrift or enjoyment of the moment more exalted?
- Is work viewed as an end in itself or as a necessary evil to be kept to a minimum?
- Is face considered more important than fact?
- Is politeness regarded as more important than factual honesty?
- Is it believed that destiny is controlled by one's actions or subject to impersonal forces?
- What killing, if any, is sanctioned (capital punishment, war, killing of adulterer, infanticide during famine, etc.)?
- How is "friend" defined? What are the responsibilities of friendship?
- What are the injunctions taught to children?
- Who are the traditional heroes or heroines? From what field of endeavor? Who are the popular idols of the day? What values do they symbolize?
- How would the virtues and vices be defined?
- How would work as compared to play be defined?

Note: As you accumulate information to answer the above questions, it is extremely helpful to pose the question "why" with each entry. Familiarity with the outward manifestations of a cultural context is helpful, but even more helpful, obviously, is an understanding of why certain behavior patterns prevail. By asking "why" such and such a custom is characteristic, you will be able to direct your attention to the values underlying behavior. When you can organize your observations in a framework, you will begin to develop an understanding of how the culture functions and how you can relate to it.

Adapted from Joan Wilson and Margaret Omar, *A Guide to Self-Taught Skills in Cross-Cultural Communication.*

Debriefing

When you have completed your discussion of the list describing the target cultural context, you and your resource person may want to respond to the following questions:

- How are you and your resource person partner similar?
- How are you and your resource person partner different?
- Did you discover any surprises as you went through the list and, if so, what did they teach you?
- Which patterns have remained the same and are unlikely to change?
- Which patterns are changing and why?
- How will reviewing these behaviors in their cultural context help you manage, change, or influence the cultural context of your client from this cultural background?

PART

II

Specific Culture-Centered Contexts

This second section examines specific cultural contexts in their similarities and differences as a demonstration of how culture is necessarily complex and dynamic. The alternative Asian and non-Western contexts demonstrate a clearly contrasting context to the Euro-American envelope that helps one understand oneself and others (Chapter 4). The spiritual context demonstrates the cosmic dimension in which boundaries of cultural contexts are defined (Chapter 5). The international student context demonstrates a population needing to adapt to two cultural contexts—in the host and home country—at the same time (Chapter 6). The family context demonstrates the complicated ways that a family cultural context shapes people's lives (Chapter 7).

Asian and
Non-Western Contexts

- ■ **Primary Objective** Describe selected contrasting cultural contexts from Asian and non-Western cultures for managing the functions of counseling

- ■ **Secondary Objectives** (1) Identify patterns of counseling in selected Asian societies and (2) Discuss 13 selected psychological assumptions in the Asian context

If we view culture-centered counseling in a global perspective we become aware that (a) the functions of counseling have a history of several thousand years and (b) the alternatives to "talk therapy" include many different means of restoring a healthy balance in the client's cultural context. Asian cultures provide a useful contrast to Western alternatives for identifying culture-centered perspectives. This chapter describes some of the Asian and non-Western alternatives and the notion of asymmetrical balance as a metaphorical outcome measure (Pedersen, 1991a, 1993a).

If you asked most Western-trained social service providers to describe what they do, most would agree that they make people feel more pleasure and less pain, more happiness and less sadness, and more success and less failure. This is a one-directional approach to social services. An alternative criterion that this chapter attempts to describe is a two-directional balance where both pain and pleasure, both happiness and sadness, and both success and failure are equally important accommodations. This "balanced" perspective introduced in Chapter 2 is now discussed as a means for distinguishing Western and non-Western alternative perspectives.

CULTURE NOTE

The most widely understood example of balance in relationships is the Yin and Yang symbol, where light and darkness are part of the same sphere and are inseparable from one another.

By helping define or restore balance in a person's life, social services can help that person integrate both pain and pleasure in a meaningful way. The models for defining and restoring balance as a criterion for social services are best found in Asian and Pacific models of health (Blowers & Turtle, 1987; Bond, 1986; Pedersen, 1983a; Roland, 1988; Sheikh & Sheikh, 1989; Tseng & Wu, 1985).

THE WESTERNIZATION OF COUNSELING

The label "Westernized" reflects more of a political than geographic reality in the counseling literature, with many Westernized influences in non-Western geographic areas and vice versa. The obvious colonial division of cultures as Western and non-Western is perhaps less relevant today than North/South differences reflecting a coincidence of more industrial development in the Northern Hemisphere and agricultural or less industrial development in the Southern Hemisphere. In any case, here the term *Westernized methods* refers to those derived from research in Europe and the United States and disseminated elsewhere in what Berry et al. (1992) call "scientific acculturation."

CULTURE NOTE

In Australia, a "corrected" version of the world map is available where the South Pole is on top and the Northern Hemisphere is below. North/South issues become clarified when looking at this "upside down" map by highlighting land mass and ocean mass ratios.

A "Westernized" description of the self presumes a separate independent and autonomous individual guided by traits, abilities, values, and motives that distinguish that person from others. Western cultures are described by Berry et al. (1992) as more "idiocentric," emphasizing competition, self-confidence, and freedom, whereas collectivistic cultures are more allocentric, emphasizing communal responsibility, social usefulness, and acceptance of authority. Westernized beliefs grew out of a naturalistic understanding of the physical world of the Enlightenment in Europe, describing human behavior in objective expressions of "mass and extension" rather than in categories of color, temperature, sound, and taste that were more subjective "created sensations" (Taylor, 1989). The Westernized perspective has traditionally defined the optional outcomes of counseling.

THE SPREAD OF WESTERNIZED THINKING

Westernized thinking spread through cultural diffusion of language, education, legal systems, and the media in the past several decades. Westernized thinking became synonymous with modernization in the schools, language, research, and interpretations of the social sciences around the world. This Westernized influence, however, has also inhibited the development of "appropriate psychologies" in many developing countries (Moghaddam & Taylor, 1986), especially when counseling interventions were adapted superficially to the indigenous ideological backgrounds of different cultures:

On the one hand psychology is only a small part of Western thought and may not have direct and widespread impact on a functioning culture. On the other hand psychology may be part of a broader package of acculturative influences that affect many of the core institutions (educational, work, religious) through which all or most people pass in the course of their development. (Berry et al., 1992, p. 380)

These problems of Westernized versus non-Westernized thinking are most vivid in majority/minority culture relationships. Counseling and therapy have a history of protecting the status quo against change, as perceived by minority cultures. These attitudes are documented in "scientific racism" and "Euro-American ethnocentrism" (Pedersen et al., 1989). Cultural differences were first explained away by a "genetic deficiency" model that promoted the superiority of dominant cultures. This evolved into a "cultural deficit" model that wrongly described minorities as deprived or disadvantaged by their culture. Minorities were underrepresented among professional counselors and therapists, the topic of culture was trivialized at professional meetings, minority views were underrepresented in the research literature, and consequently the counseling profession was discredited among minority populations.

The dangers of applying Westernized methods inappropriately are particularly important in clinical applications. Segall et al. (1990) contrast Western individualism with non-Western collectivism to demonstrate the significant differences. These two complementary perspectives demonstrate how collectivist and individualist methods are being influenced as well as doing the influencing in modern counseling interventions. Kleinman (1988) points out the importance of this reciprocity of influence:

> Whether or not psychiatrists in the developed societies gain a serious interest in the problems faced by their colleagues in the Third World, who are fashioning new approaches to remake psychiatric diagnoses and treatments so that they are more appropriate to the pressing problems of poor non-Western populations, those colleagues will be exerting an influence on international health bodies and programs. (pp. 184-185)

Refugees, for example, are an "at risk" population suffering from pressures of acculturative stress in Westernized cultures, where primary prevention is called for (Williams & Berry, 1991). Williams (1987) and Owan (1985) provide extensive annotated bibliographies on special problems in counseling refugees.

Walsh (1989) also describes the relationship between Asian and Western psychologies as complementary to one another, with the Asian systems focusing on advanced stages of development in a more "transpersonal" sense and on well-being and the Western systems focusing on psychopathology and on physical/mental development. According to Walsh,

> From a multiple-states-of-consciousness model, the traditional Western approach is recognized as a relativistically useful model provided that, because of the limitations imposed by state-specific relevancy, learning, and understanding, it is not applied inappropriately to perspectives and states of consciousness and identity outside its scope. (p. 549)

Pathologizing mystical experiences is an example of Western models going beyond their boundaries in some cultures.

Turtle (1987) describes the rapid movement of psychology from the "West" toward the "East." Given the theoretical dependence on principles of materialism, empiricism, and determinism in Western psychology, this transition is difficult at best:

> To offer practical solutions to problems of social planning, to advise on maximal utilization of capacities of individuals, to claim the ability to counsel, to comfort and to cure those in trouble and distress, in the face of firmly established beliefs about the proper forms of social organization and the relation of the individual thereto, and of highly valued practices of guidance, consolation and spiritual healing, gives evidence either of remarkable self-confidence and/or powers of salesmanship in modern psychologists, or of extraordinary social disruption in the East, or of both. (p. 1)

CULTURE NOTE

Why is English the only language that capitalizes first-person singular? Many non-Western people think it is because English speakers are so extremely individualistic.

Counseling and therapy have been dominated by the individualistic assumptions and worldview of the "Protestant ethic" (Sampson, 1977; Wrightsman, 1992) that are inappropriate, expensive, technology dependent, and frequently destructive in non-Western host cultures. It is essential to consider the non-Western alternatives. Nakamura (1964) rightly cautions that the polarization of Asian and Western cultures sometimes obscures more than it illuminates, with assumptions in one hemisphere being imperfectly or stereotypically understood elsewhere.

Chinese writings and thought were introduced in Japan in the 6th century, with particular emphasis on Confucianism and Buddhism. The Japanese selectively adapted these viewpoints to develop their own unique way of thinking, emphasizing what Nakamura (1964) calls the limited social nexus of the Japanese people themselves.

Non-Western Assertions

Some unique Asian points of view about counseling emerge as we examine assertions that differ significantly from Western points of view. Many of these assertions challenge the basic assumptions of counseling theory as we know it, substituting concepts we have normally relegated to the areas of philosophy or religion. The Asian psychologies do not fit easily into Western categories, sometimes providing answers to questions not being asked by Western psychologists. Of the 13 assertions listed below, the first 3 describe basic assumptions that define reality and the goals of personality development in Indian and Chinese society, the next 3 describe assumptions in parent-child relationships, and the final 7 deal with maintenance strategies.

It is appropriate first to establish the nature of individuality itself. The construct of *personality* assumes a particular view of the individual as a basic unit in the structure of psychology. Some examples from Indian, Chinese, and Japanese thought clearly contrast with Western psychologists' thinking on this.

1. *A newborn infant, as a result of its previous lives, has certain personality and character traits which, after its present life, are transmitted to its next existence.*

We think of an individual's personality beginning at birth and ending it at death. The Hindu concept is that the personality extends before the birth and after the death of a particular individual, a process of identity that extends over many generations. The Sanskrit equivalent of "individual" is *vyakti*. However, the concept is defined as a transitional state. To the extent that the individual is a self, it has independent reality. The ultimate end of spiritual freedom guides that individual's behavior in a particular way. To the extent that the self is embodied in the particular body as a product of nature, with a capacity to produce offspring, there is an indissolvable bond between the embodied individual and all other individuals. An individual caught in an otherwise hopeless web of misery can always hope for a better world after rebirth. To the contrary, there is the possibility that an individual will be reincarnated into a more painful existence. There is also the frustrating possibility that in spite of noble aspirations, one's unavoidable *karma* will shape one's destiny through a long series of rebirths before the basic "badness" within can be purged. Thus, the individual is important because he or she has the metaphysical status of "permanent substance coeternal with God" (Nakamura, 1964, p. 46).

CULTURE NOTE

If you believe in reincarnation, then whose personality are we talking about? The person(s) you were, the person you are, or the person(s) you will become in the future?

The implications of that doctrine are the rejection of the reality "mine," or personal possessions including one's own body. All these possessions are regarded as changeable, passed on to others after death and therefore impermanent or temporary. What, then, is left to transmigrate from one existence to the next? "Life is like fire: its very nature is to burn its fuel. When one body dies it is as if one piece of fuel were burned: the vital process passes on and recommences in another, and, so long as there is desire of life, the provision of fuel fails not" (Murphy & Murphy, 1968, p. 22).

2. *Self, the substance of individuality, and the reality of belonging to an absolute cosmic self are intimately related.*

The self, or *Atman,* is regarded as identical with the Absolute or ultimate Self throughout Indian philosophy. Although there is disagreement among the various Indian religions about the essence of the *Atman* as a metaphysical principle, there is no disagreement regarding the *Atman's* significance as the moral agent for individual action. Mastery of self is only a means to reach one's inner nature and is not "heaven" itself. The ultimate goal of the process of emancipation is the recovery or discovery of one's true self. "Hell" is continued bondage to others and to the desire of the senses; "heaven" is mastery of one's self and the blissful realization of one's divine nature. Thus, the true *Atman* is the ultimate or pure wisdom without internality or externality, indestructible and imperishable. The self therefore participates in this condition of unity with all things, with the changing manifestations of the phenomenal world being illusory and temporary. Humanistic conceptions of self-realization are far more individualistic than Buddhists or Hindus could accept.

CULTURE NOTE

When these Asian conceptions are "imported" through Westernized humanistic theories they are typically distorted and given an ego-oriented flavor. In Buddhist thought, however, the ego is the "enemy." In Buddhism, there is no self; the term *individual* is thus misleading or an illusion.

In the contemporary emphasis of humanistic psychology on rediscovering the nature of the "real self," some religio-philosophical teachings of Indian thought have demonstrated their attractiveness. The emphasis is less on individual or particular surface qualities of the self and more on the relational meaning of personality to all other realities. This provides an unchanging stability at the core of personality that is genuinely eternal, participating in ultimate reality and demonstrating the unity of all things. Consequently, the more an object is individualized, the less it participates in the essence of reality. This basic monistic view was developed in the Rg-Veda and developed to the Upanishads as a major theme throughout most of Indian thought.

The Indian view of self takes an ontological rather than an epistemological view of truth, leaning in the direction of monistic idealism and contending that all reality is ultimately One and ultimately spiritual. The emphasis is on the underlying features or "essence" of the individual rather than on surface qualities of the self. The individual or particular self is dependent on the universal that supports and defines reality, emphasizing the *relational* meaning of a person or thing rather than its fundamental uniqueness. By fixing limits between self and nonself, the person limits and defines a place in the universe that gives that individual an identity. There is thus a balance due to the harmonious tension between self-affirmation and self-negation.

In terms of modern psychology, the tendency of self-affirmation is extraversive (i.e., directed toward the external world), whereas the tendency of self-negation is introversive (i.e., directed toward the inner world), with which the ego illusion is dissolved (because an ego can only be experienced in contrast to an external world). The extraversive and introversive movements are as necessary in the life of humanity as inhalation and exhalation are in the life of an individual (Govinda, 1961, p. 29).

3. *Asian theories of personality generally de-emphasize individualism and emphasize social relationships.*

In Buddhism, there is a tremendous emphasis on "self effort" and the individual's disciplined efforts to bring about salvation through a kind of self-reliance that is frequently glossed over in describing Asian cultures as relatively collectivistic.

Western views of personality see it as a separate entity, distinct from society and culture (Hsu, 1971, p. 23). Individuals express and create society. The extreme Eastern view concentrates on relational cultural differences without specific reference to individuals. Traditional Western definitions of personality move from a central core of the unconscious to the expressible conscious (i.e., behavior). Hsu (1971), representing Asian thought, substitutes the term *psychosocial homeostasis* in place of personality to describe the balance of relationships as the basic unit to be studied. These relationships are central in the Chinese concept of *jen,* which translates as "person" but emphasizes the person's transactions with fellow human beings. Western concepts of personality emphasize what happens within an individual's psyche, whereas external behavior is seen as the overall effects or expressions of these forces. *Jen* emphasizes interpersonal transactions and evaluates the central core of individuality according to how well it serves to enhance interpersonal adjustment. Both Confucius and Mencius emphasized the universal principle of *jen,* and both were adamant that morality based on fear of public censure was not only not "true" morality but also contemptible behavior (Gielen, 1994). *Li* is desirable but must be based on *jen,* or the quality of being human. *Jen* is the universal principle, whereas *li* represents only what needs to be done in specific situations. Without *jen, li* is empty of true morality. This humanistic trend caused the Chinese to de-emphasize discrimination between the individual and human organization to which the individual belongs.

CULTURE NOTE

Jen defines the core of morality and humanity itself. A person is considered a person only when he or she observes the right behavior, so birds, animals, barbarians, and extremely immoral individuals are excluded from *jen*.

Hsu (1971) contends that the concept of *jen* is superior to the Western concept of personality. The locus of cultural change or resistance is not in the individual personality but in the circle of humanity, ideas, and things that define goodness in interpersonal relationships. This notion is close to a field theory concept of personality in the Western world, most specifically like Kurt Lewin's Gestalt concept of personality as the summation of vectors of force.

Whereas Indian psychology describes the world as impermanent and mortal, with very little difference between persons and other living things, Chinese thought attaches considerable importance to individual human beings as the highest form of existence. As a result, Chinese psychology emphasizes practical ethics, whereas Indian psychology makes individuals subject to discipline of a spiritually religious character. Chinese psychology is "situation centered" and socially controlled, with less "inward" introspection.

4. *The Hindu ideal of maturity emphasizes continuous dependency relations.*
In the Hindu extended family, the child, and to a lesser degree, the adolescent, occupies special status, rarely being required to wait for anything or to tolerate prolonged frustration. The child is praised and compared favorably to other children. This permissive style of child rearing results in adults with a lower tolerance for frustration and a consuming need for reassurance:

If no one has the time or patience to say that he is a good lad, then he himself has to proclaim it. Friends, events, and the like exist and are valued only to the extent that they supply these narcissistic needs. Deep, durable friendships become difficult and threatening especially outside the family ingroup. (Surya, 1969, p. 388)

A therapist working with a person of this culture would seek to reconcile independency strivings or to submerge the individual's complex interdependence. The concept of "mine, not mine" applied to material objects, time, thoughts, and emotions is branded as selfishness inside the extended family.

In the Indian extended family, social relations are diffused among parents, aunts, uncles, grandparents, and siblings. Each stage of the person's development marks a new network of dependency relations, with no final emergence into "adulthood" as implied in that concept in the Western sense. Each dependency relation is marked by a more or less rigid inherent status, perhaps most apparent in the caste system. Caste places strict limitations upon the liberty of the individual and constrains that person to unalterable conformity with what is called *jatidharma,* the rule of the caste. As a result, different personality patterns emerge for each of the different caste groups.

The *Kshatriyas* tend to be dominant, the *Brahmins* to be devoted to religious duties, the *Vaishyas* to be parsimonious, and the *Sudras* to be authoritarian. Rapid social change has diffused these caste distinctions, but the intricate network of dependency relations is still active in modern India.

The goal of maturity in traditional India is the achievement of a satisfying and continuous dependency. Independency longings are seen as leading to neurosis, contrary to Western concepts of mental health and adjustment. The notion of dependency is viewed positively in the Indian notions of *bandha, sambandha,* or *bandhavya* (bond, bondship, or kinship, respectively) and does not have the negative connotations of immaturity.

5. Interdependence in parent-child relationships is the Chinese ideal for personality development.

Differences between Chinese and American cultural child-rearing practices are reviewed by Chiu (1972). Chinese elders employ more severe discipline than American parents; Chinese parents emphasize mutual dependence in the family rather than self-reliance and independence; Chinese children see the world in terms of relationships rather than with an individualistic self-orientation; Chinese are more strongly tradition oriented and more situation centered as well as more sensitive to environmental factors—all of which result in a more passive than active attitude toward life. Consequently, Chinese children develop a cognitive style attuned to interdependence of relationships, whereas American children prefer to differentiate, analyze, and classify a stimulus complex in a more independent manner (Chiu, 1972). A key aspect to understanding these cultural differences lies in the parental role.

Chinese babies are normally breast-fed whenever they cry, even in public, and are carried on their mother's back and sleep in their parents' bed. Breast-feeding is prolonged, and the mother is typically extremely protective of the baby's bodily health, giving it herbs or medicines even when the baby is not sick. Continuous and immediate gratification is the ideal form of child rearing. Toilet training is very permissive: "It is the mother who 'trains' herself and sensitizes herself to the baby's rhythm. She does not train the infant to control himself. The Chinese mother assumes that she is responsible for her baby's function" (Tseng & Hsu, 1972, p. 7).

The Chinese child is taught to handle hostility without expressing anger. Aggressive behavior is severely punished. Sharing and collaterality are encouraged, thereby developing at first a "shame oriented" conscience in the child that later must lead to "internalized shame." There is little, or at least more subtle and controlled, sibling rivalry for parental favoritism, as siblings are punished for aggressive, competitive behavior toward one another. The handling of the child changes abruptly by about school age (6 years old), at which time the teacher is expected to assume control over the child's discipline. The contrast between indulgence for young children and subsequent harshness to instill discipline in maturing youngsters indicates a way of handling aggressive impulses through the basic social rhythm of *ho-p'ing* (harmony) and *hun-luan* (the confusion of vented aggression). The earlier permissiveness instills a strong sense of self-esteem and feelings of self-worth in children, and subsequent discipline teaches commitment to a family above self:

> Thus, the subsequent harsh disciplines of youth represent the parents' effort to arrest the development of that self-esteem which is the legacy of an indulged infancy. The child matures with a "selfish" longing to recapture the oral pleasures and the sense of power known early in life. (Solomon, 1971, p. 80)

The system of filial piety resembles a mutual exchange. Parents devote themselves to children, who in turn are expected to support the parents in old age. Relationships among family members provided a model for a moral virtue in all areas of society, with the ideals of family government becoming the basis of national statesmanship, sanctioned not merely by the family's emotional needs or political necessity but also by intellectual rationales with inherently religious meaning. Western parents send their maturing child into the world to gratify hostile or pleasure-seeking impulses outside the family:

> The Confucian solution, however, rejects "abandonment" as a solution to generational conflict in favor of the greater ends of parental security and the integrity of the family group. The son is to realize his social identity in a lifelong prolongation of his original state of dependency. (Solomon, 1971, p. 36)

In this interdependent relationship, children depend on parents, and later the aged adults depend on their children in a full cycle of reciprocity. The *Tao* of Taoism is not really otherworldly but emphasizes that humans should see themselves as embedded in an evolving creative cosmos.

CULTURE NOTE

As a child is totally dependent on the parent, the aged parent is totally dependent on the grown child. All other relationships are healthy to the extent that they reflect this level of dependency according to tradition.

Currently, in the People's Republic of China the breakdown of authority relations and equalization of the power of men over women or parents over children is expressed in new kinship terminology. The husband and wife now refer to each other as *ai jen,* or "loved one," suggesting equality. The wife now normally retains her maiden name, and children may assume either the mother's or father's name. Although traditional concepts of filialism are still evident, particularly in overseas and Nationalist Chinese society, through respect and obedience of children to parents, the arbitrary authority of parents over children has diminished. The child is encouraged to become relatively independent at an early stage, and this lack of parental supervision is reinforced by the mainland regime's manuals on child rearing (Vogel, 1969).

6. *Japanese personality is molded by sanctions of obligation through parental self-sacrifice.*
   The principal controversy in the field of Japanese culture and personality has revolved around different interpretations of child-rearing prac-

tices on the formation of adult personalities. Recent explanations have shifted from emphasizing formal customs, such as use of the cradle or toilet training, to less formalized but more complicated factors. The current emphasis favors affective relations between parents and child, measured by the length of time a child sleeps with its parents, who bathes a child, and other means of gratifying or expressing affective impulses (Norbeck & DeVos, 1961).

In Japan, mothers view their babies as extensions of themselves, with the psychological boundaries between mother and child more blurred than in Western cultures. Compared with Western models, there is less emphasis placed on verbal communication and more on physical contact, with the expectation that the mother will be totally devoted to the child. For the first five years of life, Japanese children experience unconditional love for what they are rather than for what they do. As they approach school age and must represent the family to the outside world, children's obligation is then emphasized. The duty to repay implies a duty to achieve in a cooperative framework on behalf of the family and within the family, contrasted with a competitive stance toward outsiders. The Japanese mother contributes to this sense of obligation: "By exhibiting an uncomplaining striving and endurance on behalf of her family, and by taking upon herself responsibility for their failures, she demonstrates that there is really something which deserves repaying" (DeVos, 1973, p. 156).

These obligations continue throughout the adult Japanese person's life until retirement. When old age is reached, the individual is again free. As Benedict (1946) points out, this developmental curve allows the most freedom at infancy and old age and the most control during the middle range of years, and so it is the *opposite* of the developmental responsibility curve of Western society. The Japanese concept of *ie,* or "family system," implies closely guarded family relationships as a model of total involvement with and commitment to a group, with other social commitments added in. Although modernization has eroded the *ie* tradition, it still serves as an ideal in Japanese society (Nakane, 1972).

As a consequence of rapid social change, presently there are coexisting traditional and modern family styles in Asia. Traditional values are less rigidly adhered to in a nontraditional family, and self-direction displaces passive compliance to parental commands; differential role expectations are allowed for men and women; and role differences of age-graded siblings place less responsibility on the eldest son. At the same time, the traditional values are maintained to some extent as ideals and continue to influence the development of personality.

The categories of development and maintenance assume a dichotomy that to some extent forces Asian psychologies along some artificial continuum, and a uniformity that disguises the tremendous variation among Asian cultures is implied. Several of the assertions presented here reflect the development of personality as well as its maintenance. The first three deal with maintenance of interpersonal relationships in Japan, the next two with authority relationships and consciousness in India, and the final two emphasize the importance of balance in applied psychology for Chinese personality maintenance.

7. *Japanese social behavior patterns are maintained through modeling the unique relationship between parents and children.*

In Japan, *amae* means to expect and depend upon another's benevolence and nurturence. The term is generally used to describe a child's relationship emphasizing its emotional qualities toward parents, particularly the mother, but it can also describe a special relationship between two adults, such as husband and wife or master and subordinate. There is no such concept in English, which reflects a difference in psychological viewpoint between the two cultures.

The unique aspect of Japanese dependency is the fluidity of relationships without fixed roles of inferiority and superiority. There is rather a mutuality in the bond of *amaeru,* implying the tendency and necessity to presume upon another person. This dependency need is both accessible and acceptable to the consciousness of a Japanese adult, and in fact social sanctions encourage it. The positive value of dependency sharply contrasts with Western views that characterize dependency negatively (Doi, 1969, p. 339). This positive attitude toward dependency is greatly influenced by an emphasis on immediate personal relations as a basic principle of Japanese culture.

Doi (1969) reviews the importance of *amae* relationships for understanding Japanese culture. With the decline of loyalty to the emperor and de-emphasis on repaying one's *on,* or spiritual debts to emperor, parents, and ancestors, that had regulated the psychology of *amae,* the delicate balance of powers maintaining Japanese personality is being disrupted. *On* strengthens in-group bonds but ultimately defines out-group members as beings for whom one does not need to show any moral consideration whatsoever.

8. *Personality maintenance in Japan depends on role-playing socially approved interactional patterns.*

Relationships in Japanese culture stress collectivism rather than individualism. Whereas the basic social unit in the West is the individual, and groups of individuals compose the state, Japanese society is more accurately understood as an aggregation of family units. Considerable importance is attached to esteem of the hierarchical order, with each person well defined in his or her role. Special attention is given to the family, clan, and nation as instrumental in defining loyalty through the mutual exchange of obligation.

In abstract terms, human relations are divided into "vertical" categories, such as the parent-child and superior-inferior relationship, and "horizontal" ones, such as that between siblings or collegial associates. Whereas the horizontal relationship has contributed to the formation of concepts of caste, as in India, or of class, as in America, the vertical relationship in Japan has taken the form of *oyabun-kobun,* as, for example, patron and protégé, landlord and tenant farmer, or master and disciple in Japanese bureaucracy. Hierarchy in the group is usually determined by seniority, and this frustrates modern Japanese management systems that emphasize individual competency. The sense of Japanese honor is closely tied to high esteem for hierarchical order. Nakamura (1964) claims this hierarchy motivates the moral faculty of Japanese self-reflection and identity:

> It posits before man the ideal of the infinite good that he should strive for, it induces him to reflect, by contrast, upon the sorry fact that he himself is too weak and helpless to refrain from doing evil; and thus it awakens within him the consciousness of man's sinfulness. (p. 513)

Nakane (1972) contrasts the notion of *attribute,* or any specific quality of an individual, with the notion of *frame,* or groups of individuals who share the same situation by living in the same neighborhood, working in the same company, or belonging to the same organization. The practical significance of a Japanese individual identifying oneself according to one's personal frame reference rather than one's individualized attributes is readily seen.

Role behavior, therefore, becomes the means of self-realization for even the modern Japanese. One is dedicated to and inseparable from one's role, probably dating back to basic Confucian values embodied in the *samurai* elite of the 19th century. Carefully prescribed role relationships, beginning with the family, have significantly contributed to the stability of Japanese society in spite of rapid social change but at the cost of de-emphasizing a sense of personal self. Achievement is not considered an individual phenomenon but, rather, the result of cooperation, both collaterally and hierarchically, in the combined and collective efforts of individuals. DeVos (1973) notes that "internalized sanctions make it difficult to conceive of letting down one's family or one's social groups and occupational superiors. In turn, those in authority positions must take paternal care of those for whom they have responsibility" (p. 185).

The importance of human relations is further evidenced in elaborate rules of propriety. The exchange of greetings, for example, is elaborate rather than simple. There is an abundance of honorific words and phrases in the Japanese language.

CULTURE NOTE

"It is said that if all such honorific words were taken out of Lady Murasaki's classic novel *Tale of Genji*, the book would be reduced to one half its length" (Nakamura, 1964, p. 407).

At the same time, there is an acknowledgment and acceptance of natural desires or sentiments as they are. It is in the social realm that conduct is carefully regulated; within one's inner self one can think whatever one pleases. The strong collectivity orientation in Japanese culture stresses stability and security but can result in stagnation, whereas the American adjustment, through self-orientation and individual freedom, can result in anomie.

9. *Internal contradictions in Japanese culture result in paradoxical personalities from the non-Japanese point of view.*

Nakakuki (1973) discusses the psychodynamic mechanisms in Japanese culture that are reconciled in a balance of contrasting tendencies. In the title of her book on Japan, Benedict (1946) juxtaposed the symbolism of a "chrysanthemum" for the soft, tranquil delicacy of aesthetic character in tension with the militaristic, authoritative attitude of a "sword." There is a similar dynamic balance throughout Japanese culture that reconciles self-expression with conformity. These contrasts are related to a basic tension between narcissism and masochism (Nakakuki, 1973).

The narcissistic element is indicated by achievement orientation, competitiveness, and ambitiousness in a self-centered, omnipotent, and grandiose manner. The Japanese self-consciously strive for higher goals to realize their ego ideal and are further motivated in this direction by a family-related, shame-oriented drive to be successful. The masochistic lifestyle is demonstrated in attitudes toward work, illness, and death whereby the person is duty bound to repay obligations. The ideals of self-denial are prominent in Japanese culture. The traditional Japanese family provides models in a narcissistic father through his omnipotence in the household and a masochistic mother whose task it is to maintain harmony in the family. The narcissistic pattern is related to shame and the masochistic pattern to guilt, as these two tendencies coexist in Japanese culture. The individual reconciles this tension by living in accord with prescribed roles within both family and society. The source of conflict most likely to occur is between individual ambition and role responsibility.

Mental health therefore depends on keeping these two opposing tendencies in balance so that the individual can move freely from masochistic hard work in the daytime to narcissistic relaxation at home without either tendency taking control. The notion of balance is also familiar in other Asian cultures—for example, the harmonious tension between *Yin* and *Yang*, the female and male principles of Chinese philosophy. This emphasis on the harmonious balance of forces once more underlines the basic theme of this chapter: that human behavior in Asian countries requires an understanding of *relational* units instead of the individualistic assumptions of Western personality theory.

10. *Rigid authority relationships do not necessarily inhibit achievement-oriented individuality.*

Although motivation patterns are greatly affected by family structure and ecology in any culture, the studies of families in non-Western countries have not confirmed predictive findings from Western research on the family (Chaubey, 1972). This may relate to the different role and function of the family in different societies. The Indian extended family, for example, usually consists of the husband, his wife and children, the husband's brothers, their wives and children, sisters, parents, and so on, all living corporately. This system has been cited as an obstacle to economic development because it inhibits the growth of personalities' motivation and even reduces incentives for hard work, which promotes idleness and irresponsibility among its members. The joint family is associated more with a dependency than an achievement orientation.

However, there is evidence that extended families may lead to enhancement of family agricultural success (Chaubey, 1972), and large families also may contribute to the entrepreneurial spirit in a village. Cooperation is required to achieve harmony in the shared living accommodations of a joint family. This cooperation is assumed to be voluntary, for members of a joint family are always able to separate with honor. Also, there is no clear evidence that the joint family is more favorable than the nuclear family in promoting achievement-oriented personality types. Still, the support provided in this joint family system and caste-based social organization maintains uniquely Indian personality traits of respect for authority and conformity. Sundberg, Rohila, and Tyler (1970) discovered that Indian adolescents were higher than Americans on deference and conformity but that Americans were not significantly more individualistic or autonomous.

In analyzing Indian school textbooks for orientations toward authority, Kakar (1971) found the "traditional-moral" source of authority to be the most popular. *Dharma* is the Hindu counterpart of traditional-moral, which prescribes duties through modes of conduct at different stages of the human life cycle. This traditional-moral base is supported by the "person" of the superior, as illustrated in the *Mahabharata* and other classical Hindu legends. The image of the superior in Kakar's findings was modeled after the paternal image of control or the maternal image of support but rarely the fraternal mode. The sanctions to maintain obedience included the arousal of guilt and the promise of emotional rewards. The "nurturant" mode appeared more effective than "assertive" styles of enforcement, resulting in an "actively submissive" mode of dependency in the core personality of Indian youths. Authority, often associated with the inhibition of freedom in Western psychology, is in India and elsewhere in Asia considered a liberating element.

11. *Experience rather than logic can serve as the basis for interpreting psychological phenomena.*

Whereas Western psychology seeks to integrate personality functions, the Indian ideal is toward dissociation and even detachment of higher from lower functions. The ego has a "witness function" in Indian thinking through watching the body suffer but essentially as a nonparticipant. This structure requires explicit acceptance of a higher consciousness beyond human control, with a capacity to influence behavior, as well as the individual's capacity to be in communication with power.

The more subjective method can be compared to a man looking out over the landscape from a high mountain watchtower, searching for the route he must travel to get where he wants to go. He does not study the total landscape but only those aspects pertinent to his route, which is almost certainly not going to be a straight line. Thus, although "reality" in the higher sense might be unobtainable within the confines of logical thought and reason, the alternative criteria, through experience, seek to go beyond the boundaries of logically abstract cognition. Even abstract ideas are expressed in concrete terms, endowed with substantiality in most schools of Indian philosophy. The idea of "being" is more important than the more abstract notion of "becoming." The universal tendency is more important than the individualistic attitude. By looking at psychological phenomena in terms of experience rather than logically, Buddhist psychology deals with criteria of reality that do not always differentiate between actual and ideal or fact and fantasy.

CULTURE NOTE

Existence is compared to a river, which has its source in birth and its mouth in death, winding through a continuous process of existence in which consciousness unites persons with one another and brings together the different moments or phases within one's life.

All components are constantly changing in relationship to one another, giving the illusion of constancy, of "ego identity," or of an unchangeable personality:

> The relation between subject and object is that of two moving systems: if their movement is exactly of the same kind, it creates the impression of non-movement; if their movement is of different kinds, that system which is the object of perception appears to move, while the system of the perceiving subject seems to be stationary. (Govinda, 1961, p. 130)

The aim of spiritual training is to achieve higher stages of consciousness through experience and exploring inner potentials through meditation.

Once one understands the relativity of the objectively perceived world and the facility of consciousness to expand beyond this ordinary level of experience, one is moving toward liberation. By participating in higher and higher levels of consciousness, one ultimately approaches the final state of *Nirvana*.

12. *Life is a dialectical, paradoxical process reconciling opposing forces.*

Although authority provides security against conflict and material deprivation through reliance on a united, dominant, and personalized political leadership, there are limits to the manipulative or harsh qualities of that authority. The five moral or natural relationships of the Chinese (*wu-lun*) describe a pattern of deference and obligation between ruler and subject, father and son, husband and wife, brothers and friends. Solomon (1971) differentiates between this expectation and the notion of an individual's social role because, unlike a role, which is defined in terms of the action of the *individual,* Chinese emphasis is on the *relationship* between individuals. The Confucian tradition defined an individual's social identity not so much by what he had achieved as by those to whom he was related through ties of kinship or personal loyalty.

A dependence on hierarchical authority rather than self-assertion reflects the authoritarianism of China's social tradition, wherein order is maintained through a structured, hierarchical series of relationships. The need for social harmony and peace is balanced with the need to express hostility and aggression. Children develop a fear of expressing hostility toward those in authority through their early experiences with harsh parental authority. They learn to "put into [the] stomach" the pain of parental discipline and to "eat bitterness" rather than act out dangerous emotions when provoked by an older family member. At the same time, children learn that hostile feelings can be appropriately released against those subordinate in status or power. In status-equal relationships, the intense expectations of friendship to embody the gratification of dependency needs, especially in times of difficulty, are so strong that even friendship takes on the flavor of a hierarchical obligation (Solomon, 1971, p. 133).

The irony is that the strength of authority, or dependent submission to it designed to create harmony, actually generates tension attributed to holding in resentment and hatred of oppressive authority. At some point, the critical flash point will be reached and the system will explode into unrestrained conflict, overthrowing the superior authority and allowing another power to reorganize the confusion in a new hierarchical ordering of social relationships. In China, early-life experiences and political ortho-doxy are combined in tension to give cyclic and balanced coherence to otherwise contradictory forces.

13. *Changes in political systems affect the interpretation of personality structures.*

China's revolution grew out of a potential for unrestrained mass violence. It stressed political education as a way of redirecting conscious-ness of the aggressive response to purposeful political action. The revolu-tion combined emotional manipulation and political education as comple-mentary dimensions of mass mobilization. By 1949, those on the Chinese mainland were experiencing an idealized, nonhierarchical brotherhood of friendship as a solution to problems of anger. However, the possibility of peer conflict, even in this idealized system, gives renewed meaning to the need for strong political authority, and the sense of ambivalence and tension remains unalleviated (Solomon, 1971, p. 122).

The Confucian order stressed emotional restraint and "eating bitter-ness" as the appropriate response of subordinates, but the revolution rejected this dependency orientation. Where Confucianism alluded to the virtues of tranquility and interpersonal harmony, Mao (Tse-Tung) made activism the key to the behavior of the ideal Party cadre. Where fear and avoidance of conflict characterized the "cultivated" response to social tension in the traditional society, Mao stressed the importance of criticism and controlled struggle in resolving those issues that have blocked China's social advance (Solomon, 1971, p. 513).

CONCLUSION

Yum (1994) distinguishes between North American and East Asian perspectives on interpersonal relationships. Whereas the East Asian perspective depends on relationship and context, the North American perspective depends on objective and universal rules. East Asian relation-ships are long term, with asymmetrical reciprocity; North American relationships are symmetrical or contractual in reciprocity. East Asians distinguish more sharply between in-groups and out-groups. They prefer informal intermediaries who are personally known, whereas North Americans prefer professional intermediaries on contract. East Asians have more overlap of personal and public relations than North Americans. East Asians pay more attention to the process; North Americans are more outcome oriented. East Asians have more differentiated linguistic codes depending on the situation than North Americans and are more likely to use indirect than direct communication as a norm. Kim (1994) summarizes the differences in terms of their meaning:

> Based on an organic, holistic and cyclic perspective the East has developed an epistemology that emphasizes direct, immediate and aesthetic components in human nature's experience of the world. The ultimate aim of human learning is to transcend the immediate, differentiated self and to develop an integrative perception of the undifferentiated universe, that is, to be spiritually one with the universe and to find the eternal within the present moment. On the other hand, the West, founded on the cosmology of dualism, determinism and materialism, encourages an outlook that is rational, analytic and indirect. History is viewed as a linear progression from the past into the future. The acquisition of knowledge is not so much for spiritual enhancement as for utilization to improve the human condition. (p. 421)

The Eastern and Western viewpoints are not competing but, rather, complementary views of reality, and the false dichotomy of materialism versus spiritualism and of West versus East must be transcended. Each must be understood within its own context.

These assertions indicate that the Western view of the individual as an independent person with freedom of will, entirely responsible for one's own life, and moving upward in the social scheme is not the only way of seeing life and truth. The Eastern person is surrounded by different traditions, different views of right and wrong, and different notions of proper relations and is treated differently in childhood by parents and relatives. Consequently, the Asian personality can be expected to develop a worldview guided by relationship strategies rather than individualistic strivings, family and group identity rather than selfish ambitions, and submission to authority rather than rebelliousness.

EXERCISE

WESTERN AND NON-WESTERN ASSUMPTIONS

Objective

The labels "Western" and "non-Western" relate less to geography and more to a culturally learned personal style. The scaled dimensions below allow you to identify your own personal style on dimensions of Western and non-Western contrasting assumptions discussed earlier.

Instructions

Rate your own culturally learned tendency toward one or another of the extreme Western or non-Western contrasting alternatives in the scaled dimensions below. Compare your profile of tendencies with the profile of a trusted colleague completing the same exercise. Discuss the similarities and differences between you and your colleague as well as the sources of your tendencies.

WESTERN		RATE YOURSELF						NON-WESTERN
Life before death	1	2	3	4	5	6	7	Life after death
Individualized self	1	2	3	4	5	6	7	Spiritualized self
Self-centered	1	2	3	4	5	6	7	Social centered
Independence as healthy	1	2	3	4	5	6	7	Dependence as healthy
Child is free	1	2	3	4	5	6	7	Child is interdependent
No obligation toward parent	1	2	3	4	5	6	7	Big obligation to parents
Child/parent independency	1	2	3	4	5	6	7	Child/parent dependency
Individualism	1	2	3	4	5	6	7	Collectivism
Truth is clear	1	2	3	4	5	6	7	Truth is paradoxical
Authority inhibits growth	1	2	3	4	5	6	7	Growth requires authority
Logic oriented	1	2	3	4	5	6	7	Experience oriented
One-directional goals	1	2	3	4	5	6	7	Two-directional balance
Personality is not contextual	1	2	3	4	5	6	7	Personality is contextual

Debriefing

By applying the assumptions describing Western and non-Western contrasting approaches to understanding in the previous chapter you have an opportunity to examine and clarify your own underlying assumptions. Identify specific situations or cultural contexts where you might respond differently than you have on the scale above and explain why your position would change according to the context.

What problems might come up as you work with clients and/or colleagues whose assumptions are different from your own?

As you examine textbooks on counseling, can you identify the underlying Western and/or non-Western assumptions implicit in the texts?

What are the consequences for counseling of a shift in population and socioeconomic-political power from a Western to a non-Western basis?

Religious and Spiritual Contexts

- ■ **Primary Objective** Describe endogenous resources for counseling

- ■ **Secondary Objectives** (1) Examine the importance of spiritual and religious resources for counseling and (2) Describe the psychological function of "tondi" among the Toba Batak

Counselors and therapists are frequently trained to isolate their values from the psychotherapy process. The assumption that religious and spiritual factors should be left out of counseling and counselor training seems to be based on the original Freudian assumption that counseling is a technical "surgical" procedure separate from value issues. How can religious values be expressed in therapy without abusing the therapist's power and the client's vulnerability? Counselors who choose to be noncommittal or "objective" are likely to fail because (a) silence may be viewed as supporting a value position, and (b) they unintentionally communicate values to their clients that may or may not be perceived accurately. Alternatively, counselors will benefit from training in assessing the spiritual perspective of a client's behavior. Counseling is not a value-free process, and spiritual factors may become important in the practice of counseling by complementing other approaches and providing new perspectives of empirical data.

Counselors do not typically sympathize with or understand the cultural aspects of their clients' religious and spiritual context. Although there has been increased sensitivity to issues of race, gender, and ethnicity in counseling, tolerance for religious and spiritual factors has not advanced significantly. The emphasis is on interpersonal rather than intrapsychic functioning. Bergin (1991) reviews empirical research literature that suggests religious and spiritual factors facilitate healthy functioning:

> Analysis of personality and social functioning separate from mental illness *per se* show considerable evidence that religious involvement is negatively correlated with problems of social conduct such as sexual permissiveness, teenage pregnancy, suicide, drug abuse, alcohol use and to some extent deviant or delinquent acts. There is also a positive association between religiosity and self esteem, family cohesion and perceived well being. (p. 401)

More traditional Chinese students contend that the "counselor" of first resort for them is to go inside themselves and learn from Confucian sayings learned in childhood from their parents. This inside-the-person resource applies to many—perhaps most—people of the world who depend first and foremost on spiritual and religious resources for counseling. These alternatives to talk therapy become extremely important in several ways. First, it is important for counselors with a more secular orientation to recognize the importance of spiritual resources for their more religious clients. Second, these inner resources provide an important resource that can be mobilized by good counseling for the client's benefit. Third, counselors should recognize that—in terms of numbers—talk therapy is actually the more exotic form of counseling in a world where the vast majority depend on spiritual and religious meaning for healthy functioning (Pedersen, 1993a). This has resulted in a dichotomy between science and religion, as expressed by Weiss (1995):

> Contrary to science, in religion the preexistence of a singular core of truth is not agreed to be discoverable through some regulated means by its seekers. There is little doubt that religionists believe that there is such a truth. Freedom of religion, however, permits as many "core truths" and searches for these as there are observers. Everyone is entitled to his or her own religious or private beliefs, without any necessary proof or methods to

demonstrate these, but science is a group consensus, moderated and regulated by experts. (p. 544)

When everything seems to be changing in a personal or social perspective what are the things that don't change? These unchanging elements act as a hinge on the door of change. The changing process can only occur relative to these unchanging elements. These unchanging elements are essentially "religious." There is a considerable literature on how religion inhibits change and on how religion is irrelevant to change (Bellah, 1965). Religion also facilitates change by providing a point of traditional reference through which change may occur and this suggests how religion can be viewed as the basis for counseling.

CULTURE NOTE

The Anglican Bishop Pike (personal communication) suggested that when organized religion is more popular, spiritualism and spirituality are less popular and vice versa, as though spirituality and religiosity are in some ways similar but in other ways quite different.

ACCESSING RELIGIOUS AND
SPIRITUAL RESOURCES

There is a difference between religion and spirituality. Spirituality is more inclusively defined as one's place in the universe, whereas religion refers to the specific religious faith and practice resulting from a person's spirituality. Spirituality is broader and more inclusive in meaning than religion: "A typical distinction between religion and spirituality is found in the demarcation between spirituality as a personal affirmation of a transcendent connectedness in the universe and religion as the creedal, institutional, and ritual expression of spirituality that is associated with world religions and denominations" (Kelly, 1995, p. 4).

In the following citations, the term *religion* is used with regard to specific faiths and practices, whereas the term *spirituality* is used to describe the more broad and inclusive phenomenon. Spiritual and religious factors are important to understanding cultural and value differences among clients. Along with cultural variables these spiritual and religious perspectives are frequently minimalized by counselors. Pate and Bondi (1992)

TABLE 5.1. Major Religions or Belief Forms of the World (in population)

Religion	World
Christians	1,869,751,000
Roman Catholics	1,042,501,000
Protestants	382,374,000
Orthodox	173,560,000
Anglicans	75,847,000
Other Christians	195,470,000
Muslims	1,014,372,000
Nonreligious	912,874,000
Hindus	751,360,000
Buddhists	334,002,000
Atheists	241,852,000
Chinese folk religionists	140,956,000
New religionists	123,765,000
Tribal religionists	99,736,000
Sikhs	19,853,000
Jews	18,153,000
Shamanists	10,854,000
Confucians	6,230,000
Baha'is	5,742,000
Jains	3,927,000
Shintoists	3,336,000
Other religionists	19,183,000
Total population	5,575,954,000

Encyclopaedia Britannica (1994 edition).

discuss the implications "that more than 90% of the general public profess a belief in God, compared with 40%-70% of psychiatrists and 43% of psychologists" (p. 109). Table 5.1 demonstrates the estimated membership of the larger religious groups around the world.

CULTURE NOTE

If the world were a village of 1,000 people, there would be 300 Christians (including 188 Catholics, 81 Protestants, 31 Orthodox, and 30 others), 180 Muslims, 130 Hindus, 60 Buddhists, 3 Jews, and 297 believers in other indigenous religions.

Whereas talk therapy tends to rely on exogenous or outside-the-person resources, primal alternatives to talk therapy emphasize the importance of endogenous or inside-the-person sources of spiritual empowerment. Many of these indigenous alternatives developed outside the European-American historical envelope, and their counseling functions were maintained by religious rituals. Studying these alternatives is useful not only because some remnants of these modes likely survive in our own deep unconscious understanding but also because some of the primal alternatives retain insights that industrialized society has forgotten. Smith (1991) suggests that a revival of interest in primal therapeutic approaches is under way:

> Dismayed by the relentless utilitarianism of technological society and its seeming inability to contain its power to destroy both people and planet, citified peoples have come to hope that a fundamentally different way of life is possible, and they latch onto primal peoples to support that hope. (pp. 380-381)

Religion and psychotherapy have presented contrasting perspectives of orthodox, atheistic, neutralist, and moderate viewpoints with psychological advocates of each perspective.

Torrey (1986; see also Lee & Armstrong, 1995) describes the variety of generic terms for therapists in other cultures. For example, the term *witchdoctors* is used by Westerners to describe African therapists, although the Africans themselves use other terms like *izinyanga* in South Africa, *ganga* among the Zulu, *mganga* among Swahili, *chimbuki* among the Ndembu, *mulogo* in Uganda, *bulomba* in Sierra Leone, *babalawo* among the Yoruba, and *baroom xam-xam* among the Lebou. In other cultures, *medicine man* is used for North American Indian tribes, *shaman* originated in Siberia for the Tungusian tribes, *curandero* in Latin America, *medium* in the Caribbean, *marabout* in Muslim countries, and more generic terms like *soothsayer, seer, diviner,* and *sorcerer* for different other cultures. In each case, the therapist's primary function is spiritual:

> The witchdoctors, being semi-religious in function, were especially anathematized by the colonizing whites, who often were there to spread the Christian faith. Witchdoctors quickly became equated with the devil. Thus it was, and still is, difficult for us to see them as they really are. . . . I have chosen instead to deal directly with the term witchdoctors so that psychotherapists in other cultures, performing the same function as psychiatrists

in Western cultures, cannot be dismissed with a single pejorative epithet. (Torrey, 1986, p. 8)

Understanding a client's religious development is helpful in the assessment and counseling of clients.

Interest in religion has risen recently from the popularity of Eastern religions in the late 1960s and early 1970s to the prominence of organized religious groups in the political arena in the 1980s and 1990s, the popularity of new religions and cults among the disenchanted and excluded, the appeal to moral and religiously flavored arguments in the public discussion of social issues such as abortion and equal rights, and the appeal to religious truth as a moral standard in judging the betrayal of public trust in Watergate, Iranscam, and other scandals (Lee & Armstrong, 1995).

CULTURE NOTE

The fiscal viability of televangelism and the sensitivity of public figures, from political leaders to terrorists, justifying their positions according to religious evidence demonstrates the strength of contemporary religion.

Tart (1975) describes the position of transpersonal psychology that psychology has excluded the spiritual side of human nature by minimalizing, trivializing, or labeling it pathological. As he points out, this has not been true of psychologies outside the Euro-American envelope:

We are twentieth-century Westerners, with science in general and scientific psychology in particular as important parts of our backgrounds. Some of us may be able to drop that background and accept a particular transpersonal psychology as our primary frame of reference. But for many of us, what we learn about the spiritual side of ourselves must at least coexist with, and preferably integrate with, our heritage of Western science and culture. So I think our job will be to bridge the spiritual and our Western scientific side. (p. 5)

Worthington (1989) suggests five reasons for counselors to attend to the implications of religion in their understanding of development and intervention:

- A high percentage of the population in the United States identifies itself as religious.
- Many people who are undergoing emotional crises spontaneously consider religion in their deliberations about their problem.
- Many clients are reluctant to bring up religious considerations because of their perception that therapy is an essentially secular process.
- Therapists are generally not as religiously oriented as their clients.
- As a result of being less religiously oriented than their clients, many therapists are not as well informed about religion as might be appropriate.

PSYCHOLOGICAL THEORIES OF RELIGION

Psychological-stage theories have classified religious beliefs in a variety of ways. Piaget's theory of cognitive development has been used to measure the development of religious faith as part of the maturation process. Kohlberg's theory of moral development has also been used to measure the importance of religious faith in decision making. Erickson's theory of psychosocial development provides another perspective for measuring the development of religious faith. Other psychological theories have incorporated religious factors in theories of personal transition, coping, stress management, and cognitive behavioral theories—for example, Allport's development of religious sentiments and Jung's individuation. Religious and spiritual factors influence individual behavior in several ways (Worthington, 1989). First, religious commitment and involvement influences a person's behavior. Second, religious and spiritual factors can be important to the context. Third, religious or spiritual explanations of a specific event may trigger a person's attributions.

Lomov, Budilova, Koltsova, and Medvedev (1993) describe the unique mix of scientific thinking and idealistic religious thinking in Russian culture: "One can hardly understand the development of psychological thought within the system of Russian culture, the regularities of the development connected with the spiritual tradition, and the historical way of Russia without due consideration of interaction between the secular and religious constituents" (p. 108). Psychological thought in Russia has combined data from natural sciences with the concept of a "vital force" with spiritual origins. Religious organizations in Russia have helped believers recognize the state of disagreement, discrepancy, or disintegration of spiritual life through confession, "sobering" the mind and heart, "looking into" minds, and concentrating on spiritual forces. Training in these practices is called "the inner making" of psychological states through training as distinguished from "the outer making," which is achieved through asceticism.

Worthington (1989) describes psychological issues in judging the quantity, type, and quality of religious information:

- How formal should the assessment be?
- To what degree is the content of a person's faith to be assessed versus the process of "faithing"?
- How is religion involved in the life of the client?
- How mature is the client in one's religious life as well as in one's cognitive, moral, and socioemotional life?
- To what degree, if any, is the client's religion related to the diagnosis?
- To what degree is the client's religion involved in the etiology of the problem?
- Is religion part of the client's identity?
- Is the counselor competent to deal with a client's religious and spiritual concerns?

As yet, though, there is little research on the outcomes of religious counseling or dynamic spiritual factors in a client's evolving perspective.

Bergin (1991) surveyed 800 clinical psychologists, clinical social workers, marriage and family therapists, and psychiatrists about values in mental health on which there was a high consensus as to what constitutes a healthy person:

> being a free agent; having a sense of identity and feelings of worth; being skilled in interpersonal communication, sensitivity, nurturance and trust; being genuine and honest; having self control and personal responsibility; being committed in marriage, family and social relationships; having a capacity to forgive others and oneself; having orienting values and meaningful purposes; having deepened self awareness and motivation for growth; having adaptive coping strategies for managing stresses and crises; finding fulfillment in work; and practicing good habits of physical health. (pp. 394-395)

According to Bergin's data, 77% of those surveyed agreed with the statement "I try hard to live by my religious beliefs," and 46% agreed with the statement "My whole approach to life is based on my religion."

At the same time, only 29% of these therapists rated religious content as important in counseling.

INTERPRETING RELIGIOUS EXPERIENCES

Indigenous psychology is not an easy answer to modern problems. As Katz (1993) points out, the straight path must be lived before it can be understood. Healing becomes nothing less than a transformation in the search for meaning, balance, connectedness, and wholeness:

> In the West there is an emphasis on technological intervention to cure illness, breaking the process down into isolated categories such as the "change agent" and "target population." Indigenous people, on the other hand, focus more on the emotional and spiritual context in healing the individual and the community, which are seen as inextricably interconnected. (p. 333)

Valla and Prince (1989) report that, based on three international surveys, about 20% to 40% of the population reports having had a religious or mystical experience. The more positive explanations of religious experiences are as dynamic and intelligible functions of the psyche reacting to life's problems. The religious experiences may function as a self-righting or self-healing mechanism to increase self-esteem and increase one's coping repertoire. Religious or spiritual experiences may be a self-righting mechanism for regulating mental health just as other mechanisms regulate body temperature, blood sugar, acid base levels, blood pressure, and pulse rate to facilitate health generally.

Prince (1984) divided psychotherapeutic healing systems into exogenous methods oriented to external resources and endogenous methods oriented to internal resources such as morphinelike endorphin substances in the person's physiology. Of these two systems, the exogenous is more familiar, but endogenous alternatives to talk therapy also exist:

> In this context, I argued that healers around the world have learned to manipulate and elaborate upon a number of these endogenous mechanisms, including sleep, dreams, dissociated states, religious experiences, and psychoses in a variety of ways to bring about resolution of life problems and alleviation of suffering. (pp. 60-61)

These endogenous resources are mobilized by events or trained healers.

CULTURE NOTE

Industrialized cultures have come to depend on exogenous resources such as counselors and therapists while their ability to mobilize endogenous spiritual resources has died out with the language for some Native American Indians and indigenous people elsewhere.

Eastern religions provide working models of this spiritual perspective. Eastern psychologies are radically different from traditional Western perspectives. The great religions, in their more mystical aspects, have a common core of perennial wisdom, philosophy, and psychology. By combining Eastern and Western psychologies we may better understand phenomena such as alternate states of consciousness, state-dependent learning, and meditation to suggest that psychology is a multistate discipline for understanding the full range of consciousness and corresponding worldviews. Religious experiences become one example of endogenous resources and primal alternatives to talk therapy where the individual goes inside oneself rather than to outside persons to seek healing functions.

THE COSMOLOGY OF THE
TOBA BATAKS AS A HEALING RESOURCE

One vividly contrasting example of how spiritual and religious resources can facilitate the counseling process is demonstrated by the Toba Bataks of North Sumatra in Indonesia. This tribal unit of about 3 million persons, whose traditional homeland surrounds Lake Toba in North Sumatra, is unique among the 380 different tribal groups in Indonesia. First, the Bataks have their own language and culture derived from "proto-Malay" ancestors migrating out of Asia. Second, being surrounded by strong Islamic tribal units, they have converted to Christianity in part to maintain their separate identity. Third, they have the reputation as being particularly aggressive and strong willed. Their belief system incorporates an internalized spiritual element called the *tondi* that plays an important role in Batak society for managing sociopsychological issues (Kraemer, 1958; Lumbantobing, 1956; Simon, 1914; Warneck, 1909).

The example of the Toba Bataks is likely unfamiliar to most readers and, for that reason, perhaps less controversial or political in its meaning. If one examines and judges the Batak alternative interpretation from its own traditional perspective and in its own cultural context, the meaning behind this thinking will become clear. Imagine yourself a visitor in a traditional Toba Batak community, learning this unfamiliar perspective and coming to understand its internal logic. Be aware of your own internal dialogue judging this perspective.

The "traditional" Toba Bataks experience all cosmic space as a totality of the underworld, middleworld, and upperworld, in which each layer has a special function and through which the harmony of existence is made possible. Elimination of one level or the disruption of this harmony would mean the annihilation of the cosmos. Symbolic of their interrelations is the "tree of life" (thought to be a banyan tree) reaching from the underworld to the upperworld. This tree, symbolic of the High God, unites all existence as a representation of cosmos and order (Vergouwen, 1964).

The Toba Bataks do not emphasize quantitatively measurable time but experience every space of time qualitatively and concretely. Special days are set aside for building a house, fighting a war, or getting married as either favorable, indifferent, or unfavorable. The day itself possesses its own amount of power and holiness, bliss, and doom.

Space is viewed as neither homogeneous nor neutral but with substance. Each point of the compass has its value, with power to affect the life and prosperity of people. The value of each point of the compass varies according to the time of the year, implying that the substance of space and its power is determined by time. However, the course of time can only be determined through changes in space, without which there is no notion of time. Time and space form an essential unity in the cosmic religious view.

There is no clear distinction between representation and identity in Toba Batak religious thought, with the symbol participating in the reality it represents and representation equating identity. The child is held responsible for the debts of the parent, as is the village *radja* (chief) for those of the community. The notion of symbolic power representation includes the animation of natural objects or carved god-representations that can be punished if not sufficiently efficacious. Conflicting powers lose their individual independence and are reconciled in a totalitarian unity.

The Toba Bataks do not distinguish clearly between the different powers and aspects of the High God because they experience each part as a totality, each microcosm as a macrocosm. This synthetic-concrete approach to reality of the Toba Bataks contrasts sharply with the analytic categorical approach of modern scientific thought. Belief in the High God is belief in a world order, excluding arbitrariness and identifying God and community. The High God not only created the cosmos but is the cosmos, with people the microcosms. Every Toba Batak is a manifestation of the High God and the *adat* (customary law) that guides the individual and community guards the microcosmic reflection of macrocosmic order.

Their personal and social life is permeated with religious meaning, guided by religious motives, and dominated by spiritual concepts such as the belief in gods, animistic veneration of ancestors, and fearful awareness of the dynamic cosmos in which they live. This religious element was interwoven with and interrelated to all practices and activities.

Being dependent on their own power and surrounded by potentially dangerous forces, it is natural for the Toba Bataks to seek magico-religious means of augmenting their power. Yet in their quest for nourishment and well-being, they avoid contact with supernatural powers except for self-protection. Missionaries misunderstood this as a basic materialistic anxiety for preservation of earthly goods, an exploitation of religious power for private advantage, prosperity, and prestige.

The Toba Batak conception of virtue and merit is sometimes diametrically opposed to the Judaeo-Christian ethic. They consider bravery essential for entrance into the Kingdom of the Dead. As a token of this bravery, the guardian of souls is likely to ask a male how many heads he has taken. An essential provision for posterity is the continuation of the family. To remain unmarried or, in regions where sexual intercourse between unmarried persons is no disgrace, to practice abstinence is a serious violation.

The ethical paradox is that "the murderer finds entrance to the spirit world, whereas the man he murders does not, because he stands condemned by the judgment of God; and the immoral person, because he has fulfilled his sexual obligations, is accepted whereas the chaste person is rejected" (Simon, 1914, p. 103). In like manner, warriors who die in battle cannot enter the Kingdom of the Dead because their deaths prove that supernatural judgment has ruled against them, whereas those who flee the battlefield out of cowardice are justified by the gods. The lepers and sickly deserve to have their houses burned down around them because terrible disease is a clear sign of divine judgment.

Religion for the Toba Bataks is acceptance of a higher reality as the object of their fear and worship on which they can depend as a powerful and resourceful ally. This religious view ignores any moral criterion or principle such as a person's responsibility to God or love for neighbors or even selfishness in favor of self-preservation. Although a person's life is permeated with religious motives, this is actually a cover for the desires and egotism of that person. It was the power or promise of power that first attracted the Toba Bataks to Christianity. Fear and worship of God stand beyond any moral criterion and to follow God is to share in God's superiority, power, and prestige.

Yet because the supreme law is self-preservation, egotism became self-justifying, and it is preferable to exploit power, even divine power, than to obey it. The Toba Bataks desire not only to serve God but to possess God. If an undertaking is successful, then it must be the will of God. If a marriage is childless, then God cannot have willed it and the couple must divorce.

TAKING CARE OF ONE'S *TONDI*

The spirit-peopled world of the Toba Bataks is designed around their special concern for their own personified *tondi*, which has been translated as "soul stuff." The descriptions of *tondi* give it qualities of a material object, although formless as air. A distinction is made between the static condition of the body and the dynamic mobility embodied in the *tondi*, which as a whole dwells in all parts of the body. The *tondi* and person are integral to each other and not separate entities. All experiences are ascribed to the activity of one's *tondi* much as we attribute behavior to an individual's personality. When represented as " life stuff," the *tondi* is also present in animals and plants but not as abundantly. Nearly every object of nature is thought to have a prescribed quantity of animating *tondi* that can be brought into focus by special circumstances.

The *tondi* is seen as having not only an independent existence but the ability to influence present and future happenings. The *tondi* of living persons, of the deceased, and of those still to come is with the High God in the upperworld and associated with God in such a way that through the *tondi* the High God is in all persons and beings. The entire religious life of the Toba Bataks, seeking their welfare in this world and the next, is fulfilled through nursing their own *tondi* according to its sometimes fickle whims.

The *tondi* determines each person's fate even before birth, asking for a leaf from the Tree of Life on which is written that person's destiny. The *tondi* is free to choose whichever role in life it wishes, and the Toba Bataks call their destiny that which their *tondi* asked for. If things go well, they credit their *tondi* for having made a good choice, but if things go badly, the *tondi* is blamed. A person's wishes need not agree with those of one's *tondi*, but it is the will of the *tondi*, not the person, that prevails.

The Toba Bataks might react defiantly against their *tondi* but are usually submissive, adopting a fatalistic attitude and calm resignation to whatever happens. Both God and people are bound by the lot that one's *tondi* has chosen. The *tondi* can be enticed to wander from the body by magical acts against the person, or it can be displaced by evil spirits. If it wanders or becomes sufficiently weak, the individual becomes sick and dies. To remain well and strong, a person makes an occasional offering to one's *tondi* so that it will warn one against harm, inspire one with courage in war, and become one's closet ally in the struggle against the world.

The *tondi* is neither the better self in people nor even their spiritual side as Westerners might understand it. The *tondi* does not punish or leave the person for having done evil and, unlike a conscience, has little to do with moral judgments of right or wrong. It might, however, react unfavorably toward a person's failure to comply with established tradition. The Toba Bataks believe that each person's *tondi* is asked by the High God if the person is generous (e.g., able to acquire property), is brave, and has children, judging each *tondi* according to values that prevail in the middle-world life.

The *tondi* exists in every aspect of the person—hair, fingernails, sweat, tears, urine, excrement, shadow, and even the person's name. Possession of a person's belongings enables others to secure sympathetic magical power over that person's *tondi*. For this reason, every piece of clothing, strand of hair, footprint, object on which one's shadow has fallen, and even one's name are carefully guarded. Toba Bataks do not reveal their first name and instead are typically known only by their last sib-group name.

The *tondi* of persons are mutually related to one another, with interacting influences traced to their *tondi*. The *tondi* demonstrates its strength in a person's wealth, the number of sons, daughters, or grandchildren; fidelity in carrying on ancestral traditions; and courage and eloquence. It is important that the *tondi* be kept strong and secure in the person, indicated by the greeting *Horas!* (meaning hard, strong, firm-fixed). Another common expression is *pir ma tondi mardingin, horas tondi matogu* (may your *tondi* be firm and cool, may your *tondi* be firm and strong), for coolness promotes the *tondi*'s stability. A customary farewell is *Horas be ma!* (may both of us be strong).

The *tondi* has no strong allegiance to the person it inhabits and so could be lured away if both the *tondi* and the person cannot live together peacefully. Because the *tondi* does not essentially belong to the person and might have little interest in the maintenance of its temporary dwelling, persons serve their *tondi* by honoring it and feeding it well. Occasional celebrations called *mangupa* are held either as a mark of gratitude to a *tondi* that has undergone difficulty or as encouragement to withstand approaching danger. The *mangupa* consists of a group eating a common meal together, appropriate speeches being made, and presents being exchanged. Eating is an important ceremony, for food is rich in *tondi* power and must be eaten in peace and quiet without disturbance. The important thing in eating is not the food itself but the *tondi* power the food contains. When food is sacrificed, the spirits receive the *tondi* power and the worshipers only the material portion left over.

At feasts and festivals, a meal is thought to bring one's *tondi* into a pleasant frame of mind so that blessings can be exchanged, problems resolved, important decisions made, harmony established, and a favorable atmosphere created. A meal is the appropriate ceremony preceding important decisions or judgments and a means of thanksgiving after the aims of the meeting had been achieved.

The ceremony of cannibalism formerly practiced by the Toba Bataks was designed to secure *tondi* power through consuming human parts especially potent in *tondi,* such as the blood, heart, palms of the hands, and soles of the feet. Cannibalism was appropriate punishment for adultery, robbery, intermarriage within the clan, and treacherous attacks on village houses or persons during wars of importance between villages (Wurtzburg, 1954). The accused had a regular trial, and the sentence was formally passed before a public assembly in the presence of chiefs from neighboring villages. On other occasions, a person might volunteer to be eaten as a means of gaining status among peers and immortality through the bodies of their descendants. Either as a particularly good volunteer or as a dangerous criminal, this person represented a source of extraordinary power. By eating the powerful person Toba Bataks hoped to share in the power as well as protect themselves against that person's spirit.

The Toba Bataks venerate and fear spirits as the most powerful middleworld force on which everyday welfare depends. When a person dies, the *tondi* leaves them but remains a power in the middleworld of ancestral spirits who must be appeased through the proper observance of sacred rites and customs they instituted during life. Family include both the living and the dead, with the fortunes of the living dependent on the good will of the ancestors and the welfare of those ancestors dependent on homage and sacrifices by the living for their benefit. The dead are half friend and half enemy, jealous of the living, envious of their good fortune, but entirely dependent on them for regular sacrifices because if the memory of a dead ancestor is forgotten, then existence ceases. If a Toba Batak dies without descendants, no one feels bound to serve and honor that person after death.

The descendants, however, are assured that by sacrifices they can secure assistance from the ancestors and thereby avoid disaster, illness, and misfortune. The worship of ancestors is therefore based more on fear than piety and acts as a powerful conservative force in society. Irreverent behavior toward the spirits, such as innovation and departure from traditional customs, brings immediate supernatural judgment not only on the individual but on the whole community. In practice, this means that the mighty with strong *tondi* can do as they please, whereas the moral commandments preached with such emphasis are binding primarily on the weaker multitude.

THE MODERNIZATION OF *TONDI* POWER

With the intervention of Westernization and Christianity, the opportunities and problems of rapid social change have penetrated Toba Batak society, modifying both the source of and access to power. First, missionaries and the churches dissolved traditional animistic beliefs, substituting a less rigidly enforced set of social and supernatural sanctions based on love rather than fear, voluntary rather than compulsory obedience, and separating sacred from secular spheres of society. Then, as new sources of social, economic, and political power developed, the Toba Bataks have aligned themselves to progressive innovative and change-oriented attitudes in a new and superior power source. This transformation does not contradict tradition because it still contributes to self-preservation.

Knowledge in traditional Toba Batak society is closely associated with religious meaning and power just as education in modern Toba Batak society is closely associated with progress and personal advancement. Special knowledge is the source of power. It is a village chief's knowledge that protects authority. Individuals protect their kinship rights by knowing their ancestral lineage that regulates status. Access to knowledge is possible through foreign language, foreign ideas, and foreigners themselves teaching or providing assistance through educational institutions (Pedersen, 1986a). The end goal is always increased power for the individual student and, presumably, the social betterment of the community.

Responses by 122 Toba Batak university students to a 400-item questionnaire (Pedersen, 1968, 1983b, 1985) emphasize the applicability of religious knowledge for solving secular problems in sciences, economics, politics, and especially personal behavior. Students' responses imply that all knowledge is religious knowledge in their vivid concern for God punishing those ignorant of God's will and yet capable of rewarding obedience. The student responses also demonstrate a high level of achievement orientation emphasizing self-sufficiency and directed by a need to achieve prestige status and approval from sources of religious and social authority.

The emphasis on self-sufficiency in these student responses describes typical personal problems as those involving competition and rivalry among peers, concern about personal inadequacy, and failing to achieve their own high standards of behavior (Pedersen, 1983a). Religion is an affair of personal piety based on a direct relationship with God, who either rewards or punishes the individual.

Items regarding family demonstrate the strongest area of conflict for these Toba Batak university students. The necessity for but not the specific direction of change is clearly identified by the students, who express a generalized rebellion against parental control and assert their power as the generation of the future. Family problems are most prominent in the areas where counseling is requested and among topics of personal concern. In 1965, one year after these data were collected, a national student-led revolution resulted in the downfall of President Sukarno and the overthrow of communism in Indonesia.

Mental health is not separated from the rest of life for the Toba Bataks. The person is part of the cosmology, and a well-defined role promotes health for both the cosmology and the individual. Religion becomes an internalized force to guide the individual toward a harmonious cosmic understanding much in the same way that counseling seeks to promote personal well-being. Both religion and counseling seek to empower the individual in meaningful ways, with religion reaching inside the Toba Batak's source of personal power and counseling supplementing the individual's resources with outside help.

CONCLUSION

Primal alternatives to counseling tend to depend on endogenous healing mechanisms turning to the sources of power within the person as the barometer of health. Prince (1984) has drawn attention to the importance of those alternatives for dealing with psychological problems in the modern world. Sheikh and Sheikh (1989) have likewise emphasized the importance of nonmechanistic understanding of a subjective and spiritual consciousness, emphasizing humans as reflecting the balance of power in which both pleasure and pain are meaningful components. To some extent, the importance of power, knowledge, and family as the means of increasing power has been preserved even among modern Toba Batak university students. Although counseling often seeks the elimination of pain and suffering, the primal alternative discussed in this chapter goes beyond suffering to the attainment of inner freedom and the experience of one's own divinity.

EXERCISE

PERSONAL, CULTURAL, AND PATHOLOGICAL INTERPRETATIONS OF CLIENT PROBLEMS (PCP QUESTIONNAIRE)

Objective

By completing this questionnaire you will identify the extent to which personal, cultural, or pathological factors have contributed to the very brief statement of a client's presenting problem.

Please fill in the following information before completing the questionnaire.

Name: _____

Address: _____

Number of years as a practicing counselor or psychologist (circle one)
    1 or less   1-3   4-6   7-10 over 10
Number of courses taken in counseling fields (circle one)
        1   2-5   6-10   over 10

Main area of professional interest: _____

Instructions

Twenty very brief presenting problems are described below. Identify on a 10-point scale (1 = *totally irrelevant* issue in respect to this problem, 10 = *extremely important* issue in respect to this problem) the extent to which personal, cultural, or pathological factors contributed to the client's presenting problem. Use the definitions of these terms as you currently understand them. A low score indicates that the factor contributed very little to the presenting problem. A high score indicates that the factor contributed very much to the presenting problem from your viewpoint. You will have an opportunity to compare your scores with those of your colleagues who have also completed this questionnaire to identify culturally learned patterns of diagnosis and attribution.

A 35-year-old man lives in a crowded neighborhood in a large city, yet feels isolated and alone. He feels people are cold and unfriendly.

Personal:	1	2	3	4	5	6	7	8	9	10
Cultural:	1	2	3	4	5	6	7	8	9	10
Pathological:	1	2	3	4	5	6	7	8	9	10

A female college student feels that men are interested only in sex and not in getting to know her as an individual. Although she admits to being very flirtatious, she feels angry and degraded when men respond in a sexual way.

Personal:	1	2	3	4	5	6	7	8	9	10
Cultural:	1	2	3	4	5	6	7	8	9	10
Pathological:	1	2	3	4	5	6	7	8	9	10

A caseworker indicates to a male client (head of household) that he will have to do some of the work needed to find him an apartment and a job. The client is angry and resentful as he feels the caseworker should be doing all these things for him.

Personal:	1	2	3	4	5	6	7	8	9	10
Cultural:	1	2	3	4	5	6	7	8	9	10
Pathological:	1	2	3	4	5	6	7	8	9	10

A 28-year-old unmarried woman is extremely reluctant to make any decision without the permission of her father and his full support.

Personal:	1	2	3	4	5	6	7	8	9	10
Cultural:	1	2	3	4	5	6	7	8	9	10
Pathological:	1	2	3	4	5	6	7	8	9	10

A 23-year-old woman engages in premarital sex for the first time. She subsequently comes to a counselor suffering from guilt and the fear that she will be viewed by her friends and family as promiscuous.

Personal:	1	2	3	4	5	6	7	8	9	10
Cultural:	1	2	3	4	5	6	7	8	9	10
Pathological:	1	2	3	4	5	6	7	8	9	10

A Korean woman has a baby who is delivered in a large city hospital. All aspects of the delivery are normal. The woman soon becomes depressed and also feels angry and resentful toward the hospital staff.

Personal:	1	2	3	4	5	6	7	8	9	10
Cultural:	1	2	3	4	5	6	7	8	9	10
Pathological:	1	2	3	4	5	6	7	8	9	10

A person is referred for counseling because he keeps losing jobs due to absenteeism and tardiness.

Personal:	1	2	3	4	5	6	7	8	9	10
Cultural:	1	2	3	4	5	6	7	8	9	10
Pathological:	1	2	3	4	5	6	7	8	9	10

A person goes to a counselor for help in choosing a career. As the counselor tries to help the client clarify feelings and attitudes about different careers, the client becomes very angry and frustrated.

Personal:	1	2	3	4	5	6	7	8	9	10
Cultural:	1	2	3	4	5	6	7	8	9	10
Pathological:	1	2	3	4	5	6	7	8	9	10

A person is referred for counseling because he reports having secret conversations with messengers from another planet.

Personal:	1	2	3	4	5	6	7	8	9	10
Cultural:	1	2	3	4	5	6	7	8	9	10
Pathological:	1	2	3	4	5	6	7	8	9	10

A woman sees a counselor because she feels that she has a lot of difficulty making friends.

Personal:	1	2	3	4	5	6	7	8	9	10
Cultural:	1	2	3	4	5	6	7	8	9	10
Pathological:	1	2	3	4	5	6	7	8	9	10

A man seeks help in trying to understand his teenage son's fixation with rock music. It appears that his son has trouble with absenteeism at school.

Personal:	1	2	3	4	5	6	7	8	9	10
Cultural:	1	2	3	4	5	6	7	8	9	10
Pathological:	1	2	3	4	5	6	7	8	9	10

A man approaches a counselor with feelings of depression. He feels that his job is leading nowhere and that his occupational efforts are fruitless.

Personal:	1	2	3	4	5	6	7	8	9	10
Cultural:	1	2	3	4	5	6	7	8	9	10
Pathological:	1	2	3	4	5	6	7	8	9	10

A 19-year-old sophomore complains to a counselor that she is being sexually harassed by her male professors. She claims that this has occurred throughout her academic life.

Personal:	1	2	3	4	5	6	7	8	9	10
Cultural:	1	2	3	4	5	6	7	8	9	10
Pathological:	1	2	3	4	5	6	7	8	9	10

A 32-year-old woman is reluctant to leave her parents' home to live on her own. She feels that to do so would be to lack filial responsibility.

Personal:	1	2	3	4	5	6	7	8	9	10
Cultural:	1	2	3	4	5	6	7	8	9	10
Pathological:	1	2	3	4	5	6	7	8	9	10

A 35-year-old man sees a counselor complaining of chest and neck pains.
He has sought medical help but has been diagnosed as normal.

Personal:	1	2	3	4	5	6	7	8	9	10
Cultural:	1	2	3	4	5	6	7	8	9	10
Pathological:	1	2	3	4	5	6	7	8	9	10

A 30-year-old woman has been seeing a counselor for three sessions; she
has remained attentive to the counselor but has said very little about
herself. She rarely volunteers any information during the sessions.

Personal:	1	2	3	4	5	6	7	8	9	10
Cultural:	1	2	3	4	5	6	7	8	9	10
Pathological:	1	2	3	4	5	6	7	8	9	10

An international student is confused about his feelings. He wishes to stay in
the United States and pursue an academic career, yet his sense of
nationalism and family unity have pressured him to consider returning to
his native country.

Personal:	1	2	3	4	5	6	7	8	9	10
Cultural:	1	2	3	4	5	6	7	8	9	10
Pathological:	1	2	3	4	5	6	7	8	9	10

A 28-year-old woman is referred by her husband because she is constantly
using prescription drugs to help her cope with day-to-day existence; the
woman is aware of her drug use but denies that it affects her family life.

Personal:	1	2	3	4	5	6	7	8	9	10
Cultural:	1	2	3	4	5	6	7	8	9	10
Pathological:	1	2	3	4	5	6	7	8	9	10

A 22-year-old woman approaches a counselor complaining that she cannot
focus on relevant issues. She claims that her thinking has suddenly become
"diffuse."

Personal:	1	2	3	4	5	6	7	8	9	10
Cultural:	1	2	3	4	5	6	7	8	9	10
Pathological:	1	2	3	4	5	6	7	8	9	10

A 20-year-old factory worker is referred to a counselor by his work
supervisor. It appears that the man is lazy on the job and that his
absenteeism is higher than average.

Personal:	1	2	3	4	5	6	7	8	9	10
Cultural:	1	2	3	4	5	6	7	8	9	10
Pathological:	1	2	3	4	5	6	7	8	9	10

Debriefing

The Personal Cultural Pathological (PCP) Questionnaire is made up of 20 very brief one- or two-sentence critical incidents, which were developed by James Campbell, John Lewis, and Paul Pedersen working together at Syracuse University in 1984. The critical incidents were selected to describe a wide range of situations where broadly defined cultural identities were indicated. The cultural identities were defined to include ethnographic (nationality, ethnicity, language, religion), demographic (age, gender, place of residence), status (social, educational, economic), and affiliation (formal and informal) variables. There is no systematic or consistent cultural identity common throughout the PCP questionnaire, although versions of it emphasizing different cultural groups might be a useful way to identify systematic cultural bias among respondents.

The PCP questionnaire is designed to elicit responses on three 10-point scales indicating whether the problem described by the brief critical incident is interpersonal, intercultural, or psychopathological in nature. The critical incidents are deliberately very brief, requiring the respondent to project a judgment based on extremely incomplete information. The assumption in this design is that more experienced and/or trained counselors will find clues in these incomplete critical incidents that guide their responses and that less experienced and/or trained counselors will not identify these same clues. The critical incidents allow the respondents to project their own interpretations in the judgment-making process. Presumably, the judgments made by more experienced and/or trained counselors will be significantly different from those with less experience and/or training.

Mwaba and Pedersen (1994) analyzed responses to this measure by students and professionals subscribing to a newsletter on multicultural counseling. The data indicated that those with 10 or more courses in counseling (about the equivalent of a master's degree) put more emphasis on pathology in describing the presenting problem, whereas those who had taken fewer courses put significantly more emphasis on culture. This may mean that persons trained in counseling become more skilled in identifying pathology. It may also mean that counseling courses socialize students to believe that "different" behavior is pathological.

The PCP instrument scores should be interpreted internally with reference to the pattern of priority or emphasis across the 20 items on one or another "source" of the presenting problem described in the incomplete critical incident. There are no external scoring protocols or external/absolute standards of right or wrong answers because this is essentially a projective test. The person taking the test is "projecting" one's own interpretation about what the basic cause of the problem might be. It may be useful to compare scores with colleagues who also completed the test and discuss patterns of similarity and/or difference, but it would be inappropriate to identify one profile of responses as "better" than another.

6

International Student Contexts

- **Primary Objective** Examine personal and situational factors influencing the role of international students

- **Secondary Objectives** (1) Identify the strengths and weaknesses of counseling international students and (2) Suggest applications of counseling appropriate to international students

We are still not sure how to define success in counseling international students. We know that success must be measured according to the goals of individual growth and professional advancement. However, institutional development goals and national goals of skilled leadership or resource enhancement must also be considered. The emphasis is not on the home or the new-host culture context but, rather, on the unique and personalized system of values integrated into each international students' own unique role and cultural context. Outcome measures of success usually focus on the 5 or 6 years the student studies abroad rather than on the 40 or 50 years after the student returns home.

When international students arrive at overseas universities, they suddenly must learn a variety of competing and sometimes contradictory roles. When the requirements of those roles are accurately perceived and adopted, these students' experience is likely to be "successful," but when the roles are not accommodated, the resulting identity diffusion and role conflict may affect their emotional well-being and present serious obstacles to the achievement of educational objectives. Failure to learn the roles of their new cultural context will result in confusion about their own identity and create conflicts. Role learning becomes a necessary coping strategy whether the international student intends to return home at the conclusion of studies or to stay in the host country (Pedersen, 1980; Wong-Rieger, 1984).

THE AMBIGUOUS ROLE OF
THE INTERNATIONAL STUDENT

There has been a tendency to confine international students to a rather narrowly defined role, isolated from their peers, when, in fact, there is probably as much difference between any two international students from different countries as between either of them and any American student. By making a "special case" of international students, we run the danger of isolating them, just as we might stereotype them by not recognizing those unique problems and resources that individual international students do in fact present. Although international students come from a wide diversity of cultural backgrounds, those students from non-Western countries, whose cultures are likely to be very different from the U.S. host culture, are increasing proportionately. The greater the cultural difference, the more complicated the international student's adjustment is likely to be.

CULTURE NOTE

International students at a large university asked me to train its mental health service providers because the health center was treating these students as "slightly crazy." The training was well received. Several weeks later, the international students asked me to return and "untrain" those health care providers because genuinely sick international students were now being diagnosed as "normal for an international." Underdiagnosis was just as serious a problem as overdiagnosis.

Counselors need, first of all, to examine their own values when working with international students (Dillard & Chisolm, 1983). Counselors need cultural self-awareness and sensitivity, an awareness of assumptions or values, openness to and respect for differing value systems, tolerance for ambiguity, willingness to learn with and from clients, and a genuine concern for people with different values (Cadieux & Wehrly, 1986; Wehrly, 1988). Without appropriate attitudes and motivation, there is a tendency for both the counselor and the international student to develop unrealistic expectations, stereotypes, and biases that contribute to difficulties (Althen & Stott, 1983).

The conflict between values inherent in theories of U.S. college student development and values inherent in the home cultures of international students makes it necessary for counselors to recognize each individual international student as a special case (Storey, 1982). Many traditional student development theories may not apply to those international students; for example, William Perry's model of student development has been applied to an international student population with only very limited success (Bulthuis, 1986; Stewart & Hartt, 1987). Storey (1982) attempted to apply Chickering's theories to international students, also with little success. In developing theories to understand the unique and complicated factors influencing international students' success, it may be necessary to modify those theories now in use.

The international student is confronted with two important questions: Will my cultural identity or values be retained? Do I want positive relations with the larger dominant society? The answers given will determine whether the student experiences assimilation, integration, rejection, or deculturation.

The international student who chooses to *assimilate* becomes more "American" in behaviors and preferences, even to the extent of marrying a U.S. national and immigrating. The student who chooses to *integrate* into the U.S. culture accepts some features of the host culture, such as clothing style, food, and slang expressions, while maintaining important elements from home, such as like values, beliefs, and relationships. The student who chooses to *reject* the host culture maintains home customs, dress, relationships, and language, with little or no accommodation of the host U.S. culture. The student who chooses to *deculturate* rejects both the home and the host culture, resulting in a loss of identity and high levels of stress that will likely prevent that student's successful completion of studies.

Selye (1974) suggests that our adaptive energy is finite and that psychological as well as physiological resources become depleted by excess stress. The first stage of stress, *alarm,* prepares the person for fight or flight. The second stage, *resistance,* leads to the third, *exhaustion,* if stress continues. These physiological reactions might include loss of appetite, inability to sleep, physical complaints, excessive sleep, tiredness, aching body pain, gastrointestinal problems, or a wide range of other somatic symptoms (Barna, 1983; Guthrie, 1966, 1975; Melis, 1982). It is not uncommon for foreign students under stress to report severe headaches, stomach problems, and other symptoms for which no organic basis can be found (Thomas & Althen, 1989). Although there is considerable support for the view that Third World students or persons outside the European-North American context have a greater tendency to somatize psychological stress (Kleinman, 1988), this perspective continues to be controversial.

Foreign students show more evidence of psychological problems than British students, but also nearly half of these cases are hypochondriacal. The symptoms are typically weakness, nervousness, sleeplessness, a cough or cold, lack of appetite, indigestion, constipation and/or diarrhea, a "heavy" feeling in the stomach, pain in the chest or limbs, palpitations of the heart, numbness, depression, anxiety about sexual functions, inability to concentrate, inability to think clearly, fear of serious disease, or an infection that spreads from one part of the body to another. When treating these highly anxious students, physicians are usually unable to find more than trivial signs of physical illness (Still, 1961, p. 61). Ward (1967) labels this the "foreign student syndrome," characterized by vague nonspecific symptoms, a passive, withdrawn style, and disheveled appearance. It is theorized that these symptoms of physical illness are the student's way of saving face rather than admitting to psychological symptoms of culture shock (Allen & Cole, 1987; Furnham & Bochner, 1986).

CULTURE NOTE

International students frequently comment that "Americans are very friendly . . . but there are no friends!"

The student becomes a mediator between home and the host country (Taft, 1977a). The framework of role theory and role differentiation provides a basis for theory building in predicting the intercultural adjustment of international students. We depend on group identification for a somewhat secure self-image, and our attitudes or values become the internalized role norms of the groups with which we identify. Our behavior grows out of differentiated roles modified somewhat by individual personality differences.

The role differentiation process is the extent to which membership in one role is independent of membership in any other role, with some roles more independent than others. In the international student's contacts, national membership roles will be dominant when the individual is in an alien context, confronted by another foreigner, or representing the home culture or country and when the home culture's symbols trigger practiced, nationalistic responses or one's cultural values are challenged. Consequently, the international student needs to (a) reduce the salience of the national role, (b) increase the convergence of cross-national perceptions in reasonable rather than irrational conclusions, and (c) reduce the social distance between oneself and other nationality groups (Bochner & Meredith, 1968).

CULTURE NOTE

The first night after returning home with her doctorate, a Singapore student stayed up all night describing to her less affluent parents how valuable the experience had been in bringing about changes in her to justify the considerable drain on family funds and resources. Suddenly, both parents began crying. They had not wanted her to change as a result of her experience abroad.

Even though basic cultural or religious attitudes, career goals, and attitudes toward their home country change very little, attitudes favoring open-mindedness, the value of knowledge, and greater freedom in the relationship between genders become much more important for international students who stay longer than 2 years. Those who stay less than 2 years are less likely to change their basic cultural or religious values. There is no consistent direction of change in attitudes toward the United States— favorable or unfavorable—and these attitudes are more likely a function of the student's individual social and academic experiences. The maintenance of traditional values serves an important function in protecting the student's self-esteem, sense of worth, and successful accomplishment of academic goals (Spaulding & Flack, 1976).

This ambiguous role is analyzed in three hypothetical situations that illustrate frequently occurring critical incidents involving international students (Pedersen, 1991b, 1994).

Incident 1

International student Mr. A wants to mix socially with U.S. students but has failed in his attempts to do so. All his American friends go out on dates regularly, but he has been unable to make a date with the U.S. students of his choice. He has decided that his strangeness as a foreign national is the reason why he is being avoided. Consequently, he has become very critical of his own culture and has begun avoiding fellow nationals. As a result, he is now being rejected by both the U.S. students and those from home. He is feeling very lonely and isolated from everyone and is beginning to withdraw from any contact with other students. By the time the counselor becomes aware of the problem, Mr. A has stopped going to classes and has spent almost a week without leaving his room unless absolutely necessary. He has become extremely lonely for his homeland, where he was quite popular. He is becoming very bitter about the way other students treat him and is ready to give up and return home immediately. The counselor begins working with him through Mr. A's closest friend, rather than directly, supporting the friend's efforts to help Mr. A get out more with both U.S. students and fellow nationals rather than rejecting either group.

Discussion

There is no "foreign student" as such but, rather, a collection of individuals from widely diverse cultures as far apart from one another as any of them might be from any one of the U.S. cultures. The wide diversity in viewpoints among foreign students does not lend itself to cohesiveness, except perhaps in their shared condition of being aliens in the United States. Some students are offended by being grouped in that category. In reaction, they relate to U.S. nationals, picking up the slang, clothing styles, ways of relating, and behaviors of their U.S. peers. Americanization is not wholly satisfactory because it makes the readjustment to the home culture that much more difficult. Foreign students also alienate themselves from and abandon the support of fellow nationals at considerable risk to maintaining their identity in this environment. By involving a third person trusted by both the counselor and the international student it was possible to provide support with a minimum of intrusion. In other cases, counselors have asked the international student to bring a friend to the counseling sessions to help increase the student's sense of safety.

Incident 2

A U.S. student rooming with an international student, Ms. B, in a university residence hall goes to the resident adviser to request a room change. Two previous roommates of Ms. B's had moved out because she was always entertaining guests from her home country who ate strange-smelling food she cooked in the room and who would talk for hours each evening in her home language. The U.S. student doesn't want to hurt her feelings but has found it impossible to live or study in that setting. She doesn't understand what is being talked about and can't get used to the weird-smelling food. Every time she tries to get a conversation going with Ms. B, who is normally very quiet and shy, there are awkward and embarrassing pauses. The U.S. student is ready to give up and wants to move in with another U.S. student where she will feel more at home. The resident adviser has tried talking with the international student about this, but Ms. B insists that everything is fine.

Discussion

In many ways the dorm provides an ideal atmosphere for international students. Their needs are cared for, meals are provided, and recreational facilities are available. They live within easy walking distance of campus, have a residential adviser for counseling, and other students are available for company. The situation is also ideal for maximizing the formal educational advantages for U.S. students through conversation and contact with these international students. In many cases, however, dorm living presents serious adjustment problems. The setting may be too radically different from their home country. The dorm food may be unacceptable either for religious reasons or because it is simply too different. Sometimes, these students cook in their rooms, which is usually not encouraged by the dorm, or make other arrangements to modify dorm living for themselves. In some cases, the students become even more intensely lonely in the midst of bustling dorm activity. Often, they respond by withdrawing instead of seeking counseling, advice, or help. These students will sometimes almost drop out of sight and their absence not even be noticed by the very busy students around them. Sometimes, this problem is solved by organizing an "international" unit in the dorm, but usually international programs in the dorm are at a minimum.

Incident 3

Mr. C is an international student living with his host family. He is used to a different style of living with his own family back home, and he feels the U.S. family is demanding too much of his time and attention. Assigned household chores, he feels like a servant to them, and it leaves him no time to study. His host family feels he is being discourteous for demanding special treatment even beyond what they would do for their own children. Open confrontations between him and the host family occur more and more frequently. His grades are being affected negatively. The host family is willing to keep him with them despite the problems, but he has asked to be assigned to a new host family. His family back home will allow him to study in the U.S. only if he can stay with a host family. They refuse to support him if he moves into a dormitory or rooming house.

Discussion

There are people in the community around most universities who take a lively interest in volunteering to take in foreign students. Most of them participate because they find contact with international students stimulating and exciting. Sometimes, they have traveled abroad themselves, or perhaps they have wanted to visit other cultures. Because most are volunteering their time and home, they can become very possessive of the foreign student. Sometimes, other priorities take precedence for the host family, causing last-minute cancellations or readjustments in a program. Few volunteers maintain steady contact with the student and are more likely to be intensely involved for bursts of time separated by longer periods of inactivity. Nonetheless, the host family program provides an extremely valuable link between the isolated international student and the community. They provide a temporary substitute for the family support system that the student left behind as well as a resource and retreat away from the university community.

THE PROBLEMS OF THE
INTERNATIONAL STUDENT

There is some controversy over whether international students experience more problems than students in general. Alexander, Klein, Workneh, and Miller (1981) describe international students as a high-risk group with more frequent problems, although Klineberg (1982) believes this may be an exaggeration. One of the problems in measuring the extent of problems encountered by international students is their reluctance to seek professional counseling. They typically do so only after other resources have been exhausted (Klineberg, 1982; Pedersen, 1975) because counseling may result in loss of status. Many traditional means of solving personal problems rely more on fellow nationals for assistance, but this tendency may work against international students' best interests.

CULTURE NOTE

An East Indian international student used to stop me as I walked across campus and we would spend half an hour or more doing "counseling." I asked her to please come to my office and talk where we could discuss her situation more comfortably. She exclaimed that she could never do that because if word reached her family that she had sought out "counseling" her bride price would be significantly reduced and her family would not forgive her.

Klineberg and Hull (1979) found that international students who were most comfortable and involved with Americans were more likely to be generally satisfied with regard to both academic and nonacademic areas. They conclude that contact with Americans may be an important coping mechanism for international students. Alexander et al. (1981), however, conclude that contact with conationals is the most important coping factor contributing to academic and personal success, although conflicting research is also cited.

In view of these factors, international students are likely to experience more problems than students in general and have access to fewer resources to help them. In their adjustment to those personal problems, these students have had to rely more on one another than any other source. One might speculate that their problems are so unique that counseling personnel are not prepared to understand them, or that cultural differences are so enormous that campus agencies lack the sensitivity and expertise to advise them, or that explaining their problem to a stranger in a foreign language is too anxiety provoking, or even that they themselves have no "problem" that requires "counseling" from a professional.

CULTURE NOTE

An international student claimed not to have any "problems," and only later did I learn that he was failing classes, his parents were bankrupt, his friends were turning against him, and he was out of status with immigration. Nonetheless, the student insisted that he had no "problems."

Leong (1984) reviewed the literature on counseling international students with regard to three types of problem situations. First, there are the problems common to all college students, such as being away from home, living with peers, and being autonomous. The second type involves adjustment to being away from home for a long period of time, situations similar to those experienced by diplomats, businesspeople, missionaries, military personnel, and others, such as culture shock, culture fatigue, or role shock. The third relates exclusively to international students, such as immigration difficulties. Church (1982) reviewed 30 years of research and found a consistent hierarchy of problems among international students that included language and financial difficulties, homesickness, and adjustment both to a new educational system and to social customs or norms.

Taft (1977a) suggests a framework that links the magnitude of the international student's coping task with the task itself, the abruptness of discontinuity, the salience of necessary changes, and the goodness of fit between the new environment and previous functioning. Taft (p. 124) delineates each of these factors in detail:

- *Size of the gap.* The greater the disparity between the familiar and the unfamiliar culture, the more difficult it is to bridge the gap. Highly relevant to the size of the gap are the language used and known by members of the new society, its economic structure and level of technology, the size and complexity of formal society and political structure, its specific ceremonies and rituals, and the style of primary social relationships.
- *Abruptness of discontinuity.* The abruptness of change can be modified either by a transitional stage or by lack of pressure to change. The

transitional period may be a contrived training course preparatory to making the change, such as the Peace Corps training schools. However, the effect of the abruptness of change on the style of coping is not a simple one.

■ *Salience of changes to functioning.* Whether or not an abrupt change from one culture to another is debilitating to a person's functioning will depend partly on the degree to which the change is salient to one's behavior. The definition of salience involves the concept that some areas of activity are more central to the ego than are others; that is, they are more closely associated with the person's self-esteem.

■ *Encompassing degree of new culture.* The difficulty in coping is a function of the degree to which the new culture is all-encompassing. Persons who move into new societies often do not wish to adapt any more than they need to, and it is possible to minimize this requirement by avoiding contacts as much as possible or by immersing oneself in a group in the new society that embodies the old culture.

Bochner's (1972; Furnham & Bochner, 1986) Culture Learning Model provides still another perspective of international student problems. The major task is not to adjust to the new culture but to learn its salient characteristics. These social skills help the student work and learn effectively in the new culture. Accordingly, failures and problems are not symptoms of an underlying pathology but merely the lack of learned skills. Remedial action does not involve "solving" the problems as much as training the international student in appropriate skills. By the same token, "adjustment" implies cultural chauvinism, suggesting that the student should abandon the culture of origin and embrace these new values and customs. By contrast, "learning" the customs and values of a new culture is less ethnocentric in its emphasis.

CULTURE NOTE

A number of Asian students complained to me that they were getting lower grades than their less deserving but more aggressive American classmates. The Asian students requested that I organize antiassertiveness training workshops to help them cope with more assertive American classmates without becoming like them.

International students' adaptation is a learning process in which strangers suddenly must acquire skills that native-born persons learn over a lifetime. Both the characteristics of the host environment and the characteristics of the stranger will influence how well that adaptation succeeds.

What factors might influence international students to use counseling services? Reluctance to use them is due in part to a low level of awareness of, and satisfaction with, most of these services and programs (Lomak, 1984). Host culture educational institutions tend to ignore the trauma of international students being uprooted from their home countries (Dadfar & Friedlander, 1982; Miller & Harwell, 1983; Smith & Smith, 1989; Zwingman & Gunn, 1983). Other research suggests that international students seek help from counselors and advisers on educational and vocational problems more easily than they do regarding mental health problems (Leong & Sedlacek, 1985).

Those who suggest that international students use counseling services at about the same rate as other students (Ebbin & Blankinship, 1986) emphasize the importance of counseling style. The general consensus is that international students prefer direct counseling, which supplies pragmatic information and emphasizes a shared counselor-client responsibility, over nondirective counseling, which may stress client verbalization and client responsibility (Exum & Lau, 1988; Larson, 1984; Leong & Sedlacek, 1986). These preferences differ from one culture to another, however.

The problems faced by these students are illustrated in the following four critical incidents that are typical of international student problem situations.

Incident 1

Ms. D has just finished her first quarter of classes. She realizes that she hasn't understood very much of what was said during the lectures even though her TOEFL (Test of English as a Foreign Language) score was above the minimum cutoff. She can't take notes because many of the words are new to her and the professors speak very quickly. She isn't able to complete her assignments on time. The lectures are particularly difficult to understand, requiring her to carefully translate each word into her own language and then write down the text. She is afraid to take the final exam, which she might well fail, but she is also afraid to withdraw from her courses at the end of the first term. She now realizes that she should have enrolled in English as a Second Language (ESL) for one or two terms before beginning regular classes, but she is too proud to admit this to her academic adviser because she was adamant in her earlier refusal of the ESL course. She feels trapped into certain failure.

Discussion

Students from non-English-speaking countries coming to U.S. universities are required to take the TOEFL and to score at a high level. Some schools or programs require a higher level of English competency than others, as measured by this test. Although the test is a good measure of reading ability, it is not as accurate in measuring a student's oral comprehension or ability to express ideas in class discussion. Obviously, students with problems understanding English are at a severe disadvantage. Course examinations and other tests primarily measure the student's knowledge of English and only secondarily a grasp of the course content. Some universities have a program for teaching ESL, which can benefit the failing student a great deal, but where this option is not available or not applied, even a very intelligent student might fail. Sometimes, a counselor can persuade the instructor to give the student an incomplete while the student works on English language fluency. The student's frustration at being unable to express herself quickly becomes both embarrassing and debilitating. The best solution is to anticipate the problem and encourage the student to become fluent in English before starting coursework.

Incident 2

Mr. E has just arrived at the university from an extremely conservative culture. He was welcomed by a group of U.S. and foreign students and invited to move into their International House. One of the U.S. female students is particularly warm toward him, and he enjoys talking with her alone for hours at a time. She feels sorry for him and wants to help him feel more at home. He, however, has never been alone with any other female outside his family and is encouraged by her friendliness. One night after he had been in the United States for about a week he knocked on her door late at night and asked to talk with her. She had been sleeping and was wearing a nightgown. Because he sounded so distressed she let him into her room to find out what was bothering him. Without a great deal of preliminary explanation he put his arms around her and pushed her back onto her bed. The more she resisted, the more excited he became until finally another resident, awakened by the noise, intervened. The girl, both frightened and angry, threatens to charge him with attempted rape. He is also angry and feels that she trapped him into an embarrassing situation. By letting him into her room at that hour he had assumed she wanted to have sex with him.

Discussion

Most of the foreign students attending U.S. universities are unmarried. Often, their most extensive preparation in terms of prearrival orientation has been through popular movies and, in some cases, television serials. Their expectations of a sexually permissive culture are compounded by feelings of loneliness, being away from home, and the excitement of being outside the supervision of family and friends. Some of the foreign students find this combination very threatening and anxiety provoking, expecting the worst at every contact with someone of the other sex. Others find the combination extremely frustrating and inconsistent, interpreting expressions of interest and friendliness from the opposite sex as provocative and misleading. Women's liberation further complicates relationships for foreign students from cultures where women's roles are carefully defined and to some extent more restricted. Well-designed orientation programs can help prevent such misunderstandings.

Incident 3

At a meeting of the International Student Association there is a general discussion about the apathy of U.S. students toward internationalism. Ms. F and several other foreign students describe their experiences with U.S. students who don't seem to be interested in either the problems of international students or the possible contributions and skills that foreign students bring to the university community. She points out that any slight interest by U.S. students is in the form of curiosity, particularly about how the foreign student "likes" the United States. When she tried to talk with U.S. students about her home country, it was frequently apparent that they knew nothing or were seriously misinformed and uninterested.

Discussion

Just getting persons from different cultures together is not enough to bring about spontaneous international understanding. There is a high potential for misunderstanding and a climate of apathy or even antipathy between foreign students and U.S. nationals. Host family programs, brother-sister relationships, or other planned interactions between foreign students and U.S. nationals have experienced a degree of success. For the most part, however, universities seem to lack the resources to invest in international programming. Foreign students often perceive themselves as too busy just staying in school, and the U.S. nationals are generally apathetic about getting to know the foreign students in their midst. As a result, international students are often left to their own devices either out of well-meaning "respect for their privacy" or because of their "strangeness." Informal counseling with both U.S. and foreign students might help mobilize U.S. students to learn from their international peers.

COUNSELING THE
INTERNATIONAL STUDENT

Longitudinal studies of coping behavior by international students are needed to help identify the criteria of good counseling, particularly those of a favorable adjustment. It is known that international students who dissociate themselves from their homeland values are more readily able to move into American culture, but is this a desirable outcome? Criteria are needed to help international students define a third culture, which is neither their home nor their host culture. Counseling might be a useful means of helping these students define their own identity and differentiate between the roles being thrust on them.

There are clear implications for counseling that emerge from the research on counseling international students (Pedersen, 1980):

- In working with international students, it is dangerous to overemphasize or underemphasize the cultural differences between the counselor and that student.
- To be effective, orientation requires contact with students before they arrive, during their stay, and after they have returned home because they experience a continuous process of adjustment.
- Counselors need to learn the skills most likely to be helpful for international students from specific cultures going into specific situations or filling specific roles.
- At times it may be helpful to ask an international student to bring a fellow national into the counseling interview as a "culture broker" for additional support.
- Strengthening and encouraging the bond between international students and their fellow nationals may provide a source of support.

- Helping international students monitor the ways in which their values and perceptions may be changing as a result of their stay in the United States is an appropriate counseling agenda.
- Following up on international students after they have returned home helps them deal with reentry problems or adjustments after leaving the U.S. university. Success in school may contribute to failure back home.

International students provide a convenient, inexpensive, and highly motivated resource for international education and training on most college and university campuses, but because these students are typically isolated, their international expertise is underused (Mestenhauser, 1983).

The highest-ranked barriers to good relationships with U.S. nationals are negative American attitudes toward international students, lack of sensitivity by Americans to cultural differences, and the international students' own isolation as foreigners. Spending leisure time with Americans is an important indicator of adaptation and correlates with knowledge of English, social support, and other indicators of effective functioning. Greater contact with Americans results in greater willingness to express and challenge stereotypes that international students and American host nationals have of one another (Nichols & McAndrew, 1984).

Much work needs to be done regarding measures, tests, and clinical or counseling tools that will assist counselors in their clinical work with international students. Thomas (1985) identified 21 psychological correlates of adjustment or adaptation in her dissertation research: depression, helplessness, hostility toward the host country, anxiety, overidentification with one's home country, withdrawal, homesickness, loneliness, paranoia, preoccupation with cleanliness, irritability, confusion, disorientation, isolation, tension, psychoticism, neuroticism, defensiveness, intolerance and ambiguity, impatience, and the need to establish continuity. The literature describing these correlates and the measures that identify them are discussed in Thomas and Althen (1989).

The appropriateness of testing instruments for international students is being challenged widely (Tompkins & Mehring, 1989). Wilson's (1986) extensive research with 1,353 ESL students in 97 departments at 23 graduate schools looked at scores on the Graduate Record Examination (GRE) and the extent of their appropriateness for international students. He found that for quantitative departments the first-year grade point average (GPA) was more related to the quantitative and analytical GRE scores than to the verbal scores. In the social sciences, however, the first-year GPA was more closely related to the verbal scores than to the quantitative and analytical scores. Other literature is cited regarding the appropriate interpretation of GRE scores for international students.

Clinical measures have always been difficult to interpret for work with international students. Worchel and Goethals (1989) describe how rigorous studies of adjustment have been plagued by the failure to develop reliable and valid measures of adjustment for these students. Furnham and Trezise (1983) note the problems in using a 220-item measure of psychological disturbance with international students in England, describing many of the same problems discussed about the use of this measure in the United States. Hsu, Hailey, and Range (1987) have used the Beck Depression Inventory with Chinese students at three universities with very limited success. Day and Haij (1986) have used the Mooney Problem Checklist, also with very limited success.

Another less clinically oriented measure, discussed in Spaulding and Flack (1976), is the Michigan International Student Problem Inventory (MISPI). This measure, developed by John W. Porter and A. D. Haller, is available from Porter at Eastern Michigan State University. The MISPI consists of 132 problem statements reported most frequently by international students. The student is asked to identify those that are troubling and those that the student would like help in solving. In many cases, international students unfamiliar with counseling are helped by this kind of structure to identify problem areas in which counseling might be helpful. Crano and Crano (1990) developed a refined and streamlined version of the MISPI, which they call the ADJ. Like most other measures of adjustment, this relies on self-report, which might not be the same as self-belief. The alternatives, such as behavioral observation, are so time consuming and costly that self-report measures will no doubt continue to be popular.

INSTITUTIONAL POLICY IMPLICATIONS FOR INTERNATIONAL STUDENTS

This section describes some practices that a college or university might find helpful for counseling international students.

The National Association for Foreign Student Affairs (NAFSA) provides guidelines for educational institutions admitting international students that its members are required to recognize (see Althen, 1983, pp. 159-160):

1. The institution should have a clearly stated policy, endorsed by the governing board, setting forth the goals and objectives of the international educational program or programs developed by the institution. This policy should be manifest in the institution's planning and budgeting. Personnel and program resources—administrative and academic—should be sufficient to assure that the program can be operated in ways consistent with the principles presented in this document.

2. The executive staff of the institution should discuss with the faculty and administrative staff the implications of the international educational exchange policy for the academic programs and academic staff.

3. Programs in international educational exchange should be closely related to and consistent with the basic purposes and strengths of the institution.

4. Regardless of program size, the institution should acknowledge its responsibility to demonstrate sensitivity to cultural needs—social, religious, dietary, and housing. These factors must be accounted for in the planning and execution of the program.

5. Special services required by involvement in international educational exchange should be performed by personnel who are trained for their particular responsibilities, and institutional policy should ensure that faculty and administrative staff receive appropriate training for the activities they manage.

6. Administrative staff and faculty should seek to develop and maintain respect and sensitivity toward those from different cultures in the execution of their responsibilities for international educational exchange programs.

7. The institution should periodically evaluate programs, policies, and services in light of established goals and regularly review those goals.

The NAFSA documents go on to elaborate on these principles, describing how appropriate services are defined and carried out to provide a "favorable context" for international students. This organization has served as a professional focus for persons working with international students in a variety of relationships, including those providing counseling to international students. Those persons seeking more information about counseling international students would be well advised to check with the NAFSA office in Washington, D.C. for more information of a practical nature. Foreign students are an important resource for the United States.

CULTURE NOTE

The NAFSA office has estimated that international students at the university and K-12 level are presently the third largest generator of foreign currency—following military equipment and food products—for the United States.

The following three critical incidents demonstrate the kinds of institutional policy issues that confront foreign students. The international student counselor may have to serve as an advocate or make an administrative intervention beyond the role of counselors with other clients.

Incident 1

A particularly evangelical church group has been giving students from Mr. J's country scholarship assistance, used clothing and furniture, and providing transportation as needed for him and others to get around town. The church group organizes a weekend retreat for the foreign students who have received aid. The program, conducted in an isolated setting, is largely Bible study and prayer groups. Some of the church members pray that individual foreign students might be converted to Christianity as a result of the generosity they have experienced. Mr. J and the other foreign students are uneasy at first, but by the time the weekend retreat is over he is extremely angry at the church sponsors, feeling that he has been used unfairly. The church group is also offended, considering the foreign student ungrateful and opportunistic. The church group threatens to withdraw its support and send all these students back home where they came from.

Discussion

The University Vice President for Academic Affairs claimed that most universities accept foreign students either to provide some international contact for local students or because of the status of having someone come to study from halfway around the world or out of an assumed responsibility for "less fortunate" countries that lack our higher levels of educational resources. Of these three reasons, the patronizing attempt to help foreign students is the most offensive. These efforts are typically made by highly motivated and well-meaning persons in the community. Although there is no discounting the tremendous contributions of religious organizations to foreign students, the students sometimes perceive these efforts as directed toward "saving" them, converting them, or changing them in ways they prefer were not changed. In situations where foreign students are dependent on sponsors for their support, the social exchange is particularly important. A counselor may need to work as a mediator between community sponsors and the foreign students, helping each to better understand the needs of the other.

Incident 2

Ms. K is caught working illegally by the Immigration and Naturalization Service (INS) and is called to a deportation hearing. She claims that she applied for work permission during the academic year but did not hear from the INS for two months. When summer came, she thought that international students were allowed to work without permission because they did not need to be in school. However, the INS claims that she knew accepting the job was illegal or she would not have applied for permission to work. Because she had never received a denial letter she feels the INS is being unfair. The procedure is lengthy and humiliating for her. She feels that whatever offense she might have committed does not justify the expense of time and effort by either the INS or herself. The job she had taken was in a nursing home for a small amount of pay after they had tried desperately but unsuccessfully to find someone else to work there. Finally, the INS relents and lets her stay, but they scold her about the problems this country is facing with unemployment and make it plain that international students should never displace U.S. nationals. She listens to the lecture but feels bitter about it.

Discussion

The INS has tended to interpret regulations more strictly in recent years, particularly relating to an international student's financial support. The international student is subject to INS regulations, which are interpreted administratively without the due protection afforded under the law. From the student's point of view, the INS seems to be arbitrary in interpreting these regulations according to their feelings about particular students from particular countries. International students are easily intimidated by the INS, and even routine inquiries are often perceived as harassment. The INS officers are not trained in cross-cultural communication beyond what they learn on the job. Consequently, their way of dealing with international students is not always sensitive to cultural variables. There is probably no single aspect of an international student's U.S. experience as anxiety-provoking as staying in status with the INS. This puts a great burden of responsibility on the international student adviser and counselor both to know the regulations and to develop trusting relationships with INS agents and to help train INS staff where that opportunity is available.

Incident 3

Mr. L is a U.S. student who writes the following letter to the campus newspaper suggesting that the International Student Office be eliminated:

If we have to save money and cut budgets in the university, the least painful way is to abolish the position of the International Student Adviser and the supporting budget. For one thing, we cannot really maintain a separate office for a relatively small group of students. The time has come that we must treat all students alike and not have services for any "special" group. Secondly, we really will not hurt anybody by this decision because international students are just students like any other student and thus can enjoy the same services as are available to any other student. This action might actually work better for international students because having a special International Student Adviser probably isolates international students from other students. International students will be more integrated with other students on campus. The great majority of international students on our large campus reportedly don't visit the ISO office anyway, unless they have to. It is only a small minority of international students that have difficulties, and they are often marginal students who possibly should not have been brought here to begin with. We must make sure that these students make a realistic decision about leaving here if they can't make it on their own. The International Student Office often protects these students, asking for more and more exceptions when in fact these extensions only delay a decision to terminate them eventually. The money we save by eliminating the ISO can be redirected to important programs related to the special problems of our own society.

Discussion

The International Student Office is found on most university campuses because of specialized problems arising among international students requiring specialized knowledge. To some extent, each campus office is designed as its own "Office of Student Affairs" for international students, with financial aid, housing, counseling, and other services offered. Problems with immigration forms, difficulties in cross-cultural adjustment, and special requirements that international students need to meet prompted setting up this office. Other student populations, such as ethnic minorities, object to the idea of an International Student Office because it favors one group at the expense of other groups. Closing the ISO office means that many of its services must either be eliminated or be shifted to other offices whose staff then need to be retrained to perform them.

CONCLUSION

International students experience a wide variety of newly acquired roles that compete with their more familiar back-home values in a variety of situations. Coping with these diverse roles becomes the primary problem for most international students, and helping them cope becomes the primary task of most international-student counselors. As specific skills are identified and taught, it may be possible to help international students protect their own past and future as well as mobilize resources in the present.

As suggested in this chapter, several areas have gaps in the research that require careful and comprehensive attention. Among these are the following:

- The direction and trends of international student growth and the effect of those trends on higher education
- Role-learning rates among international students
- Natural support system networks among international students and their usefulness
- Culture shock and the U-curve adjustment process of international students
- Stereotypes that international students and U.S. nationals have of one another
- Counselor values about counseling international students

- The appropriateness of theories of student development when applied to international students
- The person-versus-situation debate applied to international students
- Gender issues among international students
- Psychological patterns of somatized stress as a result of psychological problems
- The effect of training workshops or groups on international student adaptation
- Conationals as a counseling resource for international students
- Patterns of difference among national and cultural groups of international students
- Rates of international students using counseling centers and other student services
- The reentry adjustment of international students returning home
- The effect of prearrival orientation on international students
- International students' expectations of counseling
- Hierarchies of problems faced by international students
- The preferred counseling style of working with international students
- Uses of critical incidents in studying international students
- Informal counseling methods and contexts when working with international students
- Test bias when applied to international students

Looking over this albeit incomplete list of potential research topics may stimulate you to design your own research about international students.

The extent to which each of these students is able to build and develop a satisfying identity and the social roles to fulfill that identity will determine the student's degree of success. The role of counseling for international students is to facilitate that success.

EXERCISE

INTERNATIONAL STUDENT SURVEY OF STRONG FEELINGS

Objective

This survey provides a way for the foreign student to talk with a counselor about 10 areas of concern where the student may have "strong" (positive or negative) feelings. By establishing a rank ordering of the foreign student's strong feelings, the counselor is able to focus on priority areas of the student's concern.

Instructions

Individual students are asked to indicate whether the student strongly disagrees, disagrees, agrees, strongly agrees, or is uncertain about each of the following 90 items. There are 9 items for each of 10 areas of potential concern organized in such a way that the student receives a profile of responses rank ordering these 10 areas with regard to the "strong feeling" the student has about items in that area. Each student should be given a pledge of confidentiality by the person administering the test before the test is given.

Your answers will indicate the feelings you have toward selected items about the following topics:

1. Meaning of life
2. Adventure and achievement
3. Faults of Americans
4. Teachers and classmates
5. Academic problems
6. Self-confidence
7. Doubts and assurances
8. The opposite sex
9. Family
10. Community

Indicate *either* that you *strongly agree* or that you *strongly disagree* with the items as they describe 1 of these 10 topics more than any of the other topics. For one reason or another, you may have strong feelings about the topic.

Indicate a question mark for the items about a particular topic. For one reason or another, you may *not* have strong feelings about that topic.

The objective of the International Student Survey of Strong Feelings is to suggest which of the 10 topic areas arouses strong feelings and which do not. Having strong feelings is neither good nor bad, but it may influence your adjustment as a student and the achievement of your educational objectives.

As you begin to take this survey, you will need the following materials: (a) survey booklet, (b) special answer sheet for marking responses, and (c) pen or pencil.

You should be seated away from others (at least every other chair). This will help you concentrate completely on your own survey and finish sooner without distraction by working straight through. If at all possible, finish the survey at one sitting.

On the answer sheet, fill in your name, address, date, age, sex, telephone, college or major, and country of origin. After you have read the directions, begin with Item 1. Mark your answer in the corresponding space on the answer sheet. If you have any questions, raise your hand. The person giving the survey will answer your questions.

The words "family," "home," and "community" used throughout the survey may refer to either your back-home situation or your U.S. relationships. However you interpret them, be consistent throughout the survey, using either the home country or the U.S. situation.

READ THIS FIRST

Each statement in this section is a concern that some people have. Answer each statement as you "think about" those concerns in one of five alternative responses. If you are not sure, mark the answer that is closest to what you believe to be true.

SD = Strongly disagree
D = Disagree
? = Uncertain
A = Agree
SA = Strongly agree

1. I would like being an artist, musician, or writer.

2. I like exploring the unknown.

3. I do not feel free to discuss my personal problems with anyone.

4. Some teachers act as though a student knows absolutely nothing.

5. I do not take my studies seriously enough.

6. I am afraid of failure or humiliation.

7. I feel I am not living up to my convictions.

8. Some Americans think too much about sex when we are alone together.

9. We need a greater feeling of love in our family.

10. I do not feel that the law treats me the same as it might treat some other people.

11. I enjoy artistic experiences such as art displays, concerts, or plays.

12. I like making or building practical things.

13. We do not study my country enough at the university.
14. Some of my teachers are unfair.
15. I lack confidence when asking a question in class.
16. I often feel sorry for myself.
17. I wish I could really believe in something.
18. I wonder what to look for in a life partner.
19. There were not enough social activities in my home.
20. I feel left out of community affairs.
21. I want to arrive at a meaningful philosophy of life.
22. I like working in an adventuresome occupation.
23. Too few young people go abroad to study.
24. We need recreation at the university that we can all enjoy.
25. Americans tend to underestimate the abilities of foreign students.
26. I become discouraged rather easily.
27. I avoid discussions with Americans about my beliefs.
28. I wonder if I will marry someone who will give me happiness.
29. My family could have been a happier one.
30. I am bored most of my leisure time.
31. I want to help remove social injustice.
32. I like discovering a new idea.
33. Americans are always saying one thing and doing another.
34. Studies demand too much of a person's time.
35. I wish I knew how to study better.
36. I feel that I am not as intelligent as others.
37. There is no one I can go to with a really serious problem.
38. I wonder how I can know what a boy or girl expects before going out on a date.
39. It was hard to discuss my problems with my mother.
40. I hate to ask advice or help from people who might be able to give it to me.
41. I want to work full-time to benefit society.
42. I want to own a car.
43. I do not like the gossiping of Americans.
44. Classmates at the university could be more friendly.
45. I worry about examinations.
46. I am afraid of things.

47. Some friends I highly respect are not at all interested in my country.
48. I wonder if I will find the right life partner in marriage.
49. My parents would rather that I didn't go abroad to study.
50. I used to have more friends than I have now.
51. I like having time to read and meditate.
52. I want to have a good job with lots of free time.
53. Americans fail to understand why I spend so much time with my own nationality group.
54. Some of my professors do not understand my difficulties.
55. I am not satisfied with the grades I usually get.
56. My feelings are easily hurt.
57. I sometimes wonder why I came here to study.
58. I wonder if I can find a life partner to marry who has high moral standards.
59. I would like other members of my family to come here.
60. I don't want to become involved in the community.
61. I like being able to help others.
62. I want to enter a high-paying profession.
63. Some Americans act in favor of small cliques and disregard opinions of the majority of foreign students.
64. Some classmates are inconsiderate of my feelings.
65. I wonder if I have the ability to do university work.
66. I am irritated when things do not go the way I want them to be.
67. I worry about little things.
68. I wonder whether or not I could marry someone from some other country.
69. Outside of my family there is no group where I feel I really belong.
70. People I live with argue too much.
71. I want to be an important person in the community.
72. I have taken things that did not belong to me.
73. Some Americans are unwilling to sacrifice for the good of the nation.
74. I lack the personality and ability to be a leader in a group.
75. I am considering leaving the university.
76. I lack self-confidence.
77. I am afraid I am losing my cultural values.
78. I don't know the opposite-sex things.
79. My parents and I seldom agree on current issues.
80. I feel embarrassed when I have visitors.

81. I want to be able to visit unusual places and interesting people.

82. I am in danger of becoming unemployed.

83. Some Americans try to get along with foreign students by acting like a foreign student themselves and end up looking ridiculous.

84. I lack the ability to participate in sports.

85. I find it hard to concentrate on my studies.

86. I get into moods where I can't seem to cheer up.

87. It is too hard for me to give a reason for my convictions.

88. Outsiders sometimes join our nationality club to get acquainted with our girls.

89. Financial trouble creates difficulty in my home.

90. I buy things I don't need.

Answer Sheet

1. SD D ? A SA	11. SD D ? A SA	21. SD D ? A SA
2. SD D ? A SA	12. SD D ? A SA	22. SD D ? A SA
3. SD D ? A SA	13. SD D ? A SA	23. SD D ? A SA
4. SD D ? A SA	14. SD D ? A SA	24. SD D ? A SA
5. SD D ? A SA	15. SD D ? A SA	25. SD D ? A SA
6. SD D ? A SA	16. SD D ? A SA	26. SD D ? A SA
7. SD D ? A SA	17. SD D ? A SA	27. SD D ? A SA
8. SD D ? A SA	18. SD D ? A SA	28. SD D ? A SA
9. SD D ? A SA	19. SD D ? A SA	29. SD D ? A SA
10. SD D ? A SA	20. SD D ? A SA	30. SD D ? A SA
31. SD D ? A SA	41. SD D ? A SA	51. SD D ? A SA
32. SD D ? A SA	42. SD D ? A SA	52. SD D ? A SA
33. SD D ? A SA	43. SD D ? A SA	53. SD D ? A SA
34. SD D ? A SA	44. SD D ? A SA	54. SD D ? A SA
35. SD D ? A SA	45. SD D ? A SA	55. SD D ? A SA
36. SD D ? A SA	46. SD D ? A SA	56. SD D ? A SA
37. SD D ? A SA	47. SD D ? A SA	57. SD D ? A SA
38. SD D ? A SA	48. SD D ? A SA	58. SD D ? A SA
39. SD D ? A SA	49. SD D ? A SA	59. SD D ? A SA
40. SD D ? A SA	50. SD D ? A SA	60. SD D ? A SA
61. SD D ? A SA	71. SD D ? A SA	81. SD D ? A SA
62. SD D ? A SA	72. SD D ? A SA	82. SD D ? A SA
63. SD D ? A SA	73. SD D ? A SA	83. SD D ? A SA
64. SD D ? A SA	74. SD D ? A SA	84. SD D ? A SA
65. SD D ? A SA	75. SD D ? A SA	85. SD D ? A SA
66. SD D ? A SA	76. SD D ? A SA	86. SD D ? A SA
67. SD D ? A SA	77. SD D ? A SA	87. SD D ? A SA
68. SD D ? A SA	78. SD D ? A SA	88. SD D ? A SA
69. SD D ? A SA	79. SD D ? A SA	89. SD D ? A SA
70. SD D ? A SA	80. SD D ? A SA	90. SD D ? A SA

Scoring your test

The answer sheet is arranged in nine columns. Score your answers horizontally across columns using the following point scale:

SA or SD = 2
D or A = 1
? = 0

Scale	Items	Total Score
1. Meaning in life	1, 11, 21, 31, 41, 51, 61, 71, 81	
2. Adventure and achievement	2, 12, 22, 32, 42, 52, 62, 72, 82	
3. Faults of Americans	3, 13, 23, 33, 43, 53, 63, 73, 83	
4. Teachers and classmates	4, 14, 24, 34, 44, 54, 64, 74, 84	
5. Academic problems	5, 15, 25, 35, 45, 55, 65, 75, 85	
6. Self-confidence	6, 16, 26, 36, 46, 56, 66, 76, 86	
7. Doubts and assurance	7, 17, 27, 37, 47, 57, 67, 77, 87	
8. The opposite sex	8, 18, 28, 38, 48, 58, 68, 78, 88	
9. Family	9, 19, 29, 39, 49, 59, 69, 79, 89	
10. Community	10, 20, 30, 40, 50, 60, 70, 80, 90	

Debriefing

It is sometimes difficult for an international student, unfamiliar with the counseling process, to identify a presenting "problem" where counseling might be appropriate and helpful. This survey of strong feelings is an attempt to establish a priority of 10 different topical areas in the international student's experiences according to the strong positive and/or negative feelings the international student has about the 9 items in that topical area.

Because the direction (positive or negative) of the strong feeling is not scored, but, rather, the focus is on the intensity itself, an interpretation of results would require going back to the nine items in each topical area to identify areas where counseling might be appropriate and useful.

It might be useful to ask the international student to complete the questionnaire before coming to the counseling office or while waiting for an appointment at the counseling office. Having considered the list of topical areas where the student may have strong feeling encourages the student to review those areas of recent experience where counseling might be useful.

The answer sheet is organized so that a counselor should be able to scan the columns and rapidly identify those topical areas with a higher or lower priority of strong feelings. Having identified areas where there is a high level of strong feeling, the counselor may want to introduce that information into the counseling interview in a general inquiry about how the student is doing.

It may also be useful to move directly to those 9 items contributing to a higher score (relative to the scores on the other topics) and respond to the student's indication of high or low strong feeling on particular items.

In any case, the student's responses to this survey of strong feeling provide structure at the beginning of a counseling interview and reduce the student's sense of ambiguity in the systematic review of topical areas.

The measures of "strong feeling" are scored relative to one another to establish priorities within the 10 content areas where counseling might be appropriate. The highest possible score for any topical area is 18 and the lowest possible score 0. Because this is essentially a projective test, there is no absolute external measure against which these scores can be judged, but, rather, emphasis should be placed on the rank ordering of scores to indicate priority areas for counseling. The test items provide an indirect means for persons otherwise unfamiliar with counseling to identify areas of "strong feeling" (positive or negative) where counseling might be useful. In some cases, the priorities may be expressed through small differences and in other cases through larger differences in scores interpreted internally to each test. It may be useful to identify those high-scoring items that contribute to higher scores for more specific interpretation of test results. It may also be useful to discuss similarities and differences among persons completing the test, as those individuals explain those similarities and differences in their own unique context.

Family Therapy in a Systemic Context

- **Primary Objective** Apply culture-centered counseling skills to the family system

- **Secondary Objectives** (1) Demonstrate how a culture-centered counselor perspective mobilizes multicultural family resources and (2) Describe the advantages of systems theories for dealing with complexity and balance

amily systems therapy has emphasized the importance of context for a long time, recognizing that a family member's problems may (a) serve an important function for the family, (b) be a consequence of the family's transitional difficulty, and/or (c) be a symptom of dysfunctional patterns learned in the family context (Bitter & Corey, 1996). The family member client is part of a living context. The family system itself is the primary unit of treatment and not the identified patient (Goldenberg & Goldenberg, 1995).

FAMILY THERAPY

Attempts to modify relationships in the context of the family generally view dysfunctional behavior and problems as the result of faulty interactions rather than a deficiency within any one family member. Typically, family therapy takes an interpersonal more than an intrapsychic perspective, evaluating systemic interaction according to how each member plays out one's role in maintaining the family system. A particular family member may create problems, but the real cause of these problems and their corresponding solutions are located in the dysfunctional family system itself.

Each system shares responsibility for mutual causality as an interdependent member. Open systems, such as families, have a continuous changing flow of power and changing dynamics that is quite different from closed systems. The family system is constituted by interaction and connections among family members as relationships and patterns are repeated or change. In family therapy, the therapist attempts to redirect or influence those changes in a functional or healthy direction.

Pathology in the family system can result from dysfunctional relationships. Interlocking pathologies occur when the problems of one family member are entangled, interlocking, and frequently unconscious. These are problems typically dealt with by moving back and forth between the past and the present. Fusion occurs when family members cannot act independently of one another and are stuck together in a vague amorphous mass. These problems are typically dealt with by attempting to "unhook" family members from one another. Pseudomutuality refers to the loss of boundaries among family members. These problems are typically dealt with by breaking up or splitting alignments to create new coalitions that free up enmeshed or disengaged family members. The double bind refers to the severe limitations in a particularly important family relationship that family members can neither get along with nor get along without.

The major theories of family therapy are Object Relations Theory, Bowen Theory, Structural Family Therapy, and Communication Theory. Object Relations Theory suggests that interaction primarily differentiates between the self and other objects, presuming an unconscious denied projection of self or collusion between family members. The focus is on historical and transgenerational issues. Bowen Theory is an integrated system involving interlocking relationships of family members. The goal is to help individuals become differentiated or unstuck from the family through the help of a therapist as coach. The triangular relationships in a family —where two members involve a third—maintain the balance of the system. Structural Family Therapy attempts to change the structure of alliances and coalitions among family members to change their experiences of one another. The therapist joins the system to transform it. The focus is less on the past and more about ongoing interactions in the family that reinforce behaviors. Communication Theory looks at problems and patterns of communication among family members and is less focused on the causes or origins of the problems. The goal is to change the rules of the system (Foley, 1987).

THE FAMILY CONTEXT

All families—given differences of age, gender, and lifestyle—are bicultural to a greater or lesser extent, but not all families are willing or able to deal with their contrasting cultural contexts. When the families' cultural contexts include ethnocultural differences however, bicultural factors become more obvious and are more likely to attract our attention. Both the traditional family model—where the individual serves the family—and more modernized models—where the family is expected to serve the individual—have broken down in a confusion of bicultural and multicultural alternatives. This chapter discusses how we can find common ground for mediating conflict in bicultural families by focusing on the shared positive expectations in highly diversified or fragmented families while also recognizing the importance of differences:

> Different cultures had differing ways of understanding "appropriate" family organization, values, communication and behavior. Although the family perspective had revolutionized the individual view of the client by taking family context into account, it now needed to understand its own unit of analysis (i.e., the family) in light of an even larger context: culture. (Gushue & Sciarra, 1995, p. 588)

Each family is a social system that has evolved its own unique set of rules and roles for family members. The family provides an organized power structure with its own forms of special "family" communication rules at the overt and covert levels. Each family has developed special insider ways of negotiating and problem solving to perform effectively as a unit. Family relationships are special, deep, and have many levels of meaning based on a shared history together, shared internalized perceptions, and learned assumptions in a shared sense of purpose. Each family member is tied by powerful, durable, and usually reciprocal attachments and loyalties for the lifetime of that family.

Every family functions at three levels: first, the related and yet separate individuals with their own unique needs and separate perspectives; second, the family as an arena of social-psychological relationships that are more than the individual members themselves; and third, the family as a social institution or subsystem in the larger social and cultural context. Throughout this force field of transacting processes, changes in any one part are related to change in all parts. Intrapsychic conflict of a family member, for example, is closely related to social role conflicts among other family members as well as a conflict of cultural values that attach each family to a particular sociocultural environment. Traditionally, the family has served four functions: (a) provide and regulate affectional needs for intimacy and social-sexual relations, (b) provide care and rearing of the young, (c) provide units of economic cooperation, and (d) enculturate members into society. These same "common ground" functions are expressed very differently in different cultures requiring caregivers to understand each cultural context from its own culture-centered perspective.

Increased multicultural contact has resulted in increased conflict, especially for bicultural families. The nuclear family is experiencing internal conflict from a variety of sources:

- More working mothers are experiencing frustration and guilt for separating themselves from home and family.
- Conflict in redefining shared responsibility between husband and wife has increased.
- More wives are seeking careers outside the home.
- Increased pressure from media-driven idealized family and parenting models leads to a sense of failure.
- Otherwise successful families—as defined by family members—are experiencing painful separation from increased mobility when children leave or family members are displaced.
- Increased conflict in legal obligations toward one another by husbands, wives, and children has complicated family relationships.

The tensions and stress of modern society also affect the nuclear family, requiring adaptation. Parents, for one, are expected to function in many contrasting and competing roles:

- *The provider* contributes to the economic welfare and well-being of the family.
- *The celebrant* infuses family events with enthusiasm, joy, and self-presence, the aim being to promote harmony while emphasizing the purpose of the event.
- *The nurturer* provides the quality of care and comfort that society values for the family.
- *The technician* uses equipment and facilities to produce a product and cope with the technology attached to a broken appliance, a stalled car, or other technical skills required by the family.
- *The companion* makes use of leisure-time activities to reinforce family relations. It is more than just doing things together but, rather, being a part of the family adventure and experience.
- *The socializer* transmits the values, ideas, and content of culture from one generation to another. Socializing can include giving family members advice or teaching what is important.
- *The symbol* represents dominant ideas in the culture. There are both positive and negative aspects in parents as symbols for the family and society.
- *The manager* plans, organizes, carries out ideas, and evaluates the results. This might involve formal management of a group or the less formal management of decisions in the family.
- *The comforter* knows when another person needs aid and comfort and is able to determine both the nature of that person's problem and the appropriate steps to take to alleviate it.
- *The budgeter* makes careful use of resources such as time, money, endorsement, and organization rather than just managing them.
- *The promoter* translates ideas and values to the community where a particular point of view is promoted.
- *The counselor* sees a problem from different ways and helps the family deal with it.
- *The communicator* gives others instructions, information, and reasons and transmits the goals, ideals, and activities of the family to society and society's to the family.
- *The problem solver* identifies the appropriate solution to family crises, emergencies, and other situations, whether simple and routine or complicated.

Axelson (1993) describes some of the alternatives invented by multicultural and/or bicultural families:

- Single-parent families have increased among divorced, never-married, separated, and widowed persons. Temporary single-parent families might also occur due to military service, employment conditions, or other non-voluntary separation of parents and children.

- Blended families are reconstituted by the remarriage of a divorced person involving children from one or both partners. This family alternative is on the increase because most divorced persons remarry.

- Extended, or joint, families include relatives or in-laws who share the nuclear family household or may live nearby and interact as a single family unit. Members of the extended family may be single, abandoned, legally separated, divorced, or widowed as well as intergenerational.

- Augmented families include nonrelatives who share the household with a nuclear family as roomers, boarders, friends, transients, or long-term guests.

- Nonfamily shared households consist of two or more unrelated persons living together to meet personal financial and social needs in modernized, mobile, and frequently fragmented societies.

- Nonfamily sole-person households exist by choice or circumstance, an alternative that is on the increase particularly among the elderly and dispossessed.

- Homelessness among individuals and families, who are made so by financial or political conditions, is increasingly considered an accepted alternative and a chronic condition of modern society.

The variety of patterns and structures of modern families is further complicated by the increased migration of people from one cultural site or identity to another, resulting in a bicultural and multicultural family crisis. This chapter demonstrates how culturally defined common ground can help caregivers deal with both the confusion of different family structures and the complexity of different cultural identities through an inclusive definition of the cultural context.

FAMILIES IN A CULTURAL CONTEXT

The family functions quite differently in an individualist society compared to a collectivist society. Individualists have more personal choice in their memberships, careers, religious affiliation, political affiliation, and social role. Individualists can and do change roles or affiliations frequently. They are free to choose which family members stay in contact and how close that contact is. In collectivist societies, a person's group memberships are fixed. One's family of origin specifies the roles one is required to take in life (Bond, 1994). A "Westernized" description of the family presumes a separate, independent, and autonomous group guided by traits, abilities, values, and motives that distinguish each family from others. Western cultures are described by Berry et al. (1992) as more "idiocentric," emphasizing competition, self-confidence, and freedom, whereas collectivistic cultures are more allocentric, emphasizing communal responsibility, social usefulness, and acceptance of authority. Westernized beliefs grew out of a naturalistic understanding of the physical world of the Enlightenment in Europe, describing human behavior in objective expressions of "mass and extension" rather than internalized categories of color, temperature, sound, taste, and feeling, which were more subjective "created sensations" (Taylor, 1989).

Western and non-Western approaches to the family are complementary in that both focus on development. Non-Western systems focus on advanced stages of development in a more "transpersonal" focus of well-being, and Western systems focus on psychopathology and measured physical/mental changes:

> From a multiple-states-of-consciousness model, the traditional Western approach is recognized as a relativistically useful model provided that, because of the limitations imposed by state-specific relevancy, learning, and understanding, it is not applied inappropriately to perspectives and states of consciousness and identity outside its scope. (Walsh, 1989, p. 549)

Pathologizing mystical experiences is an example of Western models going beyond their boundaries in some cultures. The recent emphasis on "indigenous psychology" (Kim & Berry, 1993) and increased attention to non-Western approaches have resulted from increased international contact, a redefinition of postcolonial relationships, internationalization of the social sciences, radicalization of special interest groups, a methodological paradigm shift toward complexity, activism of contemporary social scientists, interdisciplinary cooperation, awareness of cultural diversity, and international educational exchange (Sloan, 1990).

CULTURE NOTE

The conventional habit of psychology has been to look "West" for theory and "East" for data.

The complexity of the family as an intergenerational system has inhibited research on the family in its cultural context: "Given the lack of theory in academic psychology to throw light on family functioning and family change, the prototypical Western (middle-class, nuclear) family has been adopted implicitly as 'the family'" (Kagitcibasi, 1996, p. 73). Kagitcibasi (1996) contends that the main shift of global socioeconomic development is not toward the model of individualistic independence but toward one of collectivist emotional interdependence:

> To reiterate, the distinguishing mark of the prototype of total interdependence is familial (intergenerational) and human (individual) independence is distinguished by independence at both familial and individual levels in both material and emotional dimensions. This model however, manifests interdependence in the emotional realm at both family and individual levels, but it entails independence at both levels in the material realm. (p. 87)

Healthy families have traditionally been identified as expressing emotions freely and openly, with each member having a right to be one's unique self with an equal or fair division of labor, egalitarian role relationships and with the nuclear family as the primary concern. In caregiving to bicultural families, the main goal is to achieve harmony, treating all members of the family together and perceiving the family itself as the corporate client, requiring the provider to help the family modify relationships and communication patterns in some way. Not all cultures value these characteristics in the same way and a more broadly defined list of criteria is required for bicultural families.

Szapocznik and Kurtines (1993) have designed a model called Family Effectiveness Training (FET) that views individual behavior problems within the context of the bicultural family system. Early prevention through FET strengthens the family system against these problems:

> It is our hypothesis that what makes this deviation from the normative component maladjustive in bicultural settings is that it renders the individual inappropriately monocultural in a bicultural context. The most important implication for family functioning is that in families where members are characterized by culturally related differences, the typical intergenerational differences found with families of adolescents are exacerbated by cultural differences. (p. 248)

By identifying the problem afflicting the family, the clinician is able to mobilize an intergenerational alliance against the "common enemy" of the problem, viewing the underlying problem as one of intercultural conflict rather than intergenerational strife. In this way, parents and children are able to collaborate in ways that strengthen the intergenerational alliance.

Culture-centered caregivers must consider at least six major factors when working with bicultural families (Ho, 1987; Sue & Sue, 1990). First, issues of racism and poverty are likely to dominate the lives of many minority groups and families from those groups. Second, value conflicts between majority and minority cultures often arise regarding the importance of family, ancestors, interdependencies, and self, leading to mislabeling behaviors and misattributions (Kim, 1981). Third, most minority families are bicultural, sharing at least two different cultures, one public and one private, both of which caregivers must understand. Fourth, many minorities have experienced profound oppression, as in the United States with Blacks coming out of slavery, native peoples out of colonialism, and refugee groups out of political exploitation. Fifth, common bonds of language give members of minority groups a sense of belonging and identity, particularly with regard to language issues. Sixth, class differences complicate cultural differences still more, leading to invisible boundaries and barriers that inhibit understanding even within the same ethnocultural group. Atkinson, Morten, and Sue (1993) suggest a bicultural socialization model where minority individuals experience acculturation within their separate group culture while also being socialized to the dominant culture.

CULTURE-CENTERED
FAMILY THERAPY MODELS

The culture-centered family therapist must be linguistically and culturally attuned to each family member without losing sight of the structural dynamics of the family system. Otherwise, the therapist's view becomes either ethnocentric or stereotypic, resulting in premature termination and underuse of family cultural resources. The multiple levels of family acculturation and racial/cultural identity are resources for rather than obstacles to therapy. They present opportunities for collaboration toward the family's higher levels of functioning.

Gushue and Sciarra (1995) propose a model of family therapy based on a racial/cultural interaction paradigm focused on four crucial dimensions:

- Important within-group and between-group cultural differences among and between families of the same culture
- Dynamic changes at all levels as different cultural identities or status roles become salient for the various family subsystems, changing the interaction both within and between families
- Racial/cultural identity roles of the counselors whose own racial/cultural identity will influence interaction with the family in its separate cultural context
- Cultural issues when a minority group member counselor works with a dominant culture group family or when both counselor and client-family come from the same "apparent" cultural context

The family therapist using Gushue and Sciarra's (1995) interactional paradigm asks these significant questions the authors propose:

> First, to what extent does this particular family conform to or differ from the typical patterns of family functioning for its culture? Second, what cultural differences may exist within the family itself (i.e., among the various subsystems)? If cultural differences exist within the family, what consequences do these differences have for interactions both among the subsystems and between the various subsystems and the counselor? (p. 589)

Koss-Chioino and Vargas (1992) describe another culture-sensitive family therapy model with two dimensions of culture and structure:

> The two cultural dimensions consist of content and context; the structural dimensions consist of form and process. All psychotherapies have these dimensions; however, the cultural dimensions that are embedded in most psychotherapeutic approaches pertain to Western values, concepts and traditions. Therapists usually are not fully aware of the cultural content or context in their work, or how the cultural dimensions interrelate with those of process and form. (p. 301)

It is possible to achieve cultural responsiveness through family therapy using a variety of different strategies. The strategy itself is less important than the ways in which a particular strategy becomes culturally responsive. It is this degree of culture-centered specificity of matching the therapy mode with cultural adaptations that helps achieve positive outcomes.

Wehrly (1995) reviews other culturally sensitive models of family therapy. For example, those designed for Asian families might focus on negotiation or mediation rather than confrontation, the special role of the mother in an Asian family, the importance of hierarchy in the family, being sensitive to face saving, and the role of family in Asian society. Those designed for African American families might focus on the extended family bond, the adaptability of roles, the strength of religious orientation, the values of a work ethic and/or an education, and coping skills for survival as a minority group family in a dominant culture context.

Kagitcibasi (1996) describes a general "contextual" model of family change, based on three models of family interaction patterns, that situates

> the self within the family and the family within the cultural and socioeconomic environment. The family is treated in terms of both its social and psychological characteristics. The former is examined in terms of the family structure and the latter in terms of the family system, including interaction and socialization. It is also a functional model as causal relations and the dynamics underlying the family interaction patterns and the socialization/development of the self are stressed. (p. 76)

Bemak, Cheung, and Bornemann (1996) propose a multilevel model (MLM) of family therapy to refugees in their cultural context:

> This model is a four-level intervention approach that integrates traditional Western psychotherapy with indigenous healing methods, cultural empowerment and psychoeducational training. The MLM takes into account cultural belief systems, acculturation, psychosocial adaptation and the influence of resettlement policy on mental health. It provides a holistic framework that conceptualizes an integrated strategy to meet the multiple needs of the refugee population. (p. 261)

Premigration factors might include ethnicity, country of origin, class status, cultural values, filial piety, face, and respect for authority. Migration factors might include leaving with or without other family members, whether through escape or emigration, voluntary or nonvoluntary migration, and camp experiences. Postmigration factors might include the refugee's new living environment, the social ecology of resettlement, the receptivity of the host culture, and all the normal stressors of family dynamics.

All culture-centered family therapy models involve commitment by family members to a higher or lower level of affiliation to the indigenous culture, on the one hand, and a higher or lower level of affiliation to the dominant culture, on the other hand.

All family therapy models emphasize the importance of complex relationships and interacting systems. Each family exists in a multilevel environment. Oetting and Beauvais (1991) have developed a theory of cultural identification that does not polarize cultures but instead acknowledges a multiplicity of coexisting identities. This *orthogonal* model recognizes that increased identification with one culture does not require decreased identification with other cultures.

The five most frequently used alternative models are less complex. The *dominant majority* model simply imposes a dominant culture on all minority groups. The *transitional* model presumes a movement toward the dominant culture as an appropriate adjustment. The *alienation* model seeks to avoid stress from anomie by assisting persons in transition to make successful adjustments. The *multidimensional* model presumes transition on several dimensions at the same time, with different degrees of change on each dimension. The *bicultural* model presumes that one can adapt to one culture without losing contact with the earlier culture.

The orthogonal model, however, suggests that adapting simultaneously to any culture is independent from adapting to many other cultures, providing an unlimited combination of patterns that combine the preceding five alternative models as potential identifications. This model presumes a higher level of complexity and a more comprehensive inclusion of cultural context. It also offers several advantages:

- Cultural groups may exist in association with one another without isolating themselves or competing with one another.
- Minority cultures need not be eliminated or absorbed in order to coexist.
- A permanent multicultural society may be possible that is multifaceted and multidimensional without becoming a "melting pot."
- Conflicts of value and belief do not present insurmountable barriers but may be combined in a realistic pluralism.
- Cultural conflict may become a positive rather than a negative force from the perspective of shared common-ground expectations.
- Members of minority groups may be less inclined toward militancy when their survival is not threatened.
- Interaction between minority and majority cultures may be less destructive for all parties.
- There are economic advantages of releasing resources previously consumed by cultural conflict.

- There are already models of orthogonal relationships in healthy bicultural and multicultural families or social units.

Biculturalism need not imply dysfunction. De Anda (1994) identifies several factors that contribute to biculturalism without this implication:

- There is harmonious cultural overlap.
- Cultural mediators/translators are available.
- Sufficient positive corrective feedback is given.
- The individual is bilingual as well as bicultural.
- There is one dissimilarity of physical appearance.

These factors demonstrate the importance of finding common ground across cultures as a primary tool of caregiving. Each of the strategies for giving care to bicultural families has depended on finding areas of shared salience to manage an otherwise impossibly complex tangle of relationships.

The culture-centered approach suggests that individual change must be sensitive to the cultural context in which that change occurs. Change is perceived as linked to the cultural context in such a way that training and education themselves become treatment modalities. The influence between a culture-centered caregiver and client becomes reciprocal in this cultural context, with both the caregiver and the client contributing to the construction of a shared context that is also complex and dynamic. Culture-centered caregivers are able to generate a wide variety of intentional verbal and nonverbal responses appropriate to their positive shared expectations with bicultural families. To the extent that members of a bicultural family among themselves or in their contact with outsiders interpret behaviors outside this common ground of shared positive expectations that conflict is likely to escalate in nonproductive ways. To the extent that members of a bicultural family interpret behaviors in the cultural context of shared positive expectations, the conflict in behaviors could make a positive contribution to the health of the family unit by demonstrating a variety of acceptable approaches and legitimate alternatives.

Refugee children in particular cannot be understood independently of their environment, for they are part of both the family and the larger transitional social systems. Refugee children and their parents typically experience disintegration of their original community and settlement in a totally new one.

By contrast, counseling and psychotherapy have traditionally focused on the individual's attaining optimal independent functioning, coping abilities, and adaptation. The refugee families, however, typically come from cultural contexts where the family and community social networks are essential resources for healthy lives.

A *ho'oponopono* Family Therapy Model

One working example of a family-based therapy model in a non-Western context is the system for maintaining harmony and managing conflict within the extended family through *ho'oponopono,* which in Hawaiian means "setting to right." This traditional system developed in the Hawaiian context has been adapted to a variety of other settings in useful ways (Shook, 1985). The Hawaiian context contributed a pattern of values and practices about family and child rearing that emphasized working together, cooperation, and harmony. Although many traditional Hawaiian cultural traditions have been lost—such as the *ali'i* chief system, the land, and universal Hawaiian language use—others such as a hierarchical social organization, traditional land-use patterns, and elements of the material culture have been maintained through the elders, or *kumus,* in traditional music, dancing, and singing.

The extended family, or *ohana,* is very important as a foundation of Hawaiian society. Child-rearing practices foster interdependence and opportunity to participate in adult roles contributing to the family's welfare. This structure is organized around a benevolent authoritarianism by the elders or the *kupuna,* or teachers. The value of affiliation is evident throughout the family system:

> The successful maturation of a person in the Hawaiian culture thus requires that an individual cultivate an accurate ability to perceive and attend to other people's needs, often without being asked. These are attitudes and behaviors that help cement the relationships of the *ohana* and the community. (Shook, 1985, p. 6)

Negative relationships result in "entanglements" called *hihia* that disrupt balance and harmony and require self-scrutiny, admission of wrongdoing, asking forgiveness, and restitution to restore that harmony. Negative sanctions such as illness result from negative actions or feelings toward others. The traditional *ho'oponopono* approach to problem solving was revived in the early 1970s with the publication of *Nana I Ke Kumu* by Pukui, Hartig, and Lee (1972), who along with Panglinawan (1972) have increased an awareness of this traditional strategy.

When family harmony is disturbed in any way, a senior family member, or *kahuna,* organizes the problem-solving process of *ho'oponopono* that includes prayer, identification of the problem, discussion, confession of wrongdoing, restitution when possible, forgiveness, and release.

The *ho'oponopono* ceremony begins with prayer, or *pule,* asking God for assistance and placing the process in a cosmic or spiritual context. This is followed by the identification, or *kukulu kumuhana,* which means sharing strength to solve the family's problems by reaching out to the persons causing disruption to establish a favorable climate. The problem, or *hala,* is then described in a way that ties the person who was wronged and the wrongdoer together in an "entanglement," or *hihia.* Then, the many different dimensions of the problem "entanglement" are explored and clarified, one by one. As each aspect is identified through discussion, or *mahiki,* the layers or tangles of the problem are reorganized until family relationships are again in harmony. Individuals who have been wronged are encouraged to share their feelings and perception, and honest, open self-scrutiny is encouraged. If the group discussion is disrupted by emotional outbursts, the leader may declare a period of silence, or *ho'omalu,* for family members to regain harmony in their discussion. Following this is the sincere confession of wrongdoing, or *mihi,* where the wrongdoer seeks forgiveness and agrees to restitution. Untangling the negative, or *kala,* then joins both the wronged and the wrongdoer in a mutual release and restores their cosmic and spiritual harmony together. A closing spiritual ceremony, or *pani,* reaffirms the family's strength and bond.

Mossman (1976) describes the underlying philosophy and family values that provide a favorable context for *ho'oponopono* to function effectively. The idea of *lokahi,* a natural and harmonious order in the universe, is the primary foundation for achieving harmony between God(s), nature, and people. This idea depends on *akua,* which is reverence and deep respect for the historically defined gods. Even after their conversion to Christianity, many Hawaiians still believe in family spirits. *Kanaka* means a deep respect for all human beings and the importance of maintaining good and open relationships. *Ke ao nei* means a deep respect for nature or the natural environment surrounding people, for Hawaiians are sensitive to maintaining harmony in the environment. *Mana* is a spiritual power possessed by special people and objects that is based on supernatural sources. *Aloha I ke ola* means a genuine positive appreciation for life and living to the fullest. *Hau'oli* describes the spontaneous ability to relax, enjoy life, and have a sense of humor. *Kapu* includes the laws to protect the rights of people and the environment, with clearly defined penalties and immediate punishment. *Pau'a like* emphasizes the mutual responsibility of all people to protect these ideas.

Mossman (1976) goes on to describe important family values for the *ohana*. There is a sense of unity, togetherness, shared love, shared responsibilities, and even shared material goods. All members of the *ohana* are valued, needed, and worthwhile, as the following family values in Hawaiian culture demonstrate:

- *Kupuna-makua:* Respect for the parent and grandparent generations defines how important the elders' wisdom is.
- *Keiki:* Children are important. Love and respect for children and their needs guide understanding, structure discipline, and define responsibilities.
- *Kuleana:* Expectations and responsibilities for self and others within the *ohana* are clearly defined.
- *Kokua:* Cooperation is important because everyone's survival depends on the resources that everyone contributes in providing for the *ohana*. Duties are willingly accepted and efficiently organized.
- *Laulima:* Cooperation to achieve certain specific tasks in larger projects depends on people coming together in an organized fashion to accomplish the task, led by a respected family member.
- *Mahele:* A shared exchange of one's food products and material goods is necessary for survival of the family.
- *Aloha:* Love, affection, kindness, and liking other people both inside and outside the family means accepting oneself and trusting others as important through unconditional love freely given.
- *Mai e 'ai:* Inviting others to share a meal demonstrates their value and how respected they are.
- *Ho'omalimali:* Patience and fortitude means waiting and assuming that each problem has a solution and decisions should not be rushed.
- *Manawale'a:* Being productive and skillful is a source of pride in one's own ability to accomplish.

There are, however, certain family values that describe rude and unacceptable behavior in the Hawaiian culture:

- *Kikoi:* Rude remarks, criticism, or putting other people down, which implies a wrongful sense of individual superiority

- *Holoholo'olelo:* Gossiping or telling stories about other people
- *Maha'oi:* Being too bold in asking for things, entering someone else's property without permission, and not minding one's own business
- *Niele:* Asking too many questions without watching and listening until the task has been completed
- *Hukihuki:* Wanting one's own way and refusing to cooperate with others
- *Kuhilani:* Ordering others to do something
- *Noiku:* Asking for something from someone without providing a polite way to refuse the request

Ho'oponopono provides a rare example of a non-Western indigenous strategy for family therapy being adapted to multicultural contexts. Some aspects of it that adapt more easily are (a) the importance of placing the strategy in a spiritual context, (b) channeling the discussion, with sanctions of silence should disruption occur, and (c) bringing the wrongdoer back into the community as a full member and with complete restitution.

CONCLUSION

Family therapy has been sensitive to the systemic context as an important resource for mental health long before individual therapy realized the importance of context. Approaches to understanding the family emphasized both the complex structure and dynamic process of families. To a large extent, family therapy was influenced by Westernized models of the nuclear family as the norm. As the multicultural context of families became more visible and as traditional nuclear family models changed, people began inventing other "familylike" affiliations that maintained aspects of "family rules" but did not resemble traditional families in structure.

With increased awareness of the cultural context, family therapies have begun to focus on both the similarities and the differences within the family as constituting a strong positive resource rather than an obstacle or barrier. One family therapy model has a complicated "orthogonal" perspective, allowing multiple culture-centered dimensions or even identities to exist simultaneously within the individual or family.

The example of *ho'oponopono* clearly illustrates how family therapy in a traditional non-Western context can untangle the problems confronting family members individually and the family as a unit. By demonstrating the interdependency of family members on one another, this Hawaiian model suggests ways that all therapy might be modified to fit a multicultural context.

By combining practice and theory in the field of caregiving to multicultural families, one can become more responsive to the importance of cultural similarities and differences at the same time in each cultural context. Whereas attending to the cultural context can facilitate the quality of caregiving, disregarding this context will lead caregivers toward abstract projections of their own self-referenced criteria and the fatal illusion of a monocultural future.

EXERCISE

CULTURE-CENTERED GENOGRAM

Objective

To identify similarities and differences within a person's family over a three-generation period of time according to ethnographic, demographic, status, and affiliation categories

Instructions

Identify your own family context by constructing a genogram for three generations including yourself, your parents on both sides, and both of your parents' parents. Identify each person's social system according to the following categories:

- Ethnographic: nationality, ethnicity, religion, language of preference
- Demographic: age at the time you had contact with them, gender, place(s) of residence
- Status: social, educational, economic
- Affiliation: significant formal affiliations (group or organization), significant informal affiliations (lifestyle or value)

The usefulness of this genogram will be enhanced if both you and a partner complete the genogram and compare the similarities and differences in your family backgrounds. Feel free to include qualitative commentary in each of these categories for each of your family members, especially regarding the "salience" or particular importance any of these categories had for that individual family member.

When you have completed your culture-centered genogram it will look like this:

GRANDFATHER	GRANDMOTHER	GRANDFATHER	GRANDMOTHER

1. Ethnographic
2. Demographic
3. Status
4. Affiliation

FATHER/SIBLINGS	MOTHER/SIBLINGS

1. Ethnographic
2. Demographic
3. Status
4. Affiliation

SELF/SIBLINGS

1. Ethnographic
2. Demographic
3. Status
4. Affiliation

Debriefing

- Which significant/salient identities in your family served a positive function in the formation of your own cultural identity?
- Which significant/salient identities in your family served a negative function in the formation of your own cultural identity?
- How would you describe the identity of each family member?
- What patterns were reinforced for males and/or females by family members?
- What would you say are the enduring cultural values across generations in your family?
- What will be your unique and special contribution to the family for the future?
- To what extent was career important to the cultural identity of family members?
- What are the myths or traditions that emerge from your family background?
- What boundaries are defined by your family background?
- What would you like to change about your family, and what would you like to keep the same?

You may come up with additional questions and/or topics as you compare your genogram with your partner's.

PART

Culture-Centered Skills

This third section focuses on the skilled response of culture-centered counselors to the complex and dynamic cultural contexts in which it is applied, for the complicated nature of culture-centered intervention skills goes beyond simplistic descriptions of counseling (Chapter 8). The Cultural Grid demonstrates how to find common ground in transferring skills from teachers to students (Chapter 9). Culture-centered ethical alternatives remind us of the important moral consequences of intervention in a cultural context (Chapter 10). Chapter 11 reviews current and enduring controversies of cultural contexts. The book concludes by summarizing the key issues of culture-centered counseling and the models developed in response to those issues (Chapter 12).

8

Culture-Centered Counseling Skills

■ **Primary Objective** Identify teachable/learnable skills for developing a culture-centered perspective in counseling

■ **Secondary Objectives** (1) Describe the importance of complexity in culture-centered counseling and (2) Review program training alternatives for culture-centered counselors in the Triad Training Model

Pedersen and Ivey (1993) have linked culture-centeredness with Kelly's personal construct theories to empower intentional caregivers. This approach to culture assumes that culture (a) is personal, (b) develops as a result of accumulated learning from a complex variety of sources, (c) depends on interaction with others in a context to define itself, (d) changes to accommodate a changing world context, (e) provides a basis for predicting future behavior of self or others, and (f) becomes the central control point for any and all decisions. The "constructivist" perspective is based on the premise that one has no direct access to a singular, stable, and fully knowable external reality but, rather, depends on a culturally embedded, interpersonally connected, and necessarily limited perspective of reality. The emphasis is on personal reality and constructed meaning in a subjective as well as objective understanding of knowledge (McNamee & Gergen, 1992).

Reality, according to this newly emerging contextual and constructivist view, is based not on absolute truth but on an understanding of complex and dynamic relationships in a cultural context. Relationships are understood not abstractly but through narratives and stories in an alternative to linear, stage-based, convergent hierarchies (Steenbarger, 1991). As the sociocultural context changes, so the self changes to accommodate and assist each other person to construct and reconstruct meaningful reality.

Howard (1991) also documents how culture is made up of the stories people live by and have learned over their lifetime:

> A life becomes meaningful when one seeks himself or herself as an actor within the context of a story—be it a cultural tale, a religious narrative, a family saga, the march of science, a political movement, and so forth. Early in life we are free to choose what life story we will inhabit—and later we find we are lived by that story. (p. 196)

Claiborn and Lichtenberg (1989) support the importance of such a sociocultural context for "interactional counseling," where change is reciprocal and multidirectional, each event is both cause and effect, roles are negotiated, and the participating counselor becomes aware of and participates in constructing new environments.

Sampson (1993) suggests that psychology and counseling have at best accommodated add-on eclectic strategies in response to culturally different movements and special interest groups without fundamentally transforming conventional frameworks of understanding:

> Psychology is accused of using a framework of understanding that implicitly represents a particular point of view, that of currently dominant social groups, all the while acting as though its own voice were neutral, reflecting reason, rationality, and with its ever expanding collection of empirical data, perhaps truth itself. (Sampson, 1993, p. 1221)

The legitimacy of counseling in bicultural and multicultural settings requires the inclusion of more subjective constructivist and contextual perspectives, based on the sociocultural contexts of culturally different people.

COMPLEXITY AS A BASIS FOR
CULTURE-CENTERED INTERVENTION

Culture's complexity is illustrated by the hundreds or perhaps even thousands of culturally learned identities, affiliations, and roles we each assume at one time or another. Culture is dynamic as each one of these alternative cultural identities replaces another in salience. A counselor must keep track of the client's *salient* cultural identity, as it changes even within the context of an interview (Pedersen, 1994). There is considerable interest in broadening the categories of culture in the development counseling literature (Stoltenberg & Delworth, 1987) and from the social cognitive perspective (Abramson, 1988). Counselors develop through stages of progressively more complex and adaptive facility in making decisions and processing information. Some form of complexity and dynamic balance may serve to anchor the upper levels of that hierarchy for multicultural counseling.

This chapter seeks to identify measures of complexity and dynamic balance already in the counseling literature and apply those measures to multicultural counseling as heuristic constructs applied to family counseling. *Complexity* involves the identification of multiple perspectives within and between individuals.

The following 10 examples of observable and potentially measurable "complex" counseling behaviors are, on the one hand, rooted in traditional theories of counseling and, on the other hand, particularly relevant for multicultural counseling.

1. *Clear and separate identification of multiple but conflicting culturally learned viewpoints between persons in the interview*
Research on empathy in counseling (Goldstein & Michaels, 1985) has already demonstrated the importance of distinguishing different viewpoints in the interview. If two culturally different viewpoints are in conflict, we need not assume that one is right and the other is wrong. The multicultural perspective is unique in allowing both viewpoints to be right within their own cultural context for a proper understanding.

2. *Clear and separate identification of multiple but conflicting culturally learned viewpoints within persons in the interview*
Behavioral approaches to counseling suggest that the same individual may take on different culturally relevant roles or identities, depending on the situation (Tanaka-Matsumi & Higginbotham, 1989). Stereotyping

results when a counselor assumes that all persons of a particular ethnic group, nationality, gender, or age always have the same perspective. This conflict in roles may be the very reason for seeking counseling.

3. *Ability to accurately relate the actions of different persons in the interview in ways that would explain their behavior from their own cultural perspective*

The ability to take another person's perspective has been an important goal of Gestalt therapists and a tool of psychodrama in counseling. It is also essential in accurate assessment (Lonner & Ibrahim, 1989). The more culturally different the counselor is from a client, however, the more difficult it will be for the counselor to take that culturally different perspective (Pedersen, Fukuyama, et al., 1989).

4. *Ability to listen and store information without interruption, when culturally appropriate, for introduction later in the interview*

An important microskill emphasized by Ivey (1988) involves careful listening and basic attending skills. Listening requires counselors to tolerate silence and suspend judgment until all perspectives of a culturally different client are thoroughly understood. Sometimes, though, keeping silent, even when appropriate, can be very difficult for a counselor. Otherwise, counselors may impose a self-reference criterion unfairly.

5. *Ability to shift topics in culturally appropriate ways*

Pattern recognition allows the counselor to lead the client toward increased insight by knowing when a topic is salient to the client's point of view. Ivey (1988) describes this as "observation of client verbal tracking and selective attention" (p. 75). This skill presumes knowledge of the client's culture so that each behavior can be matched with the client's culturally learned expectation and value (Pedersen & Pedersen, 1989).

6. *Accurate labeling of culturally appropriate feelings in specific rather than general terms*

Ivey (1988) discusses the microskill "reflection of feeling" as the foundation of a client's experience. Being specific and accurate in labeling a culturally different client's feelings requires learning new cues, signals, and patterns of emotional expression. Accurate feelings are at least as important as accurate facts in good counseling technique, even though this may be more difficult in a multicultural context. Lopez (1989) discusses how wrong attributions, assumed base rates, selective memory, and self-confirming hypothesis testing result in bias against culturally different clients.

7. *Identification of culturally defined multiple-support systems for the client outside the interview*

Recent attention to natural support systems as potential resources in counseling is encouraging (Pearson, 1985). In many cultures these support systems are the preferred source of counseling through informal methods and in an informal context (Pedersen, 1994).

8. *Ability to identify alternative solutions and anticipate the consequences of each solution*

Decisional counseling and other problem-solving or decision-making approaches to counseling are particularly useful in cultures where the counselor is perceived as a teacher and source of authoritative knowledge (Ivey, Ivey, & Simek, 1987).

9. *Ability to identify the culturally learned criteria being used to evaluate alternative solutions*

The personal constructs being applied by culturally different clients are based on culturally learned assumptions. Without knowing these culturally learned criteria, the counselor cannot accurately interpret or evaluate a client's behavior (Neimeyer & Fukuyama, 1984).

10. *Ability to generate insights for the other person from that person's culturally learned perspective(s) in the interview that explains the situation*

Many theories of counseling are based on insight by both the counselor and the client, using skills such as interpretation, reflection of feeling, and reflection of meaning (Brammer, 1988; Hackney & Cormier, 1988; Ivey, 1988). Insight presumes a high level of awareness, knowledge, and skill in the multicultural context (Pedersen, 1994).

These 10 examples of cultural complexity discussed as counseling skills are already familiar features of the counseling literature but not as they apply to culture-centered counseling. Rather than separate the multicultural perspective as a special branch of counseling, it is important to see it as a method, viewpoint, and perspective applicable to all areas of counseling (Sue et al., 1982).

SKILL TRAINING
PROGRAM ALTERNATIVES

Each cultural group defines its own contextual protocol of appropriateness and criteria of effectiveness that must be observed. By enlarging their repertoire of skills, counselors are more likely to match the right method with the right cultural context in the right way. Effective culture-centered change requires purposive action and training to accomplish that action.

Effectively trained culture-centered counselors demonstrate growth and development in their ability to assess, understand, and change complicated cultural relationships in a unique context. Toward this end, these trained counselors become less dependent on simplistic stereotypes when thinking about or working with culturally different people. They also have a wide range of response alternatives from which to choose in each multicultural context, aware that each context is viewed from the contrasting viewpoints of culturally different participants. Not only do trained counselors understand the source of a problem in each multicultural context, but they keep track of the changing and dynamic "salience" of a client's identity from time to time and place to place within that context and demonstrate an awareness of their own cultural identity as it helps and/or hinders culture-centered competence.

Brislin (1993) reviewed training programs that facilitate multicultural interactions and identified four general goals: positive feelings about developing intercultural relationships, reciprocation of feelings with members of other cultures, task accomplishment, and minimum stress from intercultural misunderstandings and difficulties. Brislin, Landis, and Brandt (1983) describe six basic approaches to doing cross-cultural training and meeting these goals:

- The typical "classroom model" emphasizes the transfer of information or fact-oriented learning through lectures, discussions, readings, or media materials.
- Attribution training focuses on accurately identifying the explanation behind a culturally different person's behavior from the host culture's viewpoint.
- Cultural awareness training is focused on learning about one's own culture and cultural identity.
- Cognitive-behavior modification involves identifying reinforcing aspects of the host culture that reward right behavior.

- Experiential learning involves face-to-face contact with a contrasting culture and analyzing the outcomes.
- The interactional approach involves working with resource persons from the target culture who are authentic and articulate.

Classifying these alternatives into approaches that emphasize more structured and formal didactic classroom-type lectures versus less structured and formal experiential activities and then further classifying them into culture-specific versus culture-general foci produces a grid for comparing skill training alternatives. Gudykunst and Hammer's (1983) two-dimensional paradigm demonstrates this framework, in which the culture-general and the culture-specific perspectives focus on the *content* being taught while the experiential and didactic approaches displayed on the other perspective indicate the *method* being used. As a result, the model offers four categories of training: experiential-general, experiential-specific, didactic-general, and didactic-specific.

The first quadrant of this paradigm reviews programs that are experiential and culture general. This category includes traditional human relations training approaches, the intercultural communication workshop, culture-general simulations of invented cultures, and self-confrontation techniques.

The second quadrant reviews programs that are experiential and culture specific. These approaches include modifications of human relations training to fit a particular context, bicultural communication workshops involving two specific cultural groups, and behavioral approaches. Culture-specific role-plays are also widely used in this type of training.

The third quadrant reviews programs that are didactic and culture general. These approaches include traditional courses on multiculturalism and approaches to develop cultural self-awareness. Self-help books and published materials on multiculturalism also fit into this quadrant.

The fourth quadrant reviews programs that are didactic and culture specific. All training activities that give instruction about a particular culture or group are appropriate, among them foreign language training programs, specific orientation programs, cultural assimilators, and country guide books.

Training people in skills for culture-centered change is not done without risk. The following barriers to successful skills training in multicultural settings need to be acknowledged and attended to (Pedersen & Ivey, 1993):

- Skills training has grown in many different directions so that comparability and generalizability across cultures are difficult.

- There is a danger that the clients are fitted to the skills-training technique rather than beginning with the needs of the culturally different person and cultural context.

- Generalizing skills learned in a laboratory to the outside world has been a continuing problem for successful skills-based training.

- Defining the limits of skills in solving or managing a problem is difficult to do, resulting in sometimes overestimating the importance of skills.

- Skills training is a product of Westernized cultures and reflects many of the culturally learned assumptions of a Euro-American context.

- When skills training focuses on individuals as an isolated biosocial unit, it ignores the needs of collectivist cultures.

- Where skills training requires the intervention of outsiders, it may not fit cultures that have a higher need for privacy within the family or cultural group.

- It is not always possible to accurately identify the reinforcing event or reward in another culture toward which skills are targeted.

- When expensive technical facilities are required for skills training, they may be too expensive for another culture.

To overcome these potential barriers, one must be aware of one's own cultural assumptions, be comfortable with both formal and informal methods and settings, know the appropriate competencies for working in the target culture, and be competent in the right skills-based training approaches. Multicultural skill is not an exotic specialization but, rather, the foundation of all interpersonal skills in bringing about effective change through accurate knowledge and appropriate action.

THE TRIAD TRAINING MODEL

Every counseling context involves three simultaneous conversations: first, a verbal dialogue between the client and the counselor, which both can monitor; second, the counselor's own internal dialogue exploring related and sometimes unrelated factors, which the counselor can monitor; and third, the client's own internal dialogue exploring related and sometimes unrelated factors, which the client can monitor. The counselor does not know what the client is thinking, but the counselor does know that some of the client's internal dialogue will be positive and some of it negative.

This chapter explores the usefulness of simulating the client's internal dialogue by matching the client with a coached anticounselor—to make explicit the client's negative internal dialogue—and a coached procounselor—to make explicit the client's positive internal dialogue.

CULTURE NOTE

Imagine the client with an angel (procounselor) on one shoulder and a devil (anticounselor) on the other shoulder, both whispering messages into the client's ear throughout the simulated counseling interview.

Simulations provide relatively safe ways to learn counseling skills without risk to actual clients. Simulated counseling interviews and role-playing have been used by all different theoretical approaches to practice skill building in counselor education. In the safety of a simulation, the counselor trainee can make mistakes and learn recovery skills after having said or done the wrong thing. Rehearsing skills through role-play and receiving feedback help counselors develop more confidence and higher skill levels (Pedersen & Pedersen, 1989).

The Triad Training Model is a simulation designed to make explicit the client's internal dialogue. This model matches a counselor trainee with three resource persons from the same background in a simulated counseling interview. One resource person plays the role of a coached client, who presents the problem for which he or she is seeking help from counseling. The second resource person plays the role of a coached anticounselor, who articulates the negative internal messages that the client might be thinking but not saying. The anticounselor will attempt to sabotage the counseling process by emphasizing and exaggerating these negative messages. The third resource person is in the role of a coached procounselor, who articulates the positive internal messages that a client might be thinking but not saying and facilitates the success of the counseling process and the counselor. The resulting four-way conversation between the counselor, client, procounselor, and anticounselor provides the counselor access to the client's internal dialogue during the simulated counseling interview. As the counselor becomes more familiar with the positive and negative messages that a culturally different client might be thinking but not saying, the counselor will be able to incorporate those messages into the explicit counseling interview (Pedersen, 1994). This four-way interaction is typically videotaped and the videotape reviewed by participants for debriefing and feedback on how well the counselor attended to both the explicit verbal and the more implicit internal client dialogue.

There are several theories of counseling that attend to a client's internal dialogue as an important counseling resource. Psychoanalytic and object-relations theories use identification and internalization to merge the real external world with the client's private perspective. This internalization may take several forms:

- *Introjection* describes an internal presence as an integral part of the client's self. This can be an imaginary playmate or other person who may be either friendly or unfriendly.

- *Identification* describes modifying one's self to fit a perspective of some other person or model through imitating that person or model with positive or negative consequences.

- *Incorporation* is a blurring of the distinction between the self and significant others, incorporating the other person into the self.

These internalizations become important for understanding how we feel about ourselves and others.

Cognitive therapies also acknowledge the importance of a client's internal dialogue. Gestalt "deluging" has helped clients explore mixed feelings in their thinking and decision making. Self-instruction training is a form of cognitive therapy that identifies disturbing thoughts and fosters more adaptive thinking. This approach has worked best in counseling persons with self-defeating behaviors to keep the negative thoughts from controlling the client. Clients develop internal monologues, or "think out loud," to better understand how they function in stressful situations.

In Gestalt therapy, people develop images of the "good me" and the "bad me" as mental images about themselves. The "good me" resembles the positive internal messages of a procounselor, and the "bad me" resembles the negative internal messages of an anticounselor. People have learned styles of selective inattention to develop inaccurate perceptions of reality according to these internalized personifications of themselves and others. By making these processes explicit through the anticounselor and procounselor, the counselor becomes more skilled in relating the client's internal dialogue to the client's decisions and behaviors.

Psychodrama has adapted the alter ego concept to the training of counselors through simulations and role-playing. Janis and Mann (Janis, 1982) describe the uses of psychodrama in education and counseling through "emotional role playing" for changing undesirable behaviors. One way of doing this is taking on an "as if" role as a victim in a crisis, exploring the negative messages and perspectives that an anticounselor might otherwise make explicit. Another way is called "outcome psychodrama," where clients project themselves into the future to articulate their worries, hopes, and unverbalized feelings and to better understand the potential consequences of their decisions.

Triads have been used in family therapy by Satir (1969) and others to illustrate pathogenic coalitions. The therapist then uses mediation and judicious side taking to break up and replace pathogenic relating. The use of co-counselors or counseling families and small groups, where some may be very positive and others negative, are other examples from systems theory of how this force field of positive and negative alternatives is important to the understanding of counseling.

The Triad Training Model was adapted from techniques of video self-confrontation and microcounseling for teaching interviewing and counseling skills (Ivey, 1993; Kagan, Krathwohl, & Farquhar, 1965). Videotaped interviews have proved effective in identifying and strengthening positive facilitative behaviors and changing nonfacilitative behaviors. Typically, the supervisor is brought in to interrogate and debrief the trainee after the interview. Other studies (Revitch & Geertsma, 1969; Solomon & McDonald, 1970; Walz & Johnson, 1963) have long indicated that videotaped self-confrontation promotes behavioral change. The use of coached clients in simulated counseling interviews has also been well documented (Whiteley & Jakubowski, 1969). Hosford and Mills (1983) reviewed research on the importance of videotape as a training asset. Video-augmented interventions have proved effective in treating alcoholism, drug addiction, sexual dysfunction, suicidal intent, disruptive behavior of children, anorexia nervosa, anxiety, employment interviewing skill difficulties, assertiveness difficulties, phobias, marital social skills deficiencies, and a wide range of other psychological problems.

Video has many advantages in training. It provides a permanent record for replay; includes multilevel perspectives about the counseling process, client, and counselor; is a highly personal and participative medium; captures actual events for detailed feedback and analysis; and encourages information processing in realistic situations.

APPLYING THE TRIAD MODEL

The Triad Training Model simulates a positive-negative force field of positive and negative factors from the client's viewpoint in the polarized roles of the procounselor and anticounselor, who make explicit the client's positive and negative internal dialogue. The Triad Training Model seems to work best when the following conditions apply:

- The counselor receives both positive and negative feedback during the interview.
- The simulated interview reflects actual events in realistic ways.
- The simulated interview occurs under conditions that the counselor considers "safe."
- Procounselors and anticounselors must be carefully trained to be effective.
- Feedback to the counselor and client is immediate and explicit during the actual interview.
- The resource person is both articulate and authentic to the client's background.
- The counselor learns how to focus on the client while listening to the anticounselor and the procounselor at the same time.
- The interview works best when it is spontaneous and not scripted.
- The debriefing is much more effective if the interaction is videotaped.
- The actual simulated interview is brief (8-10 minutes) to avoid overwhelming the counselor with information during or after the interview.

In describing the Triad Training Model it is important to understand the role of the procounselor and the anticounselor. The anticounselor is deliberately subversive in attempting to exaggerate mistakes by the counselor during the interview. The counselor and anticounselor are pulling in opposite directions, with the client judging which is "more right." Having an anticounselor in the simulation offers the following advantages:

- Forces the counselor to be more aware of the client's perspective
- Articulates the negative, embarrassing, and impolite comments that a client might not otherwise say
- Forces the counselor to examine his or her own defensiveness
- Points out a counselor's inappropriate interventions immediately while the counselor still has time to recover
- Attempts to distract the counselor, thus training the counselor to focus more intently on the client

There are several things that an anticounselor might do in the interview to articulate the negative aspects of a client's internal dialogue:

- Build on positive aspects of the problem and the client's ambivalence
- Distract or sidetrack the counselor, attempting to keep the conversation superficial
- Attempt to obstruct communication between the counselor and client, physically and psychologically
- Annoy the counselor, forcing the counselor to deal with defensive reactions
- Exaggerate differences between the counselor and client to drive them further apart
- Demand immediate and observable results from counseling
- Communicate privately with the client
- Identify scapegoats to encourage the counselor and client's unrealistic perspectives
- Attack the counselor's credibility and request that someone more expert be brought in

These examples of a client's negative internal dialogue are seldom addressed directly in counselor training. The Triad Training Model encourages the direct examination of these actual or potential negative messages and helps the counselor develop skills for dealing with them during the actual interview process.

The procounselor attempts to articulate the positive messages that might also be part of a client's internal dialogue. The procounselor helps both the counselor and the client articulate the counseling process as a potentially helpful activity. The procounselor functions as a facilitator for the counselor's effective responses. The procounselor understands the client and is thus able to provide relevant background information to the counselor during the interview. The procounselor is not a co-therapist but an intermediate resource person who can guide the counselor by suggesting specific strategies and information that the client might otherwise be reluctant to volunteer. In these ways, the procounselor reinforces the counselor's more successful strategies both verbally and nonverbally.

Having a procounselor in the simulation offers the following advantages:

- A resource person to consult when the counselor is confused or in need of support
- Gives explicit information about the client that might facilitate the counselor's success

- Provides a partner for the counselor to work with on the problem rather than the counselor having to work alone
- Helps the counselor stay on track and avoid sensitive issues in ways that might increase client resistance
- Provides beneficial feedback to the counselor to avoid mistakes and build on successful strategies

The procounselor attempts to build on positive and constructive aspects of the counseling interview through encouragement and support of the counselor, who may feel under attack by the anticounselor. There are several ways the procounselor might provide that support:

- Restate or reframe in a positive fashion what either the client or counselor said
- Relate client or counselor statements to the basic underlying problem, keeping things on track
- Offer approval or reinforcement to the client or the counselor when each is cooperating
- Reinforce and emphasize important insights that need to be discussed and expanded
- Reinforce client statements as the client becomes more cooperative in the interview
- Suggest alternative strategies to the counselor when necessary

The Triad Training Model has been used for approximately 20 years in hundreds and perhaps thousands of situations. Persons who have used the model report that they are better able to articulate the problem after a series of training interviews incorporating the procounselor and anticounselor teams. The client's problem—from the client's perspective—is almost always viewed differently by an outside counselor. Participants also reported increased skill in specifying resistance in the counseling interview. Immediate feedback from an anticounselor is used to confront the counselor with mistakes even before the counselor has finished a wrongly chosen sentence. Other research indicates statistically significant growth in empathy, respect, and congruence. There are indications that participants in the counselor role become less defensive after training and less threatened by working with clients. Finally, there is evidence that participants' real and ideal views of themselves as counselors become more congruent after training.

```
┌─────────────────────────────────────────────────────────────┐
│                                                               │
│                      CULTURE NOTE                             │
│                                                               │
│    The populations identified as having the best ability to   │
│    measure multiple simultaneous conversations—as the         │
│    counselor is required to do in working with a procounselor  │
│    and an anticounselor—are day care workers and mothers of   │
│    large families.                                            │
│                                                               │
└─────────────────────────────────────────────────────────────┘
```

Because direct and immediate feedback from an anticounselor and/or a procounselor has such a strong treatment effect, the Triad Training Model has many research applications. The more similarity there is between the counselor and the client, the more likely the counselor will accurately anticipate the client's internal dialogue. Conversely, the more cultural differences there are between the counselor and the client, the less likely the counselor will accurately anticipate that internal dialogue. For this reason, most of the research using the Triad Training Model has involved multicultural or cross-cultural training of counselors from one culture working with clients from a contrasting culture.

Research with prepracticum counseling students at the University of Hawaii showed that those who were trained with the Triad Model achieved significantly higher scores on a multiple-choice test to measure counselor effectiveness, had lower levels of discrepancy between real and ideal self-descriptions as counselors, and chose a greater number of positive adjectives in describing themselves as counselors than did students who were not trained with the Triad Model (Pedersen, Holwill, & Shapiro, 1978). Another study comparing dyad training models with the Triad Training Model showed significant gains by students in the triad mode on Carkhuff's measures of empathy, respect, and congruence, on the seven-level Gordon scales measuring communication of affective meaning, on Ivey's Counselor Effectiveness Scale, and on the Revised Budner Tolerance of Ambiguity Scale (Bailey, 1981).

Hernandez and Kerr (1985) trained three groups of students using a didactic mode, a didactic plus role-play with feedback mode, and a didactic plus triad training mode. The more experiential training produced counselors who were more culturally sensitive, expert, attractive, and trustworthy from the client's viewpoint. The findings supported experiential training of counselors in general and particularly the use of the Triad Training Model for training.

Neimeyer, Fukuyama, Bingham, Hall, and Mussenden (1986) compared the reactions of 20 counseling students who participated in the procounselor or anticounselor training models. Results from a self-assessment survey and an analysis of values questionnaire indicated that participants in the more confrontational anticounselor version felt more confused and less competent than did participants in the procounselor version. No differences were discovered from the more objective Global Rating Scale and the Counselor Rating Form. The more confrontational anticounselor model, when used alone, is better suited to more advanced students who already have developed some confidence for multicultural interactions.

Sue (1980) field-tested the anticounselor and procounselor training models with students at California State University, Hayward. The anticounselor model was more effective in achieving self-awareness, developing cultural sensitivity for contrasting cultural values, and understanding political or social ramifications of counseling. The anticounselor model was also more effective in giving participants an awareness of their cultural values and biases and engendering cultural sensitivity to other ethnically defined groups. The procounselor model was most effective in helping students obtain specific knowledge of the history, experiences, and cultural values of the client's ethnic group. Students were more comfortable with the procounselor model, whereas the anticounselor model was more anxiety provoking. When asked to rate the most effective model for learning about multicultural counseling in the shortest period of time, however, the anticounselor model was seen as superior. The anticounselor brought out issues of racism, bias, and conflicting values through immediate feedback to the counselor trainees, whereas the procounselor tended to facilitate acquisition of skills more gently.

Wade and Bernstein (1991) examined cultural sensitivity training using the Triad Training Model with Black female clients. Black female clients' perception of the counselors and of counseling was more affected by counselors who had gone through the Triad Training Model than by the counselor's race. Trained counselors received higher ratings on expertness, trustworthiness, attractiveness, unconditional positive regard, satisfaction, and empathy and returned for more follow-up sessions than counselors who had not experienced the Triad Training Model. LaFromboise, Coleman, and Hernandez (1991) used the Triad Training Model to help validate their Cross Cultural Counseling Inventory. Their results were favorable toward the use of the Triad Training Model.

Chambers (1992) combined the Triad Training Model with Ivey's Microskills approach. This variation of the Triad Training Model was found to be effective for increasing the frequency of good verbal counseling responses and decreasing the frequency of poor verbal counseling responses in training and afterward.

Irvin (Irvin & Pedersen, 1993) trained two groups of counselors in the Triad Training Model using procounselor training first and anticounselor training second for one group and reversing it for the other group. Results indicated a decrease in counselor trainee's sense of anxiety, apprehension, and defensiveness when the anticounselor was presented first; however, trainees reported a greater sense of control when the procounselor was presented first. Students experiencing the procounselor first were more likely to anticipate future contact with the client, seemed to understand the problem better, and were better able to absorb a confrontation with the anticounselor later. Students who experienced the anticounselor first felt less anxious and more comfortable, demonstrated more self-awareness, and demonstrated a lower level of confusion and less defensiveness. There appeared to be both advantages and disadvantages in experiencing either the anticounselor or procounselor first.

Strous, Skuy, and Hickson (1993) used the Triad Training Model in training family counselors in South Africa. The results reflected a consistent and significant preference for the procounselor over the anticounselor aspect and the anticounselor aspect over conventional training of family counselors in ways that encouraged the authors to advocate more research using the Triad Training Model in South Africa.

Murgatroyd (1995) describes a program using the Triad Training Model to prepare counselors at the University of New Orleans. First, the model helped trainees understand and explore the presenting problem of role-played clients. Second, it made negative thoughts toward counseling and the counselor more explicit. Students were divided into two groups. The 6 students in Group 1 had completed from 9 to 18 credits, and the 6 students in Group 2 had completed at least 24 credits. Third, it aided in understanding the "payoffs" a problem offers to the client:

> The model facilitates a faster and deeper exploration of presenting problems for group one counselor trainees. For group two trainees the model heightens the developmental issue of dependency versus autonomy. They struggle with an authority of positive and negative voices which in turn

allows them an opportunity to work through their developmental task and become more mature in their identity. (p. 22)

The Triad Training Model combines the complementary but distinct functions of a procounselor and an anticounselor to simulate the positive and negative messages of a client's internal dialogue. There appears to be some support for the Triad Training Model in the research done using that model. Much more research is needed to identify the strengths and weaknesses of the model in a variety of different situations.

EXAMPLES OF A CLIENT'S INTERNAL DIALOGUE

Each 3-person resource team is matched with a counselor trainee or a small group of 8-10 trainees who share the role of counselor. A 10-minute simulated interview is followed by about 10 minutes of debriefing out of role with the counselor trainee and the resource persons. Then the resource team moves to another group and a different resource team takes over. A group of 30 counselor trainees would require at least three teams of resource persons.

As an example of the resource team at work, consider a situation where a White American male counselor (CO) is working with a 24-year-old Japanese American female client (CL) who is troubled about whether or not to move out of her parents' home. The procounselor (PC) and anticounselor (AC) are also Japanese American females who articulate respectively the positive and negative messages the client is thinking but not saying in the following dialogue:

CL: What do you think I should do? I mean, what's correct? Do you think . . . ?

PC: That's right, trust him. He wants to help you.

AC: He's White and he's male. How can anyone that different from us be any help?

CO: Well, I guess if you are going to play by your parents' rules staying home and suffering, I think . . .

AC: See! He thinks you're suffering at home and that you should move out! Remember your parents and your obligations!

CL: Do you think I'm suffering at home?

PC: Something is certainly wrong, and he is trying to help you find out what it is.

CO: Well, I think something brought you here to talk to me about the dilemma you're in about wanting to move out and being very uncomfortable . . . having a rough time bringing it up to your folks in such a way that, uh . . . you can do that.

AC: Ask him when he moved out. When did he move out of his parents' home?

CL: Yeah, when did you move out of your parents' home?

PC: Keep the focus on yourself. Attacking him is not going to help you.

CO: I moved out of my folk's home when I was 16.

AC: Why did he move out so young? You know? He moved out at 16! After all that his parents did for him and everything! You know? He moved out at 16! Such disrespect!

CO: Well, I went away to school, and it was important to live at school. The school was in another town.

PC: Keep the focus on your problem, or he will never be able to help you. He wants to help you! Let him!

CL: Didn't your parents get mad that you went to another school?

PC: His family rules may be different, but they still loved one another. Focus on the positive part!

CO: No, they wanted me to go to school. Education was pretty important to them.

AC: See! He's saying that your parents don't think education is important! He is insulting your parents!

From this brief transcript one can see the internal dialogue in action within the client's mind, focusing on positive, common-ground expectations but also aware of different and possibly negative behaviors at the same time. Culture-centered counseling skill requires the ability to monitor both the client's positive and negative internal dialogue at the same time.

Multicultural counselors need to understand (a) the explicit verbal exchange between the counselor and the client, (b) the counselor's own internal dialogue, and (c) the client's internal dialogue. The more culturally different the counselor and client are from one another, the more difficult it is to understand the client's internal dialogue. It is a fair assumption, however, that part of it will be negative and part of it positive.

CONCLUSION

There are many ways of training counselors to make culture-centered interventions. The alternative training approaches reviewed in this chapter demonstrate the importance of recognizing culture's complexity and interpreting the client's behavior within the cultural context of that client's expectations (Ivey, 1993).

Of the several alternative training methods available, the Triad Training Model provides immediate and continuous feedback to the counselor during training rather than later, provides strong negative feedback to the culturally different counselor in a safe setting as part of the counselor's contract with the anticounselor ahead of time, and involves resource persons from the client population in the training of counselors who will return to that same client population as service providers. It is important to match the training to the client's cultural context through whatever training approach is selected.

EXERCISE

PROCOUNSELOR AND ANTICOUNSELOR
MESSAGES IN COUNSELING

Objective

To identify the positive (procounselor) and negative (anticounselor) messages a client might be thinking but not saying in selected brief counseling transcript excerpts.

One approach to training multicultural counselors is to match a coached client with two other culturally similar persons—one as a procounselor emphasizing the positive and one as an anticounselor emphasizing the negative side of what the client is thinking but not saying. The culturally different counselor can hear both the positive and the negative side of the client's internal dialogue in a role-played interview by listening to all three of the other participants. The two transcript examples presented earlier in this chapter demonstrate how an anticounselor and a procounselor might function in an interview.

Instructions

Review the brief counseling transcript exerpts that follow and write down (in the blanks provided) what you believe an anticounselor and a procounselor might say following the client's comment. You may want to specify the culture of the client and the counselor before responding as an anticounselor and/or a procounselor. You may want to role-play the interview with a partner, designating someone to role-play the anticounselor and someone else to role-play the procounselor.

The following exercise requires several steps, and its use assumes familiarity with all the exercises presented previously in this module. The purpose of this exercise is to familiarize trainees with how the Triad Model works when participants interact *without* prepared scripts.

1. Divide the class into 4-person groups, with any leftover persons acting as observers.

2. Within each small group, each person has the opportunity to role-play the counselor, client, procounselor, and anticounselor. As each person's turn to be the counselor comes up, the other 3 identify an area of "shared cultural identity" among them *that is not shared by the person in the counselor role.* This area of cultural similarity may relate to ethnicity, nationality, religion, language, age, gender, place of residence, social status, educational status, economic status, formal affiliations to a group or

informal affiliations to an idea, perspective, or familiarity with a special problem or population.

3. The 3-person team of client-procounselor-anticounselor creates a presenting problem based on an area of shared similarity with a shallow (more obvious/overt) and a deeper (less obvious/covert) level to the problem.

4. The counselor works with the 3-person team for 5 or 10 minutes attempting to help the client manage the problem while getting feedback from the anticounselor and procounselor. The client genuinely seeks help on the problem. The anticounselor articulates the client's positive dialogue. *There should be ways that at least two or three persons speaking at the same time can adequately simulate the dynamics of internal dialogue.* Anyone may speak with anyone during the interview, but physical violence is discouraged.

5. After the interview, the participants go out of role to discuss the interview process and content for about 5 or 10 minutes.

6. At the end of the discussion, the participants change roles and repeat the process until everyone has had an opportunity to play each role.

PART 1

The first set of statements is transcribed from an interview between a White male counselor and a Black female client discussing relationship problems she is having at the university.

1. Identity

Client: OK, my problem is that I don't seem to be able to trust the White people here on campus. Being Black, I seem to have sort of a problem with this sort of thing and I don't know what to do about it and somebody recommended you. Said that you were a good counselor, so I decided to come and get some help from you.

Counselor: Do you have any problems relating to the Black students on campus, Terry?

Client: No, not really. You know, there are people everywhere. Some you don't like, some you do like.

Anticounselor: _____

Procounselor: _____

2. Relationship

Counselor: How do you feel in terms of our relationship now? You came here and we have been talking for about 2-3 minutes. How do you feel about the way we've been talking?

Client: Well, you haven't helped me for one thing. I mean you just . . .

Anticounselor: _____

Procounselor: _____

3. Comfort Evaluation

Counselor: Do you feel uncomfortable with me?

Client: Um, not now, not yet.

Counselor: I, um . . . I, ah, . . . (pause) I don't feel any discomfort with you at all.

Client: Oh, well, cuz I'm a friendly person, I suppose. (laugh)

Anticounselor: _____

Procounselor: _____

4. Counselor's Culture

Counselor: Are you getting a little uncomfortable, Terry? Perhaps because I'm White? In sharing some of these things with me?

Client: Um . . . not really, and it's like I said, you know, I try to be pretty open-minded about what I'm talking about. But the thing I want to know is can you really understand where I'm coming from? What kind of things I'm really dealing with?

Anticounselor: _____

Procounselor: _____

PART 2

The second set of statements is transcribed from an interview between a White male counselor and a Latin American female client discussing relationship problems she is having at the university.

1. Identity

Client: Yeah, they treat me like dirt, that's it, you know? And I feel divided inside. Like they don't care for me as a whole person.

Counselor: Ummm . . . you said divided. What is the division?

Client: The division is that they just want sex. They don't want to see me as a whole person.

Anticounselor: _____

Procounselor: _____

2. Relationship

Counselor: Could you tell me what you would rather have from them? How you would like a man to treat you when you go out with him?

Client: Well, it's just that, especially the first time . . . for some time . . .

Counselor: Um mmm . . .

Client: I like to get to know the person in a different way.

Anticounselor: _____

Procounselor: _____

3. Comfort Level

Counselor: OK, I'd better ask you another question then. How comfortable are you with me? Should . . . maybe I'm not the right person to work with you . . . because I'm an American man.

Client: So far you're OK because you are far enough . . .

Anticounselor: _____

Procounselor: _____

4. Counselor's Culture

Client: Yeah, you see this thing, these things for me are very intense for me right now because I just came. I've been here for only about a month.

Counselor: Would you feel better if I got back behind the desk and we sort of had that between us?

Client: No, then you remind me of my father.

Anticounselor: _____

Procounselor: _____

Debriefing

Discuss the statements you made as a procounselor or as an anticounselor to someone else in a dyad or in small groups. Pay attention to how your response is similar to or different from the response of others in the group. Consider the following questions in your discussion:

■ Were the statements of the anticounselor and procounselor accurate? Why or why not?

■ How might the counselor respond on hearing the anticounselor or procounselor statements?

■ How might the client respond on hearing the anticounselor or procounselor statements?

■ How might it be useful for multicultural counselors to monitor the anticounselor and procounselor messages in a client's internal dialogue?

9

Finding Common Ground Using the Cultural Grid

- **Primary Objective** Demonstrate the importance of "common ground" for making positive change in a cultural context

- **Secondary Objectives** (1) Demonstrate how each culturally learned behavior is directed by expectations and values learned from culture teachers and (2) Separate expectations from values and find examples of common ground where two individuals or groups express the same positive values through different behaviors

---

Culture-centered change is accomplished by first examining underlying culturally learned assumptions, then gathering accurate and relevant facts for understanding the cultural context, and finally designing and carrying out effective and skillful action. This process "assumes" that (a) culturally learned assumptions are the foundation of knowledge, (b) culture is complex and not simple, (c) culture is inclusively and broadly defined, (d) behavior must be interpreted in its cultural context, (e) not all racism is intentional, (f) all are vulnerable to cultural encapsulation, and (g) culture is within the context (Wehrly, 1995).

The culture-centered search for knowledge looks to the history of multicultural relationships and the ways that culture has been managed—or mismanaged—to protect one from repeating the same mistakes. The racial controversies, for example, are examined to separate fact from fiction. Then, the alternative strategies for creating harmonious intercultural conflict are examined to learn from the success or failure of others.

Finally, the culture-centered transfer of skills looks at the range of training approaches that are available to fit the multiplicity of culturally different contexts, matching culture-general or culture-specific strategies appropriately with experiential or didactic methods. Managing the inevitable conflict that arises between cultures by separating expectations from behaviors becomes another essential skill. These skills are incorporated in the educational imperative to accomplish constructive change.

CULTURE NOTE

Many culture-centered skills can be learned but not taught. The teacher can, however, facilitate a context in which learning occurs by placing the student in a multicultural situation under favorable conditions.

Teaching culture-centered skills is neither easy nor quick. It is the teacher's task to develop an effective learning context that offers safety, harmony, respect for oneself, and a future for one's children. The culture-centered teacher rejects alternatives where some people win and others lose because ultimately everyone loses. The only acceptable culture-centered outcome is one in which everyone wins.

CULTURE-CENTERED TRAINING MODELS

Culture-centered teaching moves from simple to more complex thinking about multicultural counseling relationships. A trained counselor depends less on stereotypes and is better prepared to comprehend the influence of a cultural context on the counseling process, has a wider range of response alternatives to meet the needs of each cultural context, can describe each cultural context from the contrasting viewpoints of culturally different participants, can identify and understand the "source" or basic underlying cultural assumptions of a problem, can keep track of the "salient" culture for a client as it changes over time and place, and can account for one's own culturally learned assumptions in the counseling process (Midgette & Meggert, 1991).

In describing the various forms of the Multicultural Interviewer Training (MIT), Ridley, Mendoza, and Kanitz (1994) present a framework that moves from training philosophy to learning objectives, to instructional strategies, to program designs, and finally to evaluation. This model matches 10 instructional strategies—didactic methods, experiential exercises, supervised practical internships, reading assignments, writing assignments, participatory learning, modeling/observational learning, technology-assisted training, introspection, and research on multicultural counseling training issues—with 10 learning objectives, which are displaying culturally responsive behaviors, incorporating ethical knowledge and practice, developing cultural empathy, increasing the ability to critique existing counseling theories, developing an individualized theory that is culture relevant, gaining knowledge of normative characteristics of different cultural groups, gaining cultural self-awareness, gaining knowledge of within-group differences, knowing multicultural counseling concepts and issues, and respecting cultural differences. Each objective can be accomplished with any of the 10 instructional strategies. This very useful framework summarizes much of the other published materials on training with specific reference to the multicultural context.

A number of authors have been critical of the way terms such as "cultural sensitivity" have been used in the counseling literature. First, the various definitions of cultural sensitivity do not agree, resulting in confusion about the terminology and a high level of complexity. The construct indicators are not adequately described. There is no theoretical framework, and no accurate measurement is available. As Ridley, Mendoza, Kanitz, Angermeier, and Zenk (1994) point out, this definition of cultural sensitivity "grounds the construct in theory and limits it in practice to a perceptual prerequisite of culturally relevant interventions" (p. 134).

Ivey's (1990) model of training counselors has been the only one to explicitly emphasize the importance of culture and culturally effective counseling skills. Implicitly, all counselor training models are dependent on culturally learned assumptions. Behavior modification training depends on culturally defined reinforcers as motivators in a cultural context. Affective-oriented skill training depends on culturally validated relationship rules. Experiential training approaches include both formal and informal aspects of a client's context. Structured learning approaches (Goldstein, 1981) begin with practical competencies that the client has already learned to value in each cultural context. Each theoretical perspective is implicitly or explicitly accommodated to different cultural contexts.

AWARENESS-ORIENTED TRAINING

Developing an awareness of culturally learned assumptions is essential for the professional counselor (Pedersen, 1994; Pedersen & Ivey, 1993). Both the American Counseling Association and the American Psychological Association have developed competencies for multicultural counselors as targets of education and training (Sue et al., 1982; Sue, Arredondo, & McDavis, 1992). This three-stage framework of competency requires certain awareness, knowledge, and skill at each of the three stages. Four areas of cultural awareness provide a "first stage" foundation for culture-centered counseling: self-awareness about the counselor's own cultural heritage, awareness of how culturally learned assumptions shape the counseling process, recognition of the counselor's limitations when working with some cultures, and sense of "comfort" working with culturally different clients and contexts.

The second stage of awareness requires three knowledge competencies: counselors knowing accurate facts about their own culture to avoid being captured by a "self-reference" criterion, knowing how oppression, racism, discrimination, and stereotyping are perceived by minority populations, and knowing their own style and method of counseling as culturally learned and culturally specific.

The third stage of awareness requires two basic competencies: an understanding of, and knowing one's competency limits in, other cultures and defining and constructing a nonracist self-identity for working in different cultural contexts.

CULTURE NOTE

Rather than labeling persons in stereotypes according to their culture, it might be more functional to understand the ways that different cultural influences lead individuals to behave in a particular way through constructing a "personal-cultural orientation" toward each context situation or event.

Accuracy in assessment and interpretation requires understanding each person's behavior in the sociocultural context where that behavior occurred. Behaviors are frequently interpreted and changed without regard to the sociocultural context, resulting in misattribution and inaccurate data (Kagitcibasi, 1996). The Cultural Grid is an attempt to demonstrate how a personal-cultural orientation is constructed.

Hines and Pedersen (1980) developed the Cultural Grid to (a) help identify and describe the cultural aspects of a situation, (b) help form hypotheses about cultural differences, and (c) explain how to train people for culturally appropriate interactions. The Cultural Grid is an open-minded model that matches social system variables with patterns of behavior, expectation, and value in a personal-cultural orientation to each event (Pedersen & Pedersen, 1985, 1989).

The Cultural Grid provides one means of describing and understanding a person's behavior in the light of learned expectations and values. This more complicated approach to culture takes a broad and comprehensive perspective of culture beyond the traditional limits of fixed categories or dimensions. The Cultural Grid makes it easier to separate cultural from personal variables by identifying patterns of similarities and differences in the attributions or expectations attached to an action or behavior.

The 3 × 4 categories of the Cultural Grid, shown in Figure 9.1, assume that culture is so dynamic and complex that it changes for each individual from one situation to another. Rather than describe a person's "culture" in the abstract, it seeks to identify an individual's personal-cultural orientation in a particular situation through attention to one's behavior and its meaning.

CULTURE NOTE

A middle-school child was about to be transferred to a school for "troubled" children because every day at about 3 p.m. he would get into a fight and be so disruptive that he was sent home. A teacher followed the young man home and discovered his single-parent mother was visited by her boyfriend every afternoon about 3 p.m. and, unless the middle-school boy was present, the boyfriend would beat up the mother. The young man knew he had to get home early every day to protect his mother. Now that the disruptive behavior is understood in *context* the young man becomes a hero rather than a delinquent! He should be taught better behaviors than disruption at school, but his willingness to protect his mother is admirable.

SOCIAL SYSTEM VARIABLES	BEHAVIOR	EXPECTATION	VALUE
Ethnographic (nationality, ethnicity, religion, language, etc.)			
Demographic (age, gender, residence, physical ability, etc.)			
Status (social, economic, political, educational, etc.)			
Affiliation (formal like family or informal like a shared idea)			

Figure 9.1. The Intrapersonal Cultural Grid

A multicultural identity is complex (incorporating a great many cultures at the same time) and dynamic (in that only a few cultures are salient at any one point in time). The Cultural Grid presents a synthesis of the personal and social systems variables that contribute to a multicultural identity and also provides guidelines for integrating one's own multicultural identity with the identity of others through managing culturally learned behaviors and expectations. The achievement of multicultural awareness through education and training is not a trivial goal. Understanding the basic underlying assumptions that control both counselor and client is fundamental to accurate and appropriate counseling in each cultural context.

The Intrapersonal Cultural Grid combines personal features of behavior, expectation, and value with social system variables (Hines & Pedersen, 1980; Pedersen & Pedersen, 1985) in an open-ended framework to increase awareness of the "culture-teachers" and the cultural "rules" they taught that regulate each of one's many behaviors. Each *behavior* is guided by culturally learned expectations that regard that behavior as appropriate in a particular situation. Each culturally learned *expectation* is an extension of culturally learned basic and fundamental values that are not negotiable and cannot be compromised. Each *value* is learned from teachers in the different social systems as these systems become salient. The personal (behavior) combined with the social (systems) orientation provides an awareness of how culture controls behavior through culture-centered training.

The elements of the Cultural Grid are also useful for understanding the relationship between two or more individuals as the following examples demonstrate.

A person's behavior by itself does not communicate a clear message or intention. Only when that behavior is analyzed within a context of the person's salient social system variables does the person's cultural context become clear. The context is best described by what is called *expectation,* a cognitive variable that includes behavior-outcome and stimulus-outcome expectancies and guides an individual's choices: "If this . . . (behavior), then that . . . (expectation)." The social system variables are essential to both persons in a relationship for understanding one another's anticipated outcome. Extrapolating expectations from social system variables is a skill that improves with practice.

After having examined your own and the other person's most salient social system variables, it should be possible to identify both your own and the other person's *positive* expectations for an anticipated outcome such as "friendship," "trust," or "harmony." By applying the Cultural Grid to relationships, it is possible to understand and modify each person's behavior so that an appropriate step is taken toward a mutually valuable anticipated "win-win" outcome.

Behaviors do not easily reveal the learned expectations, consequences, or meaning intended through that behavior. Similar behaviors may have different meanings, and different behaviors may have the same meanings. It is thus important to interpret behaviors accurately in terms of the intended expectations, consequences, and meanings attached to those behaviors.

This framework is useful in understanding a person's personal-cultural orientation to behave in expected or unexpected ways when confronted with problems. The Intrapersonal Cultural Grid then becomes a useful tool of analysis, going from the particular and concrete to the more general and abstract.

First, identify and separate a particular behavior in yourself or someone else. The behavior should include a particular action, decision, or thought. Define that behavior narrowly enough so that it becomes specific. For example, analyze the behavior of reading this book.

Second, identify the expectations behind this behavior: "If I do this . . . then *that* will happen." What do you expect to happen as a result of that behavior? When you decided to read this book, you probably had several expectations in mind: to learn new ideas, fulfill a requirement, catch up on the literature, or prepare to work in a multicultural setting. There are many expectations, both explicit and implicit, attached to each behavior.

Third, identify the values behind each expectation. Some examples of values are learning, change, relevance, competence, and responsibility, to name just a few that might justify your behavior of reading this book.

Fourth, ask yourself from where those values came. Who taught them to you? This may require your analyzing the thousands of social system variables—ethnographic, demographic, status, and affiliations—that continue to be meaningful to you. Your personal-cultural orientation toward the decision to read this book was constructed out of the expectations and values taught to you by salient social system variables in your life.

The "one size fits all" assumption has led to severe deficiencies in training programs through institutionalizing cultural biases in the counselor education curriculum. McFadden and Wilson (1977) reported that less than 1% of their respondents from counselor education programs indicated a requirement for the study of non-White cultures. Parham and Moreland (1981) later surveyed 33 doctoral programs in counseling psychology and discovered that non-White applicants perceived those programs as nonsupportive of minority concerns. More recent research continues to note the minimal inclusion of cultural materials at the American Psychological Association's approved counselor training programs (Sue & Sue, 1990).

KNOWLEDGE-ORIENTED TRAINING

Developing an accurate and appropriate cultural awareness is not enough. One must also assemble the facts and information identified by those culturally learned assumptions as important for culture-centered counseling. The facts and information become important tools for change based on cultural assumptions. Counselors who have developed an appropriate awareness know what facts they need and are motivated to gather that information before proceeding with their counseling intervention. This second step of gathering knowledge and developing informed comprehension is the homework a culture-centered counselor must complete before an intervention, for without an appropriate foundation of awareness, the facts and information gathered have no meaning (Sue et al., 1992).

These knowledge competencies are divided into three categories also according to knowledge about awareness, the cultural context, and counseling skills.

The first stage, gaining awareness, requires two separate competencies:

■ Self-awareness of one's positive and negative reactions toward other cultural groups that might result in overinterpretation, underinterpretation, or misinterpretation of behaviors by persons from those groups. It is important to know both the similarities and the differences between the counselor's own cultural patterns and those of contrasting cultural groups.

■ Awareness of stereotypes and preconceived notions that each cultural group has about other groups. Knowledge of such stereotypes is important in compensating for those preconceptions in counseling.

The second stage, learning about the cultural context, requires three separate competencies:

■ A comprehensive understanding of the client's cultural context. The ethical guidelines described earlier clearly state that any counselor who is unaware of a client's culture is functioning in an unethical manner. This knowledge includes accurately articulating the client's cultural perspective and knowing the historical development of that perspective.

■ Understanding the process by which culturally learned assumptions influence personality formation, vocational choices, psychological patterns, help-seeking behavior, and appropriate behaviors. Without this knowledge, the counselor is unable to understand the client's cultural context.

■ Understanding sociopolitical influences in the client's cultural context. Everything the counselor does and/or does not do is interpreted in a sociopolitical context from the client's viewpoint.

The third stage, building counseling skills, requires two separate competencies:

■ Knowing a variety of strategies for making culturally accurate and appropriate interventions. Counselors must acquire a repertoire of skills so that they can match the right intervention with the right client at the right time.

■ Knowing about the client's life outside the counseling relationship, such as community events, social or political roles, celebrations, friendships, and networks that define the client's support systems. The culture-centered counselor needs to seek out and become acquainted with those support systems.

The counselors who have the required knowledge, understanding, and comprehension are better prepared to be genuine and authentic in a variety of cultural settings.

Sue and Sue (1990) point out a pervasive and enduring bias in the knowledge being taught in counselor education programs. First, even though there is much rhetoric about the importance of multiculturalism in these programs, there is little, if any, evidence of incorporating culture-centered knowledge in the core counseling curriculum. Cultural information, if covered at all, has usually been relegated to a separate course. Second, there has been no systematic approach to the teaching of culture-centered counseling skills. Until culture-centered constructs are recognized as generic and central to counseling knowledge and skill, the changes that do occur are likely to be only cosmetic. Third, media-based training packages need to be developed to demonstrate the broad and important role of culture in counselor education. These supporting materials added to the curriculum should also illustrate specific strategies for inclusion in counseling. Fourth, there is a presumption that multiculturalism in counselor education is merely accumulating additional knowledge about other cultures, without regard to the underlying assumptions or the consequent skills that are necessary.

MATCHING FORMAL
AND INFORMAL METHODS

We are never alone, for we are always surrounded by a support system of the thousands of cultural "teachers" who have significantly affected our thinking, feeling, and behavior. In each person's identity, different social support systems are woven together in a fabric where formal and informal elements, like texture or color in a weaving, provide a pattern or design that is unique. In each person's identity, a balance of formal and informal support systems is essential to good mental health. A multiculturally skilled counselor can balance formal and informal approaches in the treatment of culturally different populations (Pedersen, 1981, 1994).

The pattern or design of social systems in Western cultures is significantly different from that in non-Western cultures (Pearson, 1985). In a global perspective, the formal context of counseling and therapy is an "exotic" approach.

Counseling can occur in an informal as well as a formal mode. The place where counseling occurs and the method employed are defined by a balance of formal and informal support systems. This method-context combination creates a dynamic combination of indigenous support systems that define our personal culture.

Although most research on support contains similar assumptions, definitions of support vary greatly (Caplan, 1976; Cobb, 1976). The kinds

METHOD			
CONTEXT	Formal	Nonformal	Informal
Formal	1 Office-scheduled therapy	4 Mental health training	7 Mental health presentation
Nonformal	2 Community mental health	5 Support groups, friends	8 Family and service
Informal	3 Professional advice	6 Self-help groups	9 Daily encounter

Figure 9.2. Three-Dimensional Model of Counseling Services Methods

of support frequently mentioned are emotional support (feelings of closeness, intimacy, esteem, and encouragement), tangible goods and assistance, intellectual advice or guidance, and supportive socialization (Pearson, 1990). The accurate identification of social support networks helps prevent disorder by the early detection of problems and referral to appropriate helpers and by meeting basic human needs for affiliation and attachment. The literature on counseling is now providing more data on the importance of indigenous support systems to mediate the functions of counseling (Pearson, 1990).

Figure 9.2 shows the full range of methods and contexts through which support systems function—from the most formal (where rules, structures, and definite expectations apply) to the more informal (where spontaneity and the lack of defined structures apply). An examination of the figure reveals a paradigm for describing the range of formal and informal support systems.

The incorporation of formal and informal support systems has been noted in previously published literature. Figure 9.2 incorporates the full range of previously identified possibilities for analyzing how the formal and informal systems complement one another. These combinations include a range of alternatives appropriate in various culturally diverse settings.

Each numbered cell depicts a different combination for formal and nonformal features of counseling methods in various counseling contexts but illustrates a different meaning:

1. A formal method and formal context are involved when the counselor/specialist works with a fee-paying client in a scheduled office interview. Counseling as a professional activity occurs mostly in this setting.

2. A formal method and nonformal context are involved when the counselor/specialist works by invitation or appointment with a client in the client's home, office, or community. Semiformal meetings with individuals, families, or groups of foreign students are often best scheduled for locations outside the counseling office. A location that is more familiar to the client makes it easier to establish rapport when discussing personal problems.

3. A formal method and informal context are involved when the counselor/specialist is consulted about a personal problem by a friend or relative at a party or on the street. In some cultures, it is important that the person requesting help be accepted as a friend before it is appropriate for that person to disclose intimate problems. When I counseled foreign students at the University of Minnesota, I first would have to be "checked out" at group parties or approached about personal problems informally on street corners and only later—if I passed the test—in an office or formal setting.

4. A nonformal method and formal context are involved when a person not functioning in the "role" of counselor is asked for psychological help or provides a professional service, training, or presentation. During the 6 years I counseled in Asian universities, the functions of a counselor were not well understood. The concept of a medical doctor was clear, but the counselor was considered a special kind of "teacher." To accept help from a teacher was honorable and increased one's status in the community. Consequently, it was frequently useful to describe counseling as a special kind of teaching and learning interaction. Asian students were then quite comfortable asking me for advice and help on a personal problem.

5. A nonformal method and nonformal context are involved in the various support groups organized by persons to help one another through regular contact and an exchange of ideas, although none of the participants is trained as a therapist. When I had Asian or other international students as clients who were unfamiliar with counseling, I frequently asked them to bring a friend to the interview. The friend, although not trained as a counselor, would function almost as a co-therapist by providing constant support, clarifying the content of formal counseling interviews, and helping me to understand the client by acting as a mediator and interpreter. This can be especially useful if there is a language problem between the client and counselor.

6. A nonformal method and informal context are involved when self-help groups and popular psychology are used as resources. A frequent indicator

of culture shock is withdrawal from support groups and increased isolation from other groups as well. There are various self-help groups, such as Alcoholics Anonymous and other organizations for addicts, single persons, veterans, or those whose common bond is a traumatic experience. Similarly, the considerable literature on positive thinking or advice giving is a frequent source of help. My Chinese clients frequently first consulted the Confucian proverbs for advice and sought counseling only when the proverbs seemed inadequate.

7. An informal method and formal context are involved when a listener receives assistance in solving a psychological problem from a formal, scheduled presentation or activity, even if that was not the explicit intention of the program. In non-Western cultures, much of what we call "counseling" in Western settings occurs through religious institutions. Family meetings and activities also provide a valuable vehicle for the functions of counseling and leave a great vacuum by their absence. These institutions are not primarily psychological, nor is it their primary purpose to promote mental health. However, the ritualistic context is often formal and contributes significantly to healthy mental attitudes.

8. An informal method and nonformal context are involved when family and friends provide help to an individual. In many Asian cultures, it is unacceptable to go outside the family or a very close circle of friends to disclose personal problems. In some situations, a foreign student under stress while in the United States may be helped by making contact with relatives or close friends. These people can serve as a resource and context for casual and indirect conversations, which can promote healthy mental attitudes.

9. An informal method and informal context are involved in daily encounters in which individuals receive help spontaneously and unexpectedly from their contacts with other people, whether that help is intended or unintended. Spontaneous recovery from crises or stress takes many forms. For example, imagine that it is a nice day and you are walking down the street. Someone smiles. You smile back. You feel better. Each culture teaches its own repertoire of self-help mechanisms for healing.

A comprehensive picture of formal and informal support systems helps classify the different sources of psychological help. Without an adequate framework to identify the resources, counselors are likely to rely too heavily on more formal, obvious support systems and ignore the less obvious, informal alternatives. If counselors seek to translate counseling and therapy to culturally different populations, they need to complement the diverse informal influences in clients' indigenous support systems.

SKILL-ORIENTED TRAINING

Sue and Sue (1990) cite national conferences such as the Vail Conference, Austin Conference, and Dulles Conference that document the inadequacies of multicultural knowledge in contemporary psychology education programs:

> Selected recommendations included advocating (a) that professional psychology training programs at all levels provide information on the political nature of the practice of psychology, (b) that professionals need to "own" their value positions, (c) that client populations ought to be involved in helping determine what is "done to them," (d) that evaluation of training programs include not only the content, but also an evaluation of the graduates, and (e) that continuing professional development occur beyond the receipt of any advanced degree. (p. 16)

The successfully educated culture-centered counselor demonstrates an effective and skilled ability to make appropriate changes in a variety of culturally different contexts. This ability presumes a high degree of cultural awareness, knowledge about the client's cultural context (Sue et al., 1992), and competency achieved on the three stages of skills development.

The first stage requires three competencies of awareness:

- Learning respect for a client's religious and spiritual values and beliefs. These ideological beliefs are important to the client's worldview and must be respected even though the counselor may not share those same beliefs.
- Respecting the client's indigenous helping practices and help-giving resources. These indigenous approaches may be both formal and/or informal in ways that are very different from approaches described in the counseling literature.
- Learning the client's language and interpretation of words, which may be a foreign language, dialect, or even slang from the counselor's viewpoint.

The second stage requires five competencies related to knowledge and understanding:

- Knowing the theory and practice of counseling and how to adopt both the theory and practice of counseling in culture-centered ways
- Knowing how to penetrate institutional barriers that prevent minority clients from getting ahead
- An accurate interpretation of data from culturally biased tests and measures

- Knowing the role of a client's family structure and how to mobilize the family as a positive resource in counseling
- Managing discriminatory practices that might influence the interventions at the social and community level

The third stage requires seven competencies related to skillful interventions:

- Developing a repertoire of verbal and nonverbal helping responses to match with culturally different clients
- Changing the system when the client is right and the system is wrong
- Knowing when and how to seek consultation with traditional healers and other leaders in the client's cultural context
- Understanding the client's language, how to work with a translator, or how to refer the client to someone who does understand the client's language
- Knowing the tests and measures being used well enough to translate their function to fit the client's cultural context
- Eliminating biases, prejudices, and discrimination wherever possible
- Taking responsibility for familiarizing the client about the counseling process so that the client can make an informed choice about whether or not counseling might be appropriate

As urbanization, Westernization, and modernization spread around the world, the problems that gave rise to counseling as a profession are likely to increase globally. As village relationships are replaced by urban sprawl and as barter economies become more dependent on financial fluctuations, many of the counseling responses developed in an industrialized, urbanized context might become increasingly appropriate and important.

Nwachuku and Ivey (1991) demonstrate how culture-specific skills can be developed from awareness and knowledge through a series of steps a counselor might take. Ivey, Ivey, and Simek-Morgan (1993) discuss this approach in training skilled counselors. First, examine the culture itself to identify important personal and interpersonal characteristics of that culture. This can be done through field research, reading, and interviewing informants. This may be done formally as part of preservice training or informally as part of a counselor's ongoing in-service training. Second, translate concrete skills and strategies into testable patterns of counseling practice. Storytelling and metaphors become important means of identifying patterns in the client's cultural context. Third, test the most relevant helping theory and skills in practice. Rather than focusing directly on the problem as a more individualistic perspective might dictate, more time is

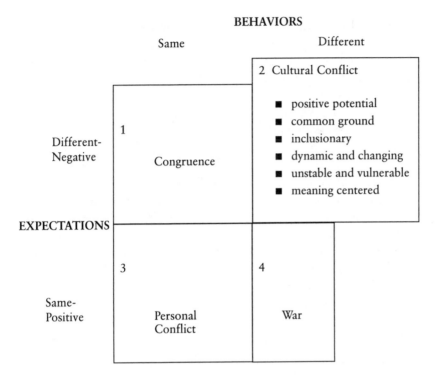

Figure 9.3. Interpersonal Cultural Grid

spent developing a relationship and informally or indirectly exploring the cultural context in which the problem exists.

THE INTERPERSONAL CULTURAL GRID

The Interpersonal Cultural Grid (Figure 9.3) describes the relationship between persons or groups by separating behaviors from expectations. Each of the grid's four quadrants explains one large or small part of this relationship. Salience may change from one quadrant to the other as the relationship changes.

In the first quadrant, two individuals have similar behaviors and similar positive expectations. There is a high level of accuracy in both individuals' interpretations of one another's behavior and the positive shared expectations behind that behavior. This aspect of the relationship is congruent and probably harmonious. Both persons are smiling, and both expect friendship.

In the second quadrant, two individuals have different behaviors but share the same positive expectations. There is a high level of agreement in that both persons expect trust and friendliness, but there is a low level of accuracy because each person perceives and incorrectly interprets the other's behavior as different and probably hostile. This quadrant is characteristic of multicultural conflict where each person is applying a self-reference criterion to interpret the other person's behavior. The conditions described in Quadrant 2 are very unstable and, unless the shared positive expectations are quickly made explicit, the silence is likely to change toward Quadrant 3. It is important for at least one of the two persons to capture the conflict in this second quadrant, where the persons may agree to disagree or adapt to one another without feeling threatened because they both have shared positive expectations.

In the third quadrant, the two persons have the same behaviors but different expectations, and at least one of them probably has a negative expectation for the relationship. The similar behaviors give the appearance of harmony and agreement, but the hidden different or negative expectations may destroy the relationship. One person continues to expect trust and friendliness, whereas the other person is now negatively distrustful and unfriendly even though they are both presenting smiling and glad-handing behaviors. If these two persons discover that the reason for their conflict is a difference of expectation, they may be able to return to Quadrant 2 and reverse the escalating conflict between them. If the difference in expectations is ignored or undiscovered, the conflict eventually moves to Quadrant 4.

In the fourth quadrant, the two people have different and/or negative expectations and they stop pretending to behave in congruent ways. They are "at war" with one another and may no longer want to maintain harmony in their relationship. This relationship is likely to result in hostile disengagement. It is very difficult to retrieve conflict from this quadrant if both parties have stopped trying to mediate or reduce the conflict.

Although the behaviors are relatively easy to identify as congruent/similar or incongruent/dissimilar, it is much more difficult to identify the expectations accurately. Rubin, Kim, and Peretz (1990) discuss the difficulties in accurately identifying another person's expectations. First, multicultural conflict might be based on misattributions and misperceptions, but both parties respond to their perception of reality, whether true or not. Second, there is a lack of reliable or complete information about what others expect, resulting in partisan or self-serving expectations by both parties. Third, both culturally different parties typically have stereotyped expectations about one another rather than accurate data. Fourth, any perceived inaccuracy or inappropriateness in assessing the other person's expectations may destroy the relationship. Fifth, selective perception, attributional distortion, and self-fulfilling prophecies might increase rather than decrease conflict.

CULTURE NOTE

As first noted in Chapter 1, smiling is an ambiguous behavior. It may imply trust and friendliness, or it may not. The smile may be interpreted accurately, or it may not be. Outside its learned context, the smile has no fixed meaning. The example of smiling provides a means to apply the four types of interaction to distinguish among ideal, multicultural, personal, and hostile alternatives.

Now, consider how the Interpersonal Cultural Grid describes two alternative sequences of events between an employer and an employee over a 5-week period. In the first example, the importance of expectation behind each behavior is not considered. You can see the relationship disintegrate as the participants move toward increasingly hostile perspectives. In the second example, the importance of the expectation behind each behavior is considered. You can see that the participants have maintained the relationship between the more workable Quadrant 1 and 2 perspectives.

Example 1

A young employee is having difficulty working with his older employer from a different country, but neither is skilled in attending to the other's cultural identity.

First Week: The employer and employee behave quite differently, with the employee being friendly and informal and the employer being formal and professionally cool toward others. The different behaviors suggest at face value that both the employer and the employee have different expectations for what constitutes "appropriate" behavior. However, in this case, both intend friendliness. (Quadrant 2)

Second Week: The differences between this employer and employee have continued to persist and have now become a source of irritation and conflict between them. As the different behavior patterns persist, both people may well conclude that they do not share the same expectations for efficiency or effectiveness in the workplace or perhaps even for liking one another as persons. (Quadrants 3 and 4)

Third Week: The employee considered modifying his behavior to become more formal because he needed the job but felt he was being dishonest in compromising his own ideals. The employer considered modifying his behavior to become less formal because he needed the employee but felt that would not be fair to his other employees or to his concept of how the office should be run. One or the other partner may compromise his beliefs and change his behavior to fit the other's, but even if their behaviors become similar, their expectations for why they are behaving as they are will become even more divergent. Compromise by either person would likely result in personal as well as professional dislike and animosity. (Quadrant 3)

Fourth Week: Both the employer and employee finally give up, saying they have tried everything humanly possible to make the situation work. As a result, the employee either leaves or is fired. This total conflict situation occurs when both behaviors and expectations are now so totally different or negative that there is little motivation to work toward harmony. (Quadrant 4)

Fifth Week: Both employer and employee conclude that there is a low level of agreement between them. Neither person is aware that there is also a low level of accuracy in his communication with the other. (Quadrant 4)

Example 2

In an alternative scenario, the young employee is having difficulty working with his older employer from a different country, but both are skilled in attending to cultural variables of interaction.

First Week: Although the employer and employee behave quite differently, they examine the reason or expectation for each other's behavior from the other person's viewpoint. The different behaviors are understood as different expressions of the same shared expectation for "excellence." (Quadrant 2)

Second Week: Because both the employer and the employee share the same expectation, they are able to interpret one another's behavior accurately and focus on the expectation they both share rather than on their differences. (Quadrant 2)

Third Week: Because they have the same expectations, the employer and employee may modify their behavior toward each other without feeling that they are compromising their principles. They may also agree to disagree and maintain their contrasting behavior style now that they know what the other's behavior means. (Quadrant 1 or 2)

Fourth Week: Both partners are likely to move toward a more harmonious situation where the similarity of expectations results in more similar behaviors, with both employer and employee modifying their behaviors somewhat to fit the other. Ultimately, both expectations and behaviors are likely to become more similar and harmonious. (Quadrant 1 or 2)

Fifth Week: By examining the cultural expectations and values behind each other's behavior, both employer and employee are now able to accurately assess the other's expectation. At this point, it is easier to decide if the two people are similar enough in their behaviors and expectations to work together and to tolerate each other's different behavior. (Quadrant 1 or 2)

The open-ended range of personal and social system categories indicated by the Interpersonal Cultural Grid provides a conceptual road map for the counselor or interviewer to interpret a person's behavior accurately in the context of learned expectations. For example, a counselor might be interviewing a Black, teenaged, wealthy, highly educated student on a personal problem. The student refers back to each of these indicated social system variables as salient to the problem during the half-hour interview. However, the counselor is so fixated on the fact that the student is in a wheelchair and is paraplegic that the counselor treats the student's handicap as the single most salient aspect of the student's culture during the whole interview. The actual problem had little or nothing to do with the student's handicap, and the counselor's assessment was inaccurate.

The introduction of a personal-cultural orientation construct provides the means to resolve a dilemma in multicultural counseling. On the one hand, data suggest that patterns of both group and individual similarities and differences must be accounted for in multicultural contact. On the other hand, attempts to describe patterns of similarities and differences through fixed dimensions or categories result in stereotyping. Although fixed data about cultures may be predictive in the form of aggregate trends in large groups that are more or less homogeneous, they are less predictive for individuals within those cultures (Atkinson, Staso, & Hosford, 1978).

An accurate assessment of another person's personal-cultural orientation is complex and dynamic but important to counselors and interviewers. The Interpersonal Cultural Grid is a useful tool for analyzing multicultural situations. It provides practical assistance in managing the complexity of culture and is also useful for analyzing case studies:

- The grid provides a framework to portray a perspective that confirms the personal and cultural orientation for each situation.
- Personal-cultural orientations can be compared across time or people to demonstrate how the same behavior can be explained by different expectations or values in different cultural settings.
- The dynamic and changing priorities of social system variables are matched with personal/cognitive variables for each time and place.
- A comprehensive description of culture includes demographic, status, and affiliation as well as ethnographic cultural variables in the range of analysis.
- The close relationship between culturally learned behaviors and culturally different expectations or values behind similar behaviors is clearly distinguished.

CONCLUSION

Effective culture-centered teaching/learning requires the identification of "common ground" between people or groups without forcing them to sacrifice their cultural integrity. This requires valuing both the similarities and differences among the population being served. The three-stage developmental approach presented in this chapter begins by reviewing the provider's cultural awareness of basic underlying assumptions. The second stage which, builds on awareness, emphasizes knowledge, facts, information, and comprehension of what that knowledge means. The third stage of the developmental sequence builds on awareness and knowledge to identify skilled and appropriate psychological interventions. All three stages are essential, and each one builds on the former.

The Intrapersonal Cultural Grid demonstrates how (a) behaviors are based on culturally learned expectations, (b) expectations are based on culturally learned values, and (c) values are learned from "culture teachers" representing salient social system variables. This "inside the person" framework shows how behaviors, expectations, values, and social system variables are linked to one another. The importance of both a broad definition of culture that includes ethnographic, demographic, status, and affiliation variables and a broad definition of counseling that includes formal and informal methods and settings are emphasized.

The Interpersonal Cultural Grid, or "between persons" framework, demonstrates how common ground can be found in the quadrant where two people share the same positive expectations or values but express those expectations and values through contrasting or different behaviors. Separating behaviors from expectations is a fundamental step in culture-centered skill leading to accurate assessment, meaningful understanding, and appropriate intervention. The ability to use this Interpersonal Cultural Grid effectively becomes the measure of excellence in culture-centered counseling as described in this book.

EXERCISE

DESCRIBING CULTURAL SIMILARITIES AND DIFFERENCES

Objective

To identify the importance of both similarities and differences in relationships of culturally different individuals

Instructions

CULTURE ORIENTATION GRID

Identify a friend or acquaintance of yours with whom you have recently had an argument or disagreement. The friend or acquaintance should be someone who shares with you as many of the following similar characteristics as possible. Check all those categories that are approximately *the same* for both of you.

Demographic: age ( ), gender ( ), neighborhood of residence ( )
Ethnographic: ethnicity ( ), nationality ( ), language ( ), religion ( )
Status: social ( ), economic ( ), educational ( )
Affiliations: formal ( ), nonformal ( ), informal ( )

Cite examples of specific similarity and differences between the two of you.

Same behaviors: _____

_____

Different behaviors: _____

_____

Same expectations: _____

_____

Different expectations:_____

_____

Same values: _____

_____

Different values: _____

_____

Debriefing

In applying the Cultural Grid in a multicultural relationship where there is apparent disagreement, it is important to emphasize both similarities and differences of behaviors, expectations, and values. Differences in behavior may or may not indicate differences in expectations or in values. The Cultural Grid is useful in "reframing" ordinary conflict into a cultural framework where two parties might disagree without one necessarily being wrong or the other one right. This exercise provides guidance for using the Cultural Grid with an acquaintance or friend whom you might not otherwise identify as "culturally different" from yourself.

First, focus on differences of behaviors, expectations, and values. The differences—particularly of expectations and values—provide each individual with a "unique" quality or integrity that one might well consider essential. The argument or conflict most likely relates to those differences. It is important to separate those differences that are fundamental or essential, particularly values, and differences, particularly of behavior, that might be negotiable and flexible.

Second, focus your discussion on similarities of behaviors, expectations, and values. The similarities—particularly of expectations and values—provide the "common ground" platform for two people to stand and discuss those things that they both expect and value. The solution to the argument or conflict will be found in the context of shared positive expectations and values achieved most efficiently by "which" behaviors.

Third, notice that different behaviors are used to express similar values. Once the common ground of shared positive expectations has been identified, the discussion can focus on which behaviors are most likely to express those positive expectations. Establishing that two persons in conflict have shared positive expectations and values allows both parties to be more tolerant or flexible in matching the most appropriate behavior.

Fourth, define the common ground without either yourself or the other party sacrificing cultural integrity. Differentiating between those expectations and values that are negotiable and those that are not negotiable provides a basis for constructive conflict management, even though the original "problem" has not been "solved."

Culture-Centered Ethics

- **Primary Objective** Provide a culture-centered basis for identifying ethical choices in culture-centered counseling

- **Secondary Objectives** (1) Identify the alternative philosophical basis for ethical decision making and (2) Separate fundamental from negotiable aspects of an ethical decision

We are better at identifying the ethical issues that face us than we are at thinking through how we should resolve them. Doing the right thing is not always easy. Because of implicit cultural bias in our social institutions, professionals working in multicultural settings sometimes have to choose between following the prescribed ethical guidelines of their profession or being ethical in a particular cultural context. This chapter discusses the ethical alternatives available to professionals working in multicultural settings so that they can become more ethically "intentional" in their decisions and actions.

Ethical principles generated in one cultural context cannot be applied to other substantially different cultural contexts without modification. However, before making any modification the counselor must distinguish between "fundamental" ethical principles that are not negotiable and "discretionary" aspects that can be modified and adapted to each setting.

CULTURE NOTE

Fundamental ethical principles are like hinges on a door, which make it possible for the door to swing open while the hinges remain fixed in place.

If the fundamental principles are compromised, the result is relativism: justice determined by whatever the common practice of a community might be. If the discretionary aspects are not modified, the result is an absolutist domination by special interest groups that benefit from the status quo (Pedersen, 1995a).

This chapter identifies the ethical actions available to culture-centered counselors and the consequences of each alternative by leading the reader through the process of making ethical choices from the general and abstract principles to the specific and practical application. The first act is to understand the three comprehensive but contrasting perspectives of relativism ("to each his own"), absolutism ("mine is best"), and universalism ("we are both the same and different") typically found throughout the literature on ethics. The second ethical act is to examine the research on cultural encapsulation and exclusionary tendencies that have characterized professional counseling and require meaningful change. The third ethical act is to look at alternative ethical guidelines that have been suggested to implement fair ethical judgments in multicultural settings. The fourth act is to demonstrate the inadequacies of professional ethical guidelines now being used. The fifth ethical act is to shape the future direction of culture-centered ethical guidelines for ourselves and the profession of counseling.

RELATIVISM, ABSOLUTISM, AND UNIVERSALISM

All ethics are guided by one of three general perspectives: divergent (relativism), convergent (absolutism), or dynamic (universalism, which accepts that all people are similar in some ways and dissimilar in others).

Berry et al. (1992) contrast relativism, absolutism, and universalism in a synthesis summary of the literature. The relativist position avoids imposing value judgments and allows each cultural context to be understood in its own terms. External descriptions of a group in the abstract or evaluations of a group's behavior by outsiders are not valid unless or until they are validated by the group's own internal criteria. There is little or no interest in similar patterns across cultures except at the most abstract level of analysis and qualitative differences are fundamental to the group's identity. Valid comparisons across groups are not possible and psychological interventions, assessments, and ethical guidelines must be based exclusively on internal group criteria. Ethical behavior would be judged by other members of the group without regard to the standards used by other groups outside this specific community. This relativist approach has more frequently been followed by anthropologists in studying cultural groups. Relativists believe in a context-bound measure of reality and discourage analysis of behavior by outside criteria.

Kierstead and Wagner (1993) divide relativism into categories. Relativism based on ethical egoism assumes that what is right for one person may not be right for anyone else. Relativism based on ethical nihilism assumes that moral concepts have no meaning (e.g., the chaos of a war context). Cultural relativism assumes that right and wrong are determined exclusively by the culture of the individual. Relativism makes moral discourse difficult and prohibits social accord toward intersubjective agreement.

The absolutist position disregards problems of ethnocentrism and applies the same evaluative criteria across cultures in the same fixed and unchanging perspective. The importance of cultural context is minimalized. Comparisons across groups are encouraged, and the same measures, strategies, theories, or ethical principles are applied in the same way regardless of cultural differences. The more powerful group defines and dominates the criteria by which ethical behavior is evaluated. Cultural differences between groups are disregarded, and cultural similarities to the dominant group are the primary criteria of judgment, as when dominant culture definitions of "normal" are imposed. Differences are typically described as deficits in intelligence, honesty, or right-mindedness as defined by the dominant and authoritarian group. Historically, psychology has often focused primarily on narrowly defined absolute principles of human behavior without regard for cultural differences. Absolutists impose a single definition of reality on the plurality of cultural contexts.

The universalist position assumes that while psychological *processes,* such as pleasure and pain, might be the same in all cultures, the way they are *manifested* is significantly different in each culture. Making friends in a foreign culture provide many examples. Comparisons are therefore possible across cultural groups by distinguishing the process from the manifestation. The application of psychological theories, measures, and ethical guidelines therefore requires understanding both the underlying, fundamental, and profound similarities as well as the essential and idiosyncratic identity features of difference. As Berry et al. (1992) state, "Theoretically, interpretations of similarities and differences are made starting from the belief that basic psychological processes are pan-human and that cultural factors influence their *development* (direction and extent) and *deployment* (for what purposes and how are they used)" (p. 258). Universalists combine culture-specific manifestations of difference with a search for fundamental similarities that link each cultural context with every other context.

Either the absolutist or the relativist position lends itself to easy answers in the search for ethical guidelines. The absolutist position imposes the criteria of the dominant culture on all other cultures without ambiguity, so that what is considered right in the dominant culture must be judged right elsewhere. The relativist position allows each group to generate its own internalized criteria for ethical judgment, so that what is considered right in one culture will be different from the judgment in every other culture. The more difficult, complex, and perhaps more accurate approach to generating ethical guidelines is the position that allows each group to manifest its own cultural identity of differences but at the same time acknowledges the common-ground psychological principles that connect each group with each other group. This is the position developed in this chapter.

In non-Western cultures, moral development has a different meaning from the traditional ethical alternatives in the Euro-American tradition. Chikuro Hiroke (1982) developed a theory of moralogy, based on the Japanese cultural context, that provides a useful example of contrasting ethical perspectives. He separated "ordinary morality" (including manners, customs, etiquette, public morality, sympathy, kindness, self-control, temperance, industry, and other moral behaviors) from "Supreme morality," which is practiced by great sages to give firm moral direction to one's spiritual life and is derived from the moral streams of Socrates of Greece, Jesus Christ of Judea, Buddha of India, Confucius of China, and Amaterasu Omikami of Japan.

There are five principles of Supreme morality: self-renunciation, realization of benevolence, precedence of duty over personal rights, respect of Otholinons, and enlightenment and salvation of others. The characteristics of Supreme morality are to emphasize the importance of mental attitudes rather than outward forms of conduct. Supreme morality describes the most rational way of living to attain beneficial purposes and goals for the individual and for society. Supreme morality is the universal moral criterion for creating peace in the world across cultural boundaries.

This example of moralogy contrasts with the more Westernized perspective in many ways. First, the main purpose of law is to encourage the performance of duty over personal rights. Second, the political basis of continuous succession by the Japanese Imperial Household is derived from the spirit of supreme morality and moral power. Third, the promotion of social progress in an orderly fashion despite political, legal, economic, and military conflict is through morality. Fourth, making people aware of the effectiveness and necessity of moral practice is the basis of scientific progress. Fifth, moral education based on precepts must parallel the teaching of other subjects based on science in the schools. Sixth, to the extent that sociology demonstrates the science of reforming society and bringing happiness to people, it demonstrates the practical effectiveness of moral practice.

It is important to realize that ethical standards are derived in a cultural context. Each culture maintains some similarity with other cultures but also is distinctively different. In the process of making moral judgments it is essential to understand the moral reasoning within the cultural context where the behavior being judged occurs. Otherwise, people, cultures, and countries will continue to be judged unfairly, inappropriately, and inaccurately.

MORAL/ETHICAL GUIDELINES

Positive guidelines are available in the American Psychological Association's (1993) publication and in Ponterotto and Casas (1991), demonstrating what can be done. Cultural bias, however, leads to encapsulation and exclusionism, the consequences of which are hurtful and profoundly dangerous. Psychology has tended to use abstractions to escape the dilemma of focusing on similarities and differences at the same time. In the abstract, nomothetic, statistical aggregate, similarities and differences can be demonstrated without difficulty, but the closer one approaches the autographic individual case, the more difficult this balance of similarities and differences becomes.

The APA (1993) guidelines provide a sociocultural framework that specifies both the core abilities and the research-based understanding essential to ethical decision making.

Core abilities include recognizing cultural diversity, understanding the socioeconomic and psychological roles of culture, understanding how socioeconomic and political factors influence cultural groups, achieving self-awareness of sociocultural identity, and understanding how culture shapes behavior. The research-based issues include the impact of cultural similarity, minority utilization of counseling, relative effectiveness of counseling style, the role of cultural values in treatment, appropriate counseling and therapy models, and competency in working with different cultures. Nine specific guidelines are provided to illustrate these examples of core abilities and the application of research-based knowledge. These general guidelines are aspirational in nature and provide goals or objectives to which the culture-centered counselor might aspire in making ethical decisions.

Ponterotto and Casas (1991) do an excellent job of demonstrating the importance of underlying philosophical assumptions in the development of multicultural ethical guidelines. The failure to define philosophical guidelines leaves the provider open to assuming one's own specific guidelines as appropriate, leading to encapsulation and exclusion. Individualistic values are presumed to be universally valid in professional guidelines, such as the APA's, and in other examples a systematic preference for the masculine perspective. Philosophical premises that tangibly translate ethical theory to practice are also identified by Ponterotto and Casas:

- The principle of altruism guides counselors toward prevailing psychosocial problems and helps identify psychocultural strengths in each cultural group. Altruism shifts the focus of counseling interventions and research from the more abstract laboratory setting to field-based sites focused on real-world problems.
- The principle of responsibility focuses on the relevance of what is done and the community involvement in the ethical decision. Responsibility requires counselors to be more reciprocal (i.e., being able to both teach and learn) in their contacts with other cultures.

■ The principle of justice deals with the quality of fairness in ethical decisions. Justice does not tolerate any one group's exploitation of any other group for its own self-interest, whether intentionally or unintentionally.

■ The principle of caring is particularly important for counselors with a sense of vocation. Caring promotes trust and a personal investment in helping culturally different clients regardless of the consequences.

Philosophical principles can guide counselors toward a more purposive and intentional basis for making ethical decisions in multicultural settings. In the absence of these principles, decisions must be made in a philosophical vacuum where counselors impose those philosophical principles most familiar to them and mistakenly presume that they are maintaining a high level of ethical standards.

Wrenn (1962, 1985) describes the dangers of cultural encapsulation among counselors seeking absolutist solutions to ethical problems. Culturally encapsulated counselors define everyone's reality according to their own cultural assumptions, minimalize cultural differences, impose a self-reference criterion in judging the behavior of others, ignore proof that disconfirms their position, depend on techniques and strategies to solve their problems, and disregard their own cultural biases. A corresponding form of cultural encapsulation based on relativism applies to counselors who segregate each group's definition of reality from any other group, minimalize cultural common-ground similarities, abstain from making judgments about behavior of other groups, escape into a subjective and nonverifiable proof of their position, disregard techniques and strategies used by other groups, and embrace cultural biases.

Neither form of encapsulation is acceptable; thus a third alternative needs to be defined. Problems in the professional ethical guidelines for counselors have resulted from the confusion entailed in distinguishing between fundamental and discretionary ethical principles. There is increased pressure to acknowledge the importance of the consumer's cultural environment in a bottom-up, consumer-driven alternative to top-down theories and approaches to counseling. Pedersen (1994) documents many different examples of professional counseling associations' inadequate attempts to mandate attention to cultural factors in the ethical practice of counseling.

Cultural encapsulation becomes most obvious in the process of exclusion, where insiders are separated from outsiders. Some individuals or groups are judged to be outside the boundaries, in which case the normal rules of fairness no longer apply to them. Those who are excluded are nonentities—expendable and undeserving—so harm to them is acceptable if not perhaps appropriate and justified. Examples of exclusion range from discrimination to genocide, "ethnic cleansing," and other means of targeting victims who are then blamed for allowing themselves to become victims! Moral exclusion occurs in degrees—from overt and malicious evil to passive and apathetic unconcern.

Opotow (1990) lists the rationalizations and justifications for moral exclusion that help identify otherwise hidden examples of moral exclusion in society, such as psychological distancing, displaced responsibility, group loyalty, and normalizing or glorifying violence. In its subtle forms, moral exclusion is so "ordinary" that it not only fails to attract attention but becomes an automatic response. It is possible to be exclusionary by what is said or done as well as by what is not said or not done. Usually, moral exclusion depends on the psychological or social principles that define unacceptable attitudes: "As severity of conflict and threat escalates, harm and sanctioned aggression become more likely. As harm doing escalates, societal structures change, the scope of justice shrinks, and the boundaries of harm doing expand" (p. 13).

CROSS-CULTURAL ETHICAL GUIDELINES

Tapp, Kelman, Triandis, Wrightsman, and Coelho (1974) developed excellent guidelines for cross-cultural research that are highly relevant to counseling. Shweder, Mahapatra, and Miller (1990) have also provided an excellent critique of moral development described in the research literature and the suggestion of positive alternatives. Other research on unintentional racism by Goodyear and Sinnett (1984), LaFromboise and Foster (1989), and Ridley (1995) demonstrates that good intentions are not enough. Lonner and Ibrahim (1989) emphasize the importance of accuracy, Miller (1994) the importance of duty, and Strike and Soltis (1985) the importance of consequences.

Tapp et al. (1974) studied psychologists' ethical responsibilities in research across cultures. In their report to the APA Committee on International Relations in Psychology, Tapp et al. pointed out that a researcher's ethical obligation goes beyond avoiding harm to the individual to include demonstrations of how the research will enrich and benefit rather than harm the host country. Generally, the benefit to the researchers is much clearer than that to the host culture providing data. Tapp et al.'s recommendation for collaboration with the host culture is also seldom observed. It is often difficult to translate psychological research into a traditional people's host culture in any meaningful way.

CULTURE NOTE

Taft (1977b) points out that "most of us are so psychologecentric that we regard ourselves as having the right to mine our data from the places where we need it, providing we pay royalties to the natives (often, incidently, in accordance with our own arbitrary concept of what is fair compensation) and provided we do not destroy the ecology irreparably. In the latter respect, we are often not really much more conscientious than is the typical multinational mining company" (pp. 11-12).

Tapp et al. (1974), who collected data on ethical guidelines for cross-cultural research over several years, note that several basic themes reappear consistently:

- Significant involvement of cross-cultural colleagues is correct, essential, and desirable.
- Criteria for informed and free consent must be determined in each cultural context.
- The ultimate responsibility for making ethical judgment lies with the individual investigator, but it is incumbent upon the investigator to check with colleagues inside and outside the culture.
- One constant responsibility is to check the benefit of the research enterprise for science and society as well as for study participants, students, and scholars.
- Advisory principles rather than a stringent ethical code can provide the necessary beginning for increased attention by individuals, institutions, and national bodies.
- Criteria for determining adequate, sufficient, or appropriate ethical standards of conduct can only be formulated through continuing exchange carried on by a transnational group drawing from an even more diverse group of cross-cultural researchers.

The search for underlying principles or standards has been a recent theme in the psychological literature. Shweder et al. (1990) reviewed the adequacy of three culturally applicable theories of moral development:

- Kohlberg's (1984) cognitive developmental theory contends that a moral obligation originates in conventional or consensus-based obligations that are rooted in convention at the lower stages but in natural law at the higher stages of development. Moral development therefore depends on the cognitive ability to construct a detached and impartial viewpoint to evaluate right from wrong.
- Turiel's "social interactional" theory separates morality from convention. Moral obligation results from social experiences related to justice, rights, harm, and protecting the welfare of others.
- A "social communication" theory combines Kohlberg's and Turiel's theories so that moral obligation is based on the universal of a learned cultural context without depending on either consensus or conviction and without universals across cultures.

A synthesis of these three alternatives differentiates between mandatory and discretionary features of moral obligation. Rationally based moral standards may be based on universal principles of natural law, justice, and harm as mandatory features and not captured by discretionary features of individualism, perceived rights, or the social contract each person has with every other person.

Bad ethical behavior is not always deliberate. Goodyear and Sinnett (1984) note that counselors might unintentionally violate ethical guidelines through misunderstanding, lack of knowledge or special skills, prejudiced attitudes that distort understanding, inattention to consequences of counseling in the client's cultural context, and apathy or disengagement from responsibility.

LaFromboise and Foster (1989) describe how institutionalized cultural bias in violation of ethical standards can result in underserved minority populations, minimalizing cultural issues in counselor education, trivializing culture in counseling texts, getting around certification requirements for cultural awareness, underrepresentation of minorities in counselor education programs, inattention to culture in research about counseling, and inadequate ethical guidelines for counselors. Ridley (1995) documents how unintentional racism can occur:

- The counselor might claim "color blindness" and claim to treat all clients equally regardless of their culture.
- Counselors might become so "color conscious" that all problems are perceived as cultural.
- Clients are likely to transfer their good or bad feelings about others to the counselor.

- Counselors are likely to transfer their good or bad feelings about others to the client.
- Counselors might misinterpret cultural ambivalence.
- The client might appropriately respond to the counselor's own unexamined racism.
- The counselor might misinterpret client nondisclosure.

Lonner and Ibrahim (1989) point out that accurate ethical assessment of a client's culture includes understanding the client's worldview and culture-specific norm group through a combined approach for clinical judgment that uses both standardized and nonstandardized methods. Even Kohlberg's (1984) measures of moral development may be culturally inappropriate. Segall et al. (1990) conclude that Kohlberg's model of moral development reflects the values of an urban, middle-class group, and Gilligan (1982, 1987) has uncovered bias favoring the male viewpoint.

Miller (1994) argues that there is no one "universal morality of caring" but, rather, alternative types of interpersonal moralities that reflect the meaning systems of different cultural groups. She describes both Kohlberg's (1984) superogatory view and Gilligan's (1987) morality of caring framework as culture bound. In her research comparing Americans and Hindus, Americans support an individually oriented interpersonal moral code stressing freedom of choice, individual responsibility, and a dualistic view of motivation, whereas Hindus support a duty-based interpersonal moral code stressing broad and socially enforceable interpersonal obligation and contextual sensitivity.

Strike and Soltis (1985) developed a taxonomy of consequentialist, nonconsequentialist, and rule-utilitarian alternatives. Consequentialism assumes that moral rightness depends on the consequences of an action, similar to utilitarism and hedonism. The problems with consequentialism are twofold: that minorities are sometimes made to suffer for the greater good of the majority and that the consequences may never be fully known. Nonconsequentialism assumes that persons' actions are judged by their intentions. The problem is that even good intentions can result in bad consequences (see Ridley et al., 1994). Even well-intentioned racism can be hurtful. The rule-utilitarian alternative is based on a reflective equilibrium, making respect for the person and human dignity a universal standard. In this more interactive mode, morality is judged both by its consequences and to the degree it treats every person or group with equal respect.

Due to scientific advancement and problems of bioethics, there is great urgency to clarify ethical obligations in multicultural social contexts because, as Murray (1993) states,

> the dominant model in bioethics assumes that moral reasoning proceeds downward, from fundamental principles to specific cases. This top-down model, deductivism, is flawed both as a description of moral reasoning, and as a prescription for how moral reasoning should be done. In recent years another model known as casuistry and based on case-centered moral reasoning has emerged to challenge deductivism. (p. 185)

The case-centered approach to moral reasoning is grounded in applications of morality as they apply to each case. This case becomes a source of moral knowledge from which principles are generated that then become guidelines for interpreting new cases. Ethical guidelines are generated from accumulated experiences in making ethical decisions and not from timeless abstract principles, however reasonable they may be.

ETHICAL GUIDELINES
FOR THE FUTURE

The future must be guided by more adequate ethical guidelines where the underlying philosophical assumptions are examined and clarified, where a relational view of responsibility guides the counselor, and where the scientific nature of counseling is validated. Counselors have a responsibility to interact meaningfully with the cultures of clients so that the methods used reflect ethical standards both explicitly and implicitly.

Even when the professional counseling association is well intentioned it functions in a culturally encapsulated framework of assumptions that constrains equity. For any ethical standard to work, the basic underlying philosophical assumptions must be identified, challenged, and clarified so that counselors will be more intentional in their ethical decisions. Self-criticism by concerned professionals will assist in overcoming the dilemma of multicultural counseling and the implicit but fundamental assumptions that function as moral absolutes in the existing guidelines.

Ivey (1987) advocates a more relational view of ethics negotiating between the client/consumer, the counselor/provider, and the cultural context variables, all of which are constantly changing. Such a relational view interprets standards of ethical behavior according to the consequences and the intention. Thus, each ethical standard is applied and interpreted differently in each cultural context but is the same principle. Absolute standards that impose one viewpoint on all others are unacceptable. A relational alternative recognizes the importance of absolute but abstract ethical principles and at the same time the multiplicity of applications in complex and dynamic cultural contexts that simultaneously reflect cultural similarities and differences.

The ethical question speaks to the scientific nature of counseling and psychology as a discipline. As a behavioral science, moral principles and ethical guidelines to counseling cannot be precisely validated. Ethical imperatives cannot be inferred from empirical data, but behavioral evidence can help identify empirical consequences. In Kendler's (1993) words,

> Natural science psychology, to be successful, must abandon two seductive myths: (a) Psychology is able to identify ethical principles that should guide humankind, and (b) the logical gap between *is* and *ought* can be bridged by empirical evidence. In spite of these limitations, psychology can assist society in settling ethical disputes by revealing the empirical consequences of different policy choices, thus allowing society to make informed decisions as to which competing social policies to adopt. (p. 1052)

Tapp (1986) reviewed her earlier research (Tapp et al., 1974) and found that the guidelines presented then also apply now. In fact, several issues remain particularly relevant.

Psychology is a culture, an institution, and increasingly a socializing agent. Psychology transmits values about health and illness and must examine the underlying principles and assumptions that guide the socializing process. As the impact of psychology grows in influence it shapes the goals of behavior for the child, parent, country, and society. Increased reliance on psychological "remedies" influences the definition of health, maturity, autonomy, dependence, intelligences, aggression, and other important social constructs. Psychology has been given the responsibility of defining "healthy" growth and development and so must become scientifically literate, socially sensitive, culturally aware, and humanely oriented, which Tapp (1986) notes "can manifest these dimensions in the way it courts scientific and social laws, shapes and sanctions ethical guidelines, seeks and applies knowledge in its multiplicity of settings" (pp. 3-4).

Counseling psychology is interactive with culture in the socializing process. By neglecting cultural variables in the ethical guidelines, by defining culture narrowly to exclude socio-political-economic factors, and in marginalizing the importance of culture in the teaching of psychology, the profession of counseling psychology has failed in its ethical obligation. The psychological impact of multiculturalism is not only indicated but required by special interest groups. Adequate ethical principles need to reflect this culturally expanded theoretical and empirical global context.

Cross-cultural psychology is both methodological and ethical in its application and concerned with a procedure or style of conduct directed toward a beneficial goal. Interaction with consumers or providers, subjects or researchers, students or teachers, and citizens or leaders depends on the equivalence of ethics and methods. The cultural component provides guidance in sharing knowledge and creating trust through ethically sensitive principles and procedures.

If counseling psychologists disregard ethical issues across cultures and ignore the connection between culture and method, the result will be careless procedures, disconnected theory, and the isolation of counseling psychology from society. The counselor then becomes a "sorcerer's apprentice, alien scientist, Blues-oriented practitioner, ivory-towered professor/teacher, research tourist, scientific imperialist and/or clinical colonist" (Tapp, 1986, p. 5). Multiculturalism must be the concern of not only cross-cultural counselors but counselors generally.

SKILL APPLICATIONS

Skill applications of applied ethics focus on aspects of human behavior important both to cross-cultural research and to morally relevant perception. How do people process social and morally relevant events? What do they attend to and use for making choices? The literature on moral development presumes that preexisting cognitive structures—the levels of moral reasoning—affect the processing of events in moral stories and, more specifically, one's recall of those stories. Narvaez (1993) applies moral perception from a multicultural perspective to the case of Kitty Genovese, who was stabbed to death in a residential neighborhood in the 1960s and, although the neighbors were aware of the ongoing crime, no one interfered. She also looks at the 1992 situation of Rodney King and Los Angeles police officers, where police brutality was recorded on videotape and still the jury found the police not guilty of using excessive force. The daily newspapers report other similar examples of human variance in moral behavior.

Rest (1995) expanded the psychological research on morality from aspects of intention and judgment to a four-component model of moral behavior: moral sensitivity to the interpretation and conceptualization of events, moral judgment to determine which potential action is the most moral, moral motivation to prioritize moral action above personal values or needs, and ego strength and implementation skills to carry out moral priorities.

In his theory of moral development, Kohlberg (1984) rejects the right of society to determine what is right and wrong for the individual. His cognitive approach presumes six problem-solving stages in moral judgment, like a staircase, based on responses to problems and observing different people's resolution of moral dilemmas. Each new stage elaborates previous ones. Rest (1995) summarizes these six stages in sequence:

- Stage 1 emphasizes obedience—"Do what you're told."
- Stage 2 emphasizes instrumental egoism—"Let's make a deal."
- Stage 3 emphasizes interpersonal concordance—"Be considerate and you will make friends."
- Stage 4 emphasizes law and duty to the social order—"Obey the law and it will protect you."
- Stage 5 emphasizes consensus-building procedures—"You have a duty to follow the due process."
- Stage 6 emphasizes nonarbitrary social cooperation—"Be rational and impartial."

In discussing these stages, Rest points out how they organize cooperation among individuals as spontaneous ways to understand each social situation to demonstrate how individuals are interconnected with other individuals. The presumption is that the deep structure of Kohlberg's (1984) six stages transcends the appearance of superficial differences across cultures. In research cited by Rest (1995), moral development scores increase with age or education, even recognizing problems of translation and dependence on samples of opportunity. Both Segall et al.'s (1990) and Berry et al.'s (1992) review of the cross-cultural research on moral development point out that the definitions of morality, the criteria of moral desirability, and prevailing moral dilemmas are likely to vary across cultures. In attempting to "do the right thing" it is important to understand how culture can shape both perceptions and interpretations of morality.

After reviewing more than 90 research studies on moral development, Gielen and Markoulis (1994) conclude that "most cross-cultural studies on moral reasoning have validated the existence and developmental properties of the preconventional and conventional levels of moral reasoning, but the cross-cultural evidence for the postconventional, principled forms of moral reasoning has been weaker" (p. 73). Both Kohlberg (1984) and Rest (1995) suggest that moral reasoning is based on the practical consequences of one's actions toward an identification of interpersonal and ultimately societal expectations implicit in moral principles.

Critics suggest that these moral principles represent a Western, male-oriented, upperclass context of individualism that minimalizes other groups. These moral principles are more than rules, for they direct us to not "use" others for our own pleasure, to respect the dignity of others, and to become more "human hearted." Gielen and Markoulis's (1994) research review found that

> whereas Western secular ideals emphasize the dignity and personhood of individuals, religious Tibetans emphasize the "Buddha-nature" inherent in everyone, Hindus uphold ideas of universal nonviolence (Ahimsa) and Confucianists focus on humanistic ideals of human-heartedness (jen). These cultural ideals are based upon different metaphysical assumptions but they all emphasize a concern for human dignity, solidarity and justice. Moral and cultural relativists have failed to perceive the underlying archtype that unites the moral imaginations of men and women living in different places and at different times. (p. 87)

Narvaez (1993) divides moral sensitivity into moral perception through preconscious and unconscious processing of data and moral interpretation through a conscious and controlled processing of data. Perception and interpretation are treated as separate and distinct processes. Whereas the criteria of interpretation are guided by culturally learned patterns, the interpretative criteria are based on culturally learned perceptions of reality. It is therefore important to first examine the "interpretations" of moral sensitivity and then to examine the "perceptions" of reality on which those interpretations are based.

CULTURE NOTE

By combining the underlying contextual perceptions with the alternative shared interpretations it is possible to demonstrate cultural variation in discretionary aspects of moral sensitivity while maintaining a constancy of moral principle.

PROFESSIONAL
ETHICAL GUIDELINES

The weaknesses of both the American Psychological Association (APA) and the American Counseling Association (ACA) ethical guidelines are that they do not identify their underlying philosophical principles, assume a dominant culture perspective, and generally minimize or trivialize the role of culture in ethical decision making. Explicit examples from the guidelines themselves as well as six implicit assumptions are identified as sources of bias and exclusionary judgment (Pedersen, 1995a).

The initial APA ethical guidelines were derived empirically from a collection of more than 1,000 ethical cases contributed by 7,500 APA members in 1948. The original ethical standards were based on members' cases from which general principles were derived, but according to Griffith (1992), the more recent revisions of the APA code of ethics have de-emphasized aspirational language and emphasized minimal standards of professional behavior:

> The minimal behavioral standards have been proposed as necessary and useful for adjudicating complaints of unethical conduct. Organizations struggling to articulate ethics, however, historically valued the primacy of their educational responsiblities. One can't help but wonder whether the age of trial lawyers, litigation and suits exploiting retributive justice has excessively influenced the document we are labeling as our code of professional ethics. (p. 15)

"Ethical Principles of Psychologists and Code of Conduct" (APA, 1992) tends to be more legal than aspirational in its framework. The code presents itself in the preamble as providing a common set of values upon which psychologists (including counselors) can build their professional work.

Each APA member is expected to supplement but not violate the code's values, as he or she is guided by personal values, culture, and experience. Principle A requires that psychologists maintain high standards of competence and work within the boundaries of their particular competence: "Psychologists are cognizant of the fact that the competencies required in serving, teaching, and/or studying groups of people vary with the distinctive characteristics of those groups" (APA, 1992, p. 1599). In those cases in which "recognized professional standards" are not specified, psychologists must protect the welfare of the client as best they can. Research on cultural bias in counseling (Pedersen, 1994) clearly demonstrates that counselors go beyond the boundaries of their competence in working with culturally different persons with few professional consequences. The lack of "recognized professional standards" for working with many different cultural groups makes it difficult to judge behavior as either following or violating Principle A.

Principle B requires that psychologists be honest, fair, and respectful of others by not making statements that are false, misleading, or deceptive: "Psychologists strive to be aware of their own belief systems, values, needs and limitations and the effect of these on their work" (APA, 1992, p. 1159). This principle does not prevent unintentional racism or many types of institutionalized racism by uninformed or naive professionals working in multicultural settings.

Principle C requires that psychologists uphold professional and scientific responsibility for their behavior and to adapt their methods to the needs of different populations. Psychologists are supposed to protect clients by monitoring their own and their colleagues' behavior. The lack of attention to multicultural issues in counseling and the tolerance for violation of the generalized guidelines that do exist demonstrate how this principle is being violated without consequences.

Principle D requires that respect be shown for people's rights, dignity, and worth. Although this principle urges meeting the needs of all clients inclusively, there are no guidelines on how that might be done.

Principle E is about concern for the welfare of others, including both human clients and animal subjects, to minimize harm. This principle deals with power differences and the tendency of the more powerful to exploit or mislead the less powerful. To the extent that multicultural relationships are defined by power differences, Principle E seeks to protect the less powerful parties, although power is itself culturally defined.

Principle F emphasizes social responsibility to the community and society in general for contributing to human welfare, preventing suffering, and serving the interests of patients, clients, and the general public. Although the general principle is clear, the application of the abstract principle in practice is difficult.

The second part of the code reviews standards of behavior, restating the general principle and often implying that the same principle will be applied in the same way regardless of the cultural context. An example of this absolutist bias is in Standard 1.08 on human differences:

> Where differences of age, gender, race, ethnicity, national origin, religion, sexual orientation, disability, language or socioeconomic status significantly affect psychologists' work concerning particular individuals or groups, psychologists obtain the training, experience, consultation or supervision necessary to ensure the competence of their services or they make appropriate referrals. (APA, 1992, p. 1601)

It is hard to imagine any psychological service or intervention in which these differences would not be significant. This standard trivializes the importance of documented differences in its "conditional" language about culture. Standard 1.10 on respecting others also warns against "unfair discrimination" based on cultural membership, suggesting that discrimination as it is usually understood might not always be unfair. Standard 1.17 prohibiting multiple relationships and Standard 1.18 prohibiting barter with clients also disregard cultural patterns in less individualistic or money-driven groups.

The second standard relates to evaluation, assessment, or intervention. Standard 2.01 requires accurate assessment to be fully implemented, presuming that the counselor can interpret the client's behavior accurately in the client's cultural context. Standard 2.02 disregards research about implicit cultural biases in tests and measures. Standard 2.04 acknowledges that assessment techniques and norms may be biased, but this standard has had little effect on the practice of assessment.

There are several problems with the APA Ethical Principles. First, in the absence of more specific guidelines, the ambiguously stated standards tend to protect the status quo. Second, if the problem is not the principles but their appropriate application in practice, then this should be clarified in the standard on education and training rather than disregarded. Third, where cultural groups are mentioned, the assumption seems to be that the longer the list the more culturally sensitive the standard. The guidelines do not deal with the fundamental ethical issues of bias in the profession and rather are designed to protect the professional/provider against the culturally different client/consumers.

The American Counseling Association's "Code of Ethics and Standards of Practice" (ACA, 1995), in a revision of the 1993 standards, also fails to guide the multicultural counselor. The weaknesses of the ACA standards are consistent with the limitations cited earlier in the APA guidelines. There are additional examples of a consistent cultural bias favoring an absolutist position (Ibrahim & Arrendondo, 1990).

First, there is a bias toward an individualistic perspective, which would not be appropriate to collectivistic cultures. These cultures would have a difficult time excluding dual relationships (Standard of Practice [SP.4]), which might be desirable or even essential to appropriate caregiving. Also, separating the rights of individuals from the responsibility of the family (SP.13) will be difficult in family-oriented cultures. Even the primary obligation to respect the integrity and promote the welfare of clients (A.1) lends itself to an individualistic interpretation without further interpretive guidelines.

Second, there is a bias toward the culturally different client who must accommodate or adjust oneself to a majority culture standard of behavior. How does the provider know a client has been "adequately informed" (SP.2)? Is it necessary for the client not only to be informed but also to comprehend the information? In very private cultures, disguising the data source as advocated in SP.16 might not be sufficient to protect the client's sense of privacy. Is the usefulness of data more important than getting the client's permission? Who defines the limits in SP.18 of a counselor's competence? What constitutes an adequate continuing education? Does accuracy in SP.21 imply not only the accurate sending of an advertising message but also the accurate receiving and comprehension of that same message?

Third, there is an elitist bias favoring the more powerful care providers' obligation to protect the profession. In SP.24, limiting the use of the term *doctor* to counselor or "closely related" professions disregards the historical fact that disciplines other than counseling psychology have frequently been more responsive to multicultural populations' needs. The provider needs to accurately identify credentials to the client and verify that the client understands those credentials regardless of disciplinary background. In SP.43, "professional" counselors are obligated to see that students and supervisees get remedial attention when necessary, but the same obligation should apply to colleagues and peers or supervisors, who may also require remedial attention with regard to cultural sensitivity.

Fourth, there is an assumption that cultural issues can be dealt with in relatively simple and objective ways. In SP.34, the simple admonition to use assessment instruments "appropriately" is so general it has no meaning until the criteria of appropriateness are made clear. In SP.35, is merely informing the client about the nature and purpose of testing sufficient, or should the client also comprehend that information? Throughout this code, the authors have tried to avoid controversy by being very general in their guidelines. The implicit assumption is that all colleagues of goodwill understand the guidelines in the same way, but this is a dangerous assumption. Cultural groups not addressed are language groups and physically disabled populations, which, by their omission, seem to be trivialized. There is frequent mention of "respecting differences" but no regard for "respecting similarities" at the same time, as though the liturgical acknowledgment of differences will protect the standards from criticism.

Fifth, there is an assumption of absolute standards for right and wrong behavior in a "one size fits all" perspective. In SP.8 and later, there is constant reference to "professional counselors," which either is redundant or suggests that the standard does not apply to "unprofessional counselors." The counselor who determines that he or she is unable to help a culturally different client should terminate contact. If the client determines that the counselor is unable to help, is termination also appropriate even if the counselor does not share the client's viewpoint? Do both counselor and client have to be hopeful for counseling to be continued? In SP.36, the need to provide culturally appropriate interpretations of culturally biased tests is emphasized. If one begins with the assumption that all tests are to a greater or lesser extent biased, then compensating for that bias through skilled interpretation is extremely important, although not included in this standard. In SP.42 and elsewhere, counselors working through interpreters or across language barriers would be hard pressed to guarantee that the client's rights were protected. In SP.44, there is an implication that classes or coursework should not contribute toward self-growth or require self-disclosure in order to be graded or evaluated. This standard seems to presume a scientific objectivity that minimizes subjective learning. In SP.47, cultures will differ on what they consider reasonable precautions to avoid causing injury. Who decides what is reasonable?

There is an underlying assumption throughout the ACA standards that what is good for the counselor is good for everyone. This "self-reference criterion" is dangerous. Client populations sometimes underuse counseling—even good counseling—because it has a resocialization effect that alienates young people from their traditions. This may be true even though the effects of counseling are judged as "positive growth" by absolutist ethical standards. There also seems to be a bias toward the medical model and away from the educational model in the language used and the quasi-scientific implications. In many cultures the role of the teacher incorporates the counseling functions more adequately than the role of a doctor. It should be important to acknowledge the appropriate role of both medical and educational models from their different perspectives. Finally, there is a bias toward a legal description of ethics and away from the philosophical or aspirational perspective. These trends do not contribute toward developing culture-centered ethical guidelines for counseling.

The best way to learn about making ethical decisions in multicultural settings is to look at actual incidents where decisions were made and then evaluate whether or not those decisions were ethically appropriate. Casebooks on ethical decisions are available from the American Psychological Association (1987) and the American Counseling Association (Herlihy & Corey, 1996) or in books like Corey, Corey, and Callahan's (1993). One can also find critical incidents in newspapers and other media. Another route is to interview samples of providers and consumers of human services who have had experience in multicultural situations. These incidents capture the complexity of multicultural relationships in which ethical decisions are made.

CONCLUSION

Another option besides relativism and absolutism is needed to guide ethical behavior in culture-centered counseling. This third alternative requires that one differentiate between those underlying fundamental and absolute truths in which one believes and will defend against change and those habits and behaviors that can be modified to fit each different cultural context. The literature on moral reasoning provides guidelines toward identifying moral principles as different from moral rules.

The professional field of counseling has tended to emphasize moral rules without identifying underlying cultural assumptions. This has resulted in ethical guidelines that direct counselors toward their own "self-reference criteria" to judge others' behavior in a "one size fits all" perspective, focus on catching and punishing the wrongdoer rather than reconciliation, blur the boundaries between ethics and law, and finally institutionalize Euro-American values such as individualism as criteria of Truth.

Guidelines for the future need to be more relational and direct the culture-centered counselor toward thinking through each cultural context for implicit guidelines of moral behavior.

EXERCISE

DEVELOPING CONTEXTUAL ETHICAL GUIDELINES

Objective

To differentiate between moral principles and moral rules in a variety of critical incidents that involve making ethical decisions

Instructions

1. Gather examples of multicultural critical incidents that occurred in a brief 5- to 6-minute period, required a decision to be made, and had serious consequences if a wrong decision was made but where no clearly right decision was obvious ahead of time.

2. Analyze each critical incident by identifying each behavior that might be interpreted in a negative or potentially hostile way by other individuals or groups but without judging or evaluating the behavior out of context.

3. Analyze each example of different and potentially negative or hostile behavior in terms of the possibility of shared positive common-ground expectations between individuals or groups as a basis of comparison and evaluating one or both individuals' or groups' behavior.

4. Develop an intervention strategy for building on the common-ground shared perceptions of trust, respect, safety, success, or ultimate effective behavior without disregarding the culturally learned interpretations by which those perceptions are manifested.

5. Collect a variety of 20 to 30 critical incidents with a brief description of the incident plus your analysis of how the individuals or groups are both similar and different and your suggested strategy for evaluating the ethical behavior of the individuals or groups.

6. Apply your critical incidents to a training setting by dividing participants into several small groups of about five persons per group. Divide the critical incidents so that each group has copies of all the incidents to work with.

7. Give each group an equal amount of time (5 to 10 minutes) to discuss each incident and evaluate your intervention strategy in terms of its ethical adequacy. If the group believes it has a more adequate ethical intervention strategy for the critical incident, ask that this strategy be identified.

Debriefing

When all the groups have evaluated each critical incident and your intervention strategy in terms of its ethical adequacy, discuss whether your solution reflects "moral principles" or "moral rules."

Moral principles will apply more or less unchanging across all situations with a minimum of modification, will reflect positive values of most if not all cultures around the world, and can be expressed in a variety of ways through contrasting behaviors.

Moral rules will be more specific and reflect unique aspects of a particular cultural context, more legalistic in their interpretation, focusing on behaviors rather than values or expectations, and controversial in other cultures and cultural contexts.

Culture-Centered Controversies

- ■ **Primary Objective** Review and discuss the controversies surrounding a culture-centered perspective in counseling

- ■ **Secondary Objectives** (1) Present both sides of the arguments for and against the culture-centered perspective and (2) Argue for a culture-centered perspective in spite of the controversies

There are many controversies being debated about how counseling interventions should be applied to multicultural settings. Although there are no conclusive and final answers to any of these controversies, it is important to be informed on the issues being debated (Ponterotto, Casas, Suzuki, & Alexander, 1995).

IS COUNSELING CULTURALLY ENCAPSULATED?

Wrenn (1962) first introduced the concept of cultural encapsulation. This perspective assumes five basic identifying features. First, reality is defined according to one set of cultural assumptions. Second, people become insensitive to cultural variations among individuals and assume their own view is the only right one. Third, assumptions are not dependent on reasonable proof or rational consistency but are believed true regardless of evidence to the contrary. Fourth, solutions are sought in technique-oriented strategies and quick or simple remedies. Fifth, everyone is judged from the viewpoint of one's self-reference criteria without regard for the other person's separate cultural context. There is evidence that the profession of counseling is even more encapsulated now than it was when Wrenn wrote his original article (Wrenn, 1985).

George Albee (1994), former president of the American Psychological Association, describes how completely psychology in the United States has been encapsulated in the past 100 years:

> Most of the early leaders in psychology embraced ideological views that stressed the natural superiority of a white male patriarchy, the acceptance of Social Darwinism, the inferiority of women and of the brunette races. Calvinism stressed economic success as the hallmark of salvation and psychology concurred. Anti-semitism and homophobia were standard. Eugenics spokesmen urged the elimination of the unfit and inferior and opposed welfare programs, decent wages, and safe working conditions. (p. 22)

These views continue to be held but in subtler forms.

Examples of cultural encapsulation are evident in the counseling literature when the following assumptions are presumed to be true and accepted (Pedersen, 1994):

- All persons are measured according to a single hypothetical "normal" standard of behavior irrespective of the different cultural contexts.
- Individualism is presumed to be more appropriate in all settings than a collectivist perspective.
- Professional boundaries are narrowly defined and interdisciplinary cooperation is discouraged.
- Psychological health is described primarily in abstract jargon, with little or no attention to the unique cultural context.
- Dependency is always considered an undesirable or even neurotic condition.
- A person's support systems are not normally considered in the analysis of that person's psychological health.
- Only linear-based "cause-effect" thinking is accepted as appropriate.

- The individual is usually or always expected to adjust to fit the system.
- The historical roots of a person's background are disregarded or minimalized.
- The counselor presumes oneself to be free of racism and cultural bias.

Ponterotto (1988) summarizes other examples of cultural encapsulation among counselors in the research about counseling:

- No conceptual theoretical framework for dealing with cultural variables
- Overemphasis on simplistic counselor-client process variables, although important psychosocial variables are disregarded
- Overreliance on experiential analogue research outside the real-world setting
- Disregard for intracultural within-group differences
- Overdependence on student samples of convenience
- Continued reliance on culturally encapsulated measures
- Failure to adequately describe the sample according to cultural backgrounds
- Failure to describe the limits of generalizability
- Lack of minority cultural output
- Failure of responsibility by researchers toward minority subject pools

LaFromboise and Foster (1989) describe other examples of institutionalized bias resulting in minority populations being undeserved by counselors, the lack of multicultural courses in the counselor education curricula, the low visibility of multiculturalism in counseling textbooks, the ways counseling programs "get around" certification requirements for multiculturalism, the underrepresentation of minorities in counselor education programs, violations of cultural values in research about counseling, and the inadequacy of ethical guidelines for multicultural counseling.

Not all racism is intentional. If one assumes that racism is reflected in what the person does rather than feels or thinks, that racist acts can be performed by prejudiced as well as apparently nonprejudiced persons, and that members of any cultural or ethnic group can be racist, then the criteria for judging an act as racist lie in the consequences rather than the causes of the behavior. Ridley (1995) describes seven forms of unintentional racism in counseling:

- Counselors who claim to be "color blind" may be avoiding their own inability to deal with cultural differences.

- Counselors who are overly "color conscious" may attribute all of a person's problem to the cultural background.
- Clients may exhibit cultural transference of positive or negative affect to the counselor and be misunderstood.
- Counselors might exhibit cultural countertransference of positive or negative affect to the client.
- A more dependent counselor might feel cultural ambivalence and guilt about exploited minorities, which can reduce that counselor's objectivity with a client.
- Pseudotransference might occur when the client discovers unexamined racism in the counselor.
- The counselor may misinterpret client nondisclosure as resistance in counseling.

Counselors have resisted cultural sensitivity mainly because conceptualizations of the term have been frustrated by differences in how it is defined, inadequate descriptions of indicators, lack of supporting theories, and difficulties in measurement (Ridley, Mendoza, Kanitz, et al., 1994). So, even though cultural sensitivity is strongly advocated in professional rhetoric, it is too frequently disregarded in counseling practice.

Counseling has a reputation in many minority communities as having been used as an oppressive instrument by those in power to maintain the status quo (Sue & Sue, 1990). This has resulted in restricting rather than enabling the well-being and development of culturally different persons through overt or covert forms of prejudice and discrimination. Many minority clients approach counseling with caution, asking "What makes you, a counselor/therapist, any different from all the others out there who have oppressed and discriminated against me?" (Sue & Sue, 1990, p. 6). Ponterotto and Casas (1991) contend that "the majority of traditionally trained counselors operate from a culturally biased and encapsulated framework which results in the provision of culturally conflicting and even oppressive counseling treatments" (pp. 7-8).

Sampson (1988) examines the importance of core cultural values for freedom, responsibility, and achievement as part of an individualistic perspective that has captured or encapsulated the process of psychological intervention from a Western perspective. He describes individualism as one—but not the only—type of "indigenous psychologies." Counseling must therefore resist cultural encapsulation, which is another form of racism, so as to become relevant in a wide range of international cultural settings.

ARE COUNSELING MEASURES AND ASSESSMENTS CULTURALLY BIASED?

Lonner and Ibrahim (1989) point out how assessment measures used in counseling have been culturally biased. They conclude that an accurate assessment must meet certain criteria:

- The client's worldview, beliefs, values, and culturally unique assumptions must be understood.
- The client's culture-specific norm grouping must be considered.
- A combination of approaches using clinical judgment as well as standardized or objective measures is appropriate.

At the same time, standardized assessment measures raise problems of distinguishing between constructs and criteria, establishing equivalence, the effect of verbal or nonverbal stimuli, the role of response sets, the tendency to infer deficits from test score differences, and other examples of embedded Westernized bias. Kohlberg's measures of moral development, for example, are biased toward an individualistic norm reflecting the values of an urban middle-class group (Segall et al., 1990) and with a bias favoring the male perspective (Gilligan, 1982, 1987).

Cultural bias in the use of tests and measurements is likely to result in over-, under-, or misdiagnosis. Although it is generally accepted that biases exist in the use of counseling tests and measures (Anastasi, 1988; Dana, 1993; Paniagua, 1994), this does not necessarily mean that those tests and measures cannot or should not be used. The search first for "culture free" tests and later for "culture fair" tests has not been successful (Irvine & Berry, 1993; Lonner & Ibrahim, 1989). Flaherty, Gaviria, Pathak, et al. (1988) suggest that any culture fair test would need to fulfill five validity criteria: content equivalence across cultures, semantic equivalence across cultures, technical equivalence, criterion equivalence, and conceptual equivalence. Escobar (1993) contends that no test or assessment can fulfill these five criteria.

Paniagua (1994) describes how the basic necessary criteria for accurate assessment and treatment in multicultural groups require that the counselor follow prescribed guidelines:

- Because there is no generally accepted definition of mental disorder—at least at less severe stages—the limitations in generalizability of data must be acknowledged.

- The need to validate measures with regard to the culturally defined population must be understood.

- The extent to which the data include an assessment of acculturation effects helps screen out differences as artifacts of the measure itself.

- The representativeness of the population being assessed compared to validating populations must be considered.

- The generalizability of data from a particular sample to the entire population must be done with extreme caution and care.

If the measures are construct related (i.e., based on psychological theory) rather than criterion referenced (i.e., based on empirical data and not tied to any particular psychological theory), they are more likely to result in misattributions (Lonner & Ibrahim, 1989). The most obvious example of such a construct-based measure is in the research on intelligence across cultures (Serpell, 1994). Jensen's (1969) research resulted in more controversy regarding sociopolitical policy, human values, morality, radicalism, and free speech than on scientific genetic theories with regard to Black-White differences in measured intelligence. Yee et al. (1993) note that "by stressing Black-White racial differences so assiduously, Jensen lost control of scholarly goals while fueling racist and sociopolitical forces" (p. 1136).

The same behavior might and frequently does serve a different function in different cultures. The conceptual meaning of a behavior also differs across cultures. The same words or sentences are not likely to convey the same meaning, especially in translation, to different cultural groups. The same level of measurement or scale is likely to be interpreted differently in each cultural context. The more equivalent the measure is assumed to be across cultures, the less likely that cultural differences will be found, and the more one looks for cultural differences, the less equivalence one will find, for "as a test item or stimulus diffuses into (is carried to) another culture, its form, function and meaning may vary in unknown and perhaps unpredictable ways" (Lonner & Ibrahim, 1989, pp. 307-308).

Until recently it was assumed that tests dependent on verbal linguistic dimensions were more likely to be biased than nonverbal measures based on figural analogies, mazes, and other formats. Response sets or response styles favoring acquiescence, social desirability, and self-disclosure are other ways that cultural bias can influence psychological measures. A longer discussion of cultural bias in particular testing instruments is available elsewhere in the counseling literature (Bamford, 1991; Dana, 1993;

Paniagua, 1994). Paniagua (1994) is drawn to conclude that all tests are to some extent biased but that a skilled interpretation can find useful meaning even in biased data.

The focus of culture-centered counseling should be on training counselors to be more skillful in their interpretation of test data to culturally different clients. Lonner and Ibrahim (1989) suggest that this can be done in three steps. The first step requires an understanding of the client's worldview and unique way of looking at that person's cultural context. The second step requires an understanding of the client's norm group with whom that client identifies. The third step is using a combination of approaches both quantitative and qualitative, both clinical judgment and standardized assessment, to verify the counselor's understanding of measurement data. Discarding or disregarding psychological measures, tests, and assessment techniques is not an acceptable solution to the problem of bias.

Even the format of testing may already be biased. Lonner (1990) demonstrates that (a) testing and assessment are not familiar procedures in much of the non-Western world, (b) psychological constructs and concepts are not universally valid, (c) the basis of comparison across cultures is often not equivalent, (d) test stimuli are more frequently in the verbal than visual mode, even though language conveys strong bias, and (e) test score differences frequently imply a "deficit" in one or another culture by the language used to describe that difference.

The problem of biased measures even applies to measuring multicultural competence of counselors. Ponterotto, Reiger, Barrett, and Sparks (1994) review four measures of multicultural co-counseling competence— Cross-Cultural Counseling Inventory-Revised (CCCI-R), Multicultural Counseling Awareness Scale-Form B (MCAS-B), Multicultural Counseling Inventory (MCI), and Multicultural Awareness-Knowledge-Skills Survey (MAKSS)—with regard to item development, psychometric properties, and pragmatic utility. Each of these four measures attempts to measure competence in multicultural counselors without imposing cultural bias.

SHOULD CULTURE BE DEFINED
BROADLY OR NARROWLY?

The broad definition of culture presumes that the salient features of a person's cultural identity may include demographic variables (e.g., age, gender, and place of residence), status variables (e.g., social, educational, and economic), and affiliations (formal and informal) in addition to ethnographic variables of nationality and ethnicity. According to the broad definition, some aspects of all counseling are multicultural, given the complexity of culturally defined salience as it adapts to each changing cultural context. From this perspective, the culture-centered perspective is generic, and culture becomes an important metaphor for counseling.

The more inclusive and broadly defined definitions of culture have been controversial. In arguing that counseling psychologists have prematurely abandoned the study of racial factors in counseling in favor of all-inclusive multiculturalism, Helms (1994) contends that

> whereas multiculturalism may be a useful construct for encouraging discussion about matters of culture in society in general, it is virtually useless as a scientific construct. In particular, the lack of specificity about which aspects of individual diversity are appropriately subsumed under the rubric of multiculturalism has contributed to considerable confusion in theory, research and practice. (p. 162)

Culture-centered counseling must be sensitive to the client's comprehensive cultural context. Segall et al. (1990) describe culture as the ecological forces that move and shape nature: "Given those characteristics of culture it becomes possible to define it simply as the totality of whatever all persons learn from other persons" (p. 26). If culture is part of the environment and all behavior is shaped by culture, then culture-centered counseling is a response to all culturally learned patterns. Cultural psychology, according to Shweder (1990), presumes that each human behavior gives meaning to the environment that changes people in response to that sociocultural environment. Cultural traditions and social practices regulate, express, and change patterns of human behavior: "Cultural psychology is the study of the ways subject and object, self and other, psyche and culture, person and context, figure and ground, practitioner and practice live together, require each other and dynamically, dialectically and jointly make each other up" (p. 1).

Recent research that includes gender and socioeconomic status as potentially salient cultural features provides examples of this broader definition. Kinloch (1979) included physical, cultural, economic, and behavioral characteristics in his analysis of cultural difference because these characteristics function in ways similar to those of nationality and ethnicity.

Erickson and Schultz's (1982) term "co-membership" involves any shared interest, status or characteristic, including nationality and ethnicity, as the basis for shared identity and solidarity. Hilliard (1986), for example, is critical of psychological research that disregards within-group differences of gender, socioeconomic status, and age in the study of cultural groups.

Warheit, Holzer, and Areye (1975) and Ambrowitz and Dokecki (1977) identify socioeconomic status as the most powerful predictor of mental health. Lorion (1974) and Lorion and Parron's (1985) review of the literature shows that counseling is provided differently to different economic class groups. Lower-income persons are less likely to be in therapy or, if they are, for shorter periods of time with symptoms similar to, although more severe than, those of clients from higher socioeconomic groups. Lower-income clients are also treated by less experienced staff and with less sophisticated modes of therapy. Goldstein (1994) attributes this prescriptive mismatch of services to the sociocultural differences between lower-class clients and typically middle-class change agents:

> Both may be of the same race, ethnicity, age, gender and city of residence. But if they are from different social classes, they are from different cultures. Further, they are from different cultures in ways that directly bear upon the form and efficacy of the intervention most appropriately offered. (p. 160)

Differences of power, prestige, and money coincide with socioeconomic differences in both how people are perceived and how they perceive themselves. Pinderhughes (1984) describes differences of feelings and behaviors between those who are powerful and those who are powerless. This is not to say that low-income persons are a homogeneous group in the discredited "culture of poverty" perspective as an inherent characteristic of being a poor person rather than as a reaction to environmental conditions. Even though a class-bound viewpoint may not be transmitted from generation to generation, it nonetheless provides a potentially powerful salience in shaping the way persons perceive themselves and how they are perceived by others.

Gender provides another example of a potentially salient cultural perspective in the broad definition of culture. Sundahl-Hansen (1985) points out six assumptions related to gender issues for counseling across cultures:

- There are differences in the career development of men and women.
- Both men and women need to reduce the negative effects of stereotyping one another on sex-role issues.
- Sex-role stereotyping pervades society throughout all aspects of culture.
- Gender is a major factor in determining life roles and options.
- The study of human development over the life span requires that we consider differential experiences and perceptions of men and women in their developmental growth.
- Intervening variables such as locus of control, self-concept and self-esteem, achievement motivation, risk taking, work orientation, and playfulness need to be considered differently for men and women.

Segall et al. (1990) document the perspective that "while sex itself (i.e., membership in one of the physiological/anatomical subgroups of humankind) is biologically determined, behaviors that are characteristic of the two sexes (masculine and feminine behaviors) however much influenced by biology are not biologically determined" (p. 239). At the same time, males and females differ behaviorally in different cultures, demonstrating that culture shapes gender roles, separating the biological "sex" from the psychosociocultural "gender" perspective. Berry et al. (1992) conclude that "while conformity and sex-role ideology are clearly patterned according to cultural factors, others (such as gender stereotypes and some shared values) are not" (p. 68).

Gender and culture interact with one another. Chodorow's (1978) work on female development and Gilligan's (1982) later work on women's moral development have demonstrated important differences in a multifaceted perspective, leading Davenport and Yurich (1991) to state that "as both researchers and practitioners, we need to move beyond our preference for looking at others through a singular lens such as gender or ethnicity and instead examine the interactive nature of various influences" (p. 70).

Sampson (1993) includes gender along with other psychological characteristics of a participant's identity, which have contributed to movements that are changing the nature of psychological interventions, in his discussion of "identity politics." Identity politics is based on the culturally learned perspectives of people seeking to be in control of their own identities despite being denied that opportunity:

The clear message is that current forms of cultural and psychological practice deny certain groups any possibility of being heard in their own way, on their own terms, reflecting their own interests and specificities, and that this condition does not reflect mere chance but rather reflects the operation of the power of those in charge to dictate the terms by which psychological and social reality will be encountered. (p. 1220)

Other examples of potentially salient features of cultural identity—broadly defined—are described in the special populations of elderly, children, adolescents, and residents of rural areas as well as other cultural and ethnic minorities. Just as the client's salient culture may change, so must the appropriate counseling intervention. The problem must be addressed at several levels including the epidemiology of mental health problems, generating appropriate help-seeking strategies, and incorporating community-based alternatives in formal counseling interventions.

Triandis et al. (1990) argue against the broad definition of culture, distinguishing between cultural, demographic, and personal constructs. Cultural constructs are shared by persons with the same dialect, from the same geographical region, and having norms, roles, values, and associations in common to explain their experiences. Demographic constructs deal with the same topics but only within a select group, such as old and young. Personal construct groups are differentiated by individual differences only. Lee and Richardson (1991) are also critical of the definition because it makes the term *culture* so broad as to be almost meaningless, including any and all constituent groups who define themselves as a culture. Locke (1992) agrees that "as the term has been increasingly stretched to include virtually any group of people who consider themselves 'different' the intent of multicultural counseling theory and practice has become unclear" (p. 6). Locke describes the broad view of culture, at best, as a prologue for a more "focused" perspective.

While Sue (1990) favors a more culture-specific approach, he acknowledges the dangers of a narrow definition of culture in counseling because it may foster technique-oriented definitions of counseling without regard to a conceptual framework and thus be distal to the goals of good counseling, limit counselors in their ability to change counseling style, and perpetuate stereotypes by focusing too narrowly on the characteristics of each ethnic group.

Ethnic cultural groups have become extremely important globally as a special interest power and force. Ethnic revival movements have been revitalized by recent migrations (Banks, 1991). Immigrants made up 7.1 of the population in Germany by 1984, with Frankfurt housing 23.9% and immigrants making up 12.4% of West Berlin's population. There were

405,000 foreign nationals living in Sweden by 1983. Australia too has increased populations of European and Asian immigrants as has Canada. Lopez and Lopez (1993) are also critical of research that values ethnicity as only one of many important factors, their concern being that this broad definition will continue the historical trend to minimize the significance of ethnicity, culture, and race in human behavior.

CAN YOU MEASURE ETHNO-RACIAL-CULTURAL IDENTITY?

One useful area of counseling research that has grown out of the culture-specific and more narrowly defined approach to culture has been on racial/ethnic identity development models (Ponterotto & Pedersen, 1993). This research was based on a conceptual framework proposed by Thomas's (1971) six-stage "negromachy" and independently by Cross's (1971) four-stage "nigrescence" framework of Black identity development as well as Jackson's (1975) four-stage model. The Cross model became more popular, building on the first stage of pre-encounter with a world that is anti-Black, the second stage of encounter that validates being Black, the third stage of immersion rejecting non-Black values, and the fourth stage of internalization resulting in a secure Black identity.

In Jackson's (1975) four-stage Black identity development model, the first stage emphasizes passive acceptance, the second stage active resistance, the third stage redirection, and the fourth stage internalization of identity. Marcia (1980) based his research on Erickson's stages of crisis in ego identity formation through diffusion, foreclosed identity, and then achieved identity. Delworth (1989) used Marcia's (1980) work to look at gender-related aspects of identity development.

The stage model by Helms (1985) is based on Cross's early framework as expressed in five assumptions:

- Minority groups develop modal personality patterns in response to White racism.
- Some styles of identity are more healthy than others.
- Cultural identity requires new attitudes toward cognitive, affective, and conative processes.
- Styles of identity are distinguishable.
- Cultural interaction is influenced by the participant's cultural identity.

Helms (1990) traces racial consciousness from historical and sociocultural patterns, moving from "less healthy" White-defined identities to a "more healthy" self-defined racial identity. Helms describes each stage as a worldview related to maturation. In Stage 1, pre-encounter, the Black idealizes White standards and ignores or is assimilated into a White society. Stage 2, encounter, is where the Black is confronted with racial injustice. Stage 3, immersion, follows an internalized, stereotyped Black perspective. Stage 4, immersion, follows an internalized and nonstereotyped Black perspective. Stage 5, internalization, moves toward a positive internalized Black identity, and commitment to that positive internalized perspective occurs in Stage 6.

Cross (1991, 1995) modified his earlier model on which Helms's (1990) model was first based. Cross's recent framework follows his earlier work in the first three stages, but in Stage 4, internalization, a thoughtful salience shifts from nationalistic to bicultural or multicultural perspectives, so that racial identity is matched to other identity concerns about religious, gender, career, class, and role orientations. In Stage 5, internalization-commitment, there is a long-term transition of Black identity into a more broadly defined life plan focused on a wide range of potentially salient identities.

Examples of other research that focuses on racial/ethnic identity are Kim (1981) on an Asian-American identity development model, Arce (1981) on a model of Chicano identity, Atkinson et al. (1993) on a minority identity development model, and Phinney (1989, 1990) on White identity development. Phinney's (1990) model has three stages. The initial stage, ethnic identity diffusion, or foreclosure, accepts unquestioningly the values of the dominant culture. The second stage, identity search and moratorium, explores ethnic identity issues as a result of encounter experiences. The third stage, ethnic identity achievement, makes racial/ethnic identity the most salient feature. Hardiman (1982) expanded research on a five-stage White identity model, moving from no social consciousness, to acceptance, to resistance, to redefinition, and finally to internalization. Helms (1990) also developed a White identity model, moving from the lower-level abandonment of racism toward a higher level defining a nonracist White identity. Ponterotto's (1988) four-stage model of White racial identity relies on Helms's earlier work, moving from pre-exposure, to exposure, to the zealot-defensive, to integration, and finally to a balanced perspective.

Both the broad and the narrow perspective of culture are useful to a culture-centered counseling perspective. Both perspectives emphasize the importance of salience in determining the person's culturally defined identity. Both perspectives emphasize the process of growth and change over time in a developmental process. It would be unfortunate if the broad and narrow perspectives of culture were seen as polarized, mutually exclusive, dichotomous alternatives.

SHOULD CULTURE-CENTERED COUNSELING EMPHASIZE SIMILARITIES OR DIFFERENCES?

To distinguish universal and shared aspects of all cultures from unique and particular aspects of a single culture—as previously discussed—Pike (1966) borrowed from the linguistic term *phonemics* (emic), referring to sounds unique in a particular language, and the linguistic term *phonetics* (etic), or universal language sounds. The "emic/etic" distinction has led some counselors to focus only on cultural similarities and others to focus only on cultural differences, ignoring the essential complementarity of both.

Although the labels are culture specific, the functions of counseling may be universal. Brislin (1993) identifies six universal aspects of counseling:

- Counselors give each problem a name.
- The qualities of caring, competence, and concern of the counselor are important.
- The counselor must establish credibility.
- The client's problems are classified in a familiar framework.
- Techniques or treatment should give relief to the client.
- Counseling or treatment occurs at a special time and place.

The applications of counseling, however, are always unique. Brewer (1991) describes social identity as deriving from a tension between similarity and unique individuation at the same time. Brewer documents the importance of this dual emphasis in "uniqueness theory" and other models of individuation: "In general these models assume that individuals meet these needs by maintaining some intermediate degree of similarity between the self and relevant others" (p. 477). Segall et al. (1990) also emphasize the interaction of similarities and differences. A counselor begins with an "imposed etic," applying one's own culture "as though" it were a universal rule while refining and adapting those rules in practice to identify cultural differences. As a result, the two cultures are distinguished by their differences, and a "derived etic" describing their similarities is constructed. The emic approach has been associated with relativism and the etic approaches with universalism. Berry et al. (1992) distinguish the relativist from the universalist positions in cross-cultural psychology, pointing out the different implications of each for counseling interventions.

The relativist position grew out of anthropological research and attempts to understand people from their own perspective or in their own terms without imposing any external judgments. First, cultural factors are basic to understanding behaviors and defining roles. Second, similarities exist only at a very abstract level and differences are defined by cultural rules in each specific cultural context. Third, it is not possible to accurately assess behavior out of context, and fourth, assessment is best done qualitatively with indigenous measures. Making comparisons across cultures is difficult and requires a high level of skill. The universalist position attempts to understand people according to standard criteria that focus on shared or similar aspects across all cultures. First, biological and cultural factors are basic to understanding behavior and defining roles. Second, theoretical perspectives depend on basic processes of the human species, with differences accounted for in culture-organism interactions within the boundaries of a "derived etic," even though it is difficult to define concepts outside their cultural context. Third, it is sometimes impossible and always difficult to assess concepts outside their cultural context, and fourth, outside measures must be adapted to the indigenous setting to allow nonevaluative comparisons in a controlled context.

Some models of multicultural counseling emphasize culture-general features; others emphasize culture-specific ones. Locke (1992) describes a culture-specific perspective where each counselor begins by understanding self, then family, community, and finally, global influences for a comprehensive awareness. Lee and Richardson (1991) describe a culture-specific perspective for counseling focused on the cultural dynamics of 13 specific cultural groups. Ramirez (1991), Vargas and Koss-Chioino (1992), and Cheatham and Stewart (1990) each focus on specific minority group populations as separate cultures. Atkinson et al. (1993) focus on diversity issues as primary to the process of culture-centered counseling in the reaction against the "melting pot" perspective in which specific cultural groups are forced to abandon their identity to acculturate. Othman and

Awang (1993) review the problems of counselor identity, drugs, moral values, stress, and breakdown of the family in eight specific Asian-Pacific cultures, demonstrating how the same problem is dealt with differently in each culture.

There is also a literature on multicultural counseling emphasizing universal features. One set of universal patterns is based on value frameworks that describe dispositions among culturally different peoples. Ibrahim and Kahn (1985) have applied the Kluckhohn-Strodbeck five value orientations to measure a counselor's awareness of culturally different value orientations across cultures. Carter (1991) reviews the multicultural counseling literature on these value orientations for studying within-group and between-group patterns of cultural similarity and difference. Sue and Sue (1990) describe the Kluckhohn-Strodtbeck framework as "one of the most useful frameworks for understanding differences among individuals and groups" (p. 138).

Other universal patterns are derived from different patterns of behavior by culturally different peoples (Fukuyama, 1990). Sue (1978) presents a worldview paradigm based on locus of control and locus of responsibility that matches patterns of behavior with specific populations (Sue & Sue, 1990). Persons with a high internal locus of control and internal locus of responsibility believe they are masters of their fate and can control their environment by their own actions. Persons with an external locus of control and internal locus of responsibility accept being controlled by a dominant culture like Stonequist's (1937) "marginal man" and blame themselves. Persons with external locus of control and external locus of responsibility feel helpless and controlled by those in power beyond their capability to change things. Persons with internal locus of control and external locus of responsibility believe in their own ability to change their situation, but it is not their fault if prejudice and discrimination prevent positive change.

Pedersen and Ivey (1993) developed four dimensions of "synthetic culture" based on the four research dimensions of Hofstede (1991): Alpha (high power distance), Beta (strong uncertainty avoidance), Gamma (high individualism), and Delta (strong masculinity). Synthetic cultures provide a safe setting to examine and compare cultural differences and similarities on the same problem in a temporary laboratory. Both similarities and differences must be understood to clearly understand the client's cultural context in counseling. Understanding differences contributes an identity; understanding similarities defines "common ground."

ARE PROFESSIONAL ETHICAL
GUIDELINES ADEQUATE TO GUIDE
CULTURE-CENTERED COUNSELORS?

The culture-centered counselor is too often having to choose between following professional ethical guidelines or acting in an ethical manner (Casas & Thompson, 1991). All professional counselor associations with ethical guidelines emphasize the responsibility of counselors to know their clients' cultural values before delivering a mental health service to those clients, but professional guidelines continue to support the perspective of a dominant culture (Pedersen, 1994), sometimes requiring the counselor to demonstrate "responsible disobedience" (Pedersen & Marsella, 1982). The trend toward ethical consciousness in culture-centered counseling is credited to demographic changes favoring minority groups, increased visibility of ethnic minorities, pressure by civil rights and human rights groups worldwide, and the economic incentives to attract minority clients (Casas, 1984).

Payton (1994) is critical of the current APA (1992) ethical code for its lack of humanitarian consciousness:

> Ethnic minorities, women, gay men and lesbians have reason to be apprehensive about the apparent downgrading in importance of psychologists' declaration of respect for the dignity and worth of the individual. All previous codes seemed to have been formulated from the perspective of protecting customers. The new code appears to be driven by a need to protect psychologists. (p. 317)

This tendency is evident in a number of ways:

- Explicitly limiting the code to work-related activities only
- Replacing the standard opening sentence to the preamble emphasizing humanitarian issues with one dedicated to scientific knowledge based on research
- Using a qualifier in urging "appropriate" respect for the fundamental rights, dignity, and worth of all people
- Diluting the code's humanitarian standards to protect against lawsuits
- Labeling those groups "included" and by implication excluding others
- Writing the code in "legal language," with numerous exclusions and exceptions noted

Dana (1994) distinguishes between "principle ethics," where judgments are based on value systems (Keith-Spiegel & Koocher, 1985), and "virtue ethics," where ideas are based on historic content and purpose linking individuals and their community (Jordan & Meara, 1990). Dana (1994) goes on to demonstrate how the increasingly nonspecific guidelines resulted in personalized multicultural biases and to suggest alternatives:

> As a minimum requirement, cultural competence should include (a) assessment of the client as a cultural entity; (b) culture-specific delivery styles, including different cultural rules for dual roles and physical contact; (c) cultural belief systems of health and illness, values and identification of legitimate providers; (d) use of the client's first language for services and (e) familiarity with general principles, procedural details, and local examples of culture-specific assessment. (p. 351)

Dana is particularly critical of the ethical code regarding assessment. First, the guidelines lack specificity, allowing assessors to be naive, uninformed, or unintentionally biased and to project their own interpretations. Second, there is little attention to emic or culture-specific assessment methods, marginalizing the importance of cross-cultural psychology. Third, there is confusion in the multicultural literature about the role of cultural variables and what constitutes a valid cultural orientation in assessment.

June Tapp with Lawrence Wrightsman, Harry Triandis, Herbert Kelman, and George Coelho headed a subcommittee of the American Psychological Association on worldwide ethical considerations of cross-cultural research. They pointed out that ethical obligation goes beyond avoiding harm to include enriching and benefiting clients from different cultures (Tapp et al., 1974). The support for more adequate multicultural ethical guidelines has continued with heightened group consciousness, government-mandated affirmative action, court-ordered integration, and bicultural educational alternatives. From the international perspective, the U.S. perspective is unusual "in its growing salience of ethnic/racial relations, its bipolarity, its emphasis on hierarchy over cultural contrast, the casting of government in the role of protagonist for the underclass and the ethical specificity and direction of violence" (Lambert, 1981, p. 189).

The ethical imperative has been overshadowed by the need to fix blame. This polarization of society into majority versus minority orientation has resulted in moral exclusion demonstrated by psychological distancing, displacing responsibility, expressing group loyalty, and normalizing violence, any of which can occur through overt and malicious action or through covert support and passive disregard. Opotow (1990) states, "As severity of conflict and threat escalates, harm and sanctioned aggression become more likely. As harm doing escalates societal structures change, the scope of justice shrinks, and the boundaries of harm doing expand" (p. 13). Moral exclusion is most obvious in institutional racism.

Implicit examples of institutionalized bias have resulted in minority populations being underserved by counselors. Counselor education has minimalized cultural issues in curricula and texts, certification requirements for multicultural skills of counselors have been interpreted "liberally," minorities have been underrepresented among counseling students, violations of cultural values in counseling have not been acted on, and professional guidelines have protected providers against culturally different consumers (LaFromboise & Foster, 1989). Even the measures of moral development favor individualistic societies (Snarey, 1985) and urban middle-class males (Gilligan, 1987).

Most of the criticism of professional ethical guidelines presumes that the principles are valid but poorly implemented due to inadequate training and inappropriate counseling interventions. The American Psychological Association's (1992) ethical guidelines provide examples of how cultural biases are implicit within the principles themselves. Many counselors violate Principle A on competence by going beyond the boundaries of their capability in working with culturally different clients unfamiliar to them. Although explicit misrepresentation is prevented by Principle B unintentional racism is minimalized. Principle C upholds professional and scientific responsibility, but there is no application of this obligation to multicultural issues. Principle D requires respect for people's rights, dignity, and worth in a general and ambiguous sense that tends to be rhetorical. Principle E on concern for the welfare of the less powerful and Principle F on social responsibility are also frequently overlooked in the application (Pedersen, 1994).

The APA (1992) standards are even more blatant in their cultural bias, beginning with Standard 1.08, which presumes that differences of age, gender, race, ethnicity, national origin, religion, sexual orientation, disability, language, and socioeconomic status are not usually significant in all psychological interventions. The definition of unfairness in Standard 1.10, harassment in 1.12, prohibiting multiple relationships in 1.17, and prohibiting barter in 1.18 depends on the presumptions of a dominant, middle-class, urban, cultural context. Although accurate assessment is mandated in Standard 2.10, appropriate interpretation is mandated in 2.02, and biased tests are excluded in 2.04, these conditions are often not possible as counseling is currently practiced.

The patterns of ethical guidelines and standards for professional counseling reflect a consistent cultural bias (Axelson, 1993; Ponterotto & Casas, 1991). The presumption of generalized and abstract standards or guidelines for ethical behavior is that all counselors of "goodwill" share the same cultural assumptions, which one knows is not true. Escaping into abstraction has allowed the individual counselor to project self-referenced cultural assumptions into these guidelines at the expense of culturally different minority client populations.

We need to move toward pluralistic contextually sensitive ethical guidelines that accommodate different culturally learned assumptions for counselors and their clients. Cultural differences provide an opportunity to develop inclusionary perspectives to increase ethical counseling practice with persons of different ages, genders, lifestyles, socioeconomic status, and affiliations. As culture-centered counseling is understood to focus on accuracy in the theory and practice of counseling, the mandate for good practice is more and more likely to take culture seriously in defining the counselor's ethical guidelines. Corey et al. (1993) predict increased importance for the multicultural perspective in defining ethical obligations for counseling to prevent "cultural tunnel vision."

CONCLUSION

There are many controversies surrounding the interface between culture and counseling to stimulate field research and classroom teaching. The several controversies discussed in this chapter are only some of the issues that promote discussion and debate. It is important to go beyond these selected examples of controversy in adapting the counseling process to a multicultural reality.

After several decades of focus on cultural bias it may be that counseling is more culturally encapsulated now than ever in its history. The temptation of seeking easy answers in a new test or technique is just too tempting and the struggle with complex problems too painful. In the same mode, it is safe to assume that all tests and measures are culturally biased. The skilled counselor will, however, be able to compensate for that bias in an accurate interpretation of those test data to the client in the client's cultural context. The more inclusive and broad interpretation of culture seems to be gaining support as the many within-group variables of demographics, status, and affiliation are increasingly recognized as potentially salient in a specific cultural context. The controversies surrounding measurement of ethnic or racial identity have stimulated many new scales and tests to help clients clarify their own culturally learned identity issues. The controversy of whether to emphasize similarities or differences seems to be resolved in a shared and complementary relationship between both. Applications of moral reasoning to multicultural contexts raise the controversy of objectively evaluating other people's subjective reality. The ethical controversy has not been resolved in the research or professional literature and remains more difficult now than ever before.

The task of continuing research on and discussion of controversies is primarily aimed at defining the questions more precisely and clearly. Only then can one hope to find answers. Think of these controversies as the energy or fuel that runs the multicultural engines of change, not as barriers but as bridges to better understanding.

EXERCISE

TEST OF REASONABLE OPPOSITES

Objective

To challenge one's prevailing culturally learned assumptions

Instructions

1. Identify a culturally learned assumption that you have assumed to be true without examination because it is so fundamental to yourself or to what you are doing.
2. Identify an alternative position that would reverse that assumption and provide an "opposite" position.
3. Compare the two statements to see which alternative is more "reasonable." Some examples of opposites are the following:
   - Differences are important versus similarities are important.
   - Counseling descreases versus increases pain.
   - Clients should come to counseling versus counseling should come to clients.

Debriefing

Assumptions are usually so fuzzy that it is hard to find an opposite to what you assume. Once an opposite truth statement has been generated, it is often as reasonable as the original statement. The test of reasonable opposites forces one to generate new and creative alternatives that would never have been considered.

12

Conclusion

■ **Primary Objective** Speculate on the role of culture in the future of counseling

■ **Secondary Objectives** (1) Review the key issues that need to be solved and (2) Describe how culture-centered counseling can contribute to the future

---

Understanding one's own underlying culturally learned assumptions and interpreting all behaviors in their cultural context has been the primary theme of this book. The most vivid weakness of counseling multicultural client populations as it is currently taught and practiced is its inability or reluctance to identify the underlying culturally learned assumptions on which counseling functions are based and to interpret or seek to change behaviors outside their cultural context. The research gaps that have been identified in previous sections of this book can be summarized in a series of models for counseling intervention and the "key issues" raised by each alternative model from a culture-centered perspective.

Counseling is experiencing a revolutionary change although the ultimate direction of that change remains unclear. Ponterotto and Casas (1991) outline 12 areas where research is required to determine the nature of counseling in the future:

- Accurate epidemiological data on the incidence and prevalence of psychological problems for culturally defined groups as a database
- Development of identity models to guide minorities toward healthy sociopolitical development
- Historical influence of Euro-American political and educational assumptions as they continue to define access and opportunity
- How to control, manage, and prevent prejudice through counseling interventions
- The developmental progress of dominant White cultural groups
- A balanced perspective to assess the problems and opportunities within minority communities
- Within-group differences to supplement current research on between-group differences
- The definition and achievement of bicultural, biracial, or multicultural identity
- Samples that go beyond university student samples of convenience in multicultural research
- Primary prevention programs, such as parent training programs
- Development of tests and measures that accurately assess persons from different cultures
- Balancing emic (culture-specific) with etic (culture-universal) aspects of counseling

CULTURE-SPECIFIC MODELS

A culture-specific model emphasizes a special interest group defined typically by ethnicity, age, gender, or other affiliation. This model does not ignore the other aspects of a client's identity, but by focusing narrowly on one particular identity at a time, the analysis presumes to achieve a greater depth of understanding. Until recently, this model was the most popular and practically the only one for increasing a counselor's awareness of a client's particular culture. Its strength is that it provides a deeper and more comprehensive understanding of one potentially salient client identity feature. Its weakness is that it presumes that each client has only one primary cultural identity across situations and over a period of time. Culture-specific models raise key issues, such as the following, that require more research:

- *Identification of salient cultural features in a client or in a cultural context.* The research literature cited previously documents the multiplicity of potentially salient identities for each client but how does one track the rapidly changing salience as it moves from one specific cultural identity to another? How is cultural salience measured in the client's context? How can the counselor be trained to shift strategies appropriately to match the complex and dynamic cultural salience the client is experiencing? Pedersen (1994) suggests that training counselors to interpret a client's "internal dialogue" through training clients with procounselors (positive internal dialogue) and anticounselors (negative internal dialogue) might help counselors follow the changing cultural salience in the counseling interview.

■ *Definition of an appropriate role for the dominant culture relative to minority groups.* In the past, the most powerful cultural group has established the rules and defined the roles for other less powerful groups. This domination by one group has led to cultural encapsulation and an "imposed etic" when the most powerful group presumes their way is the only right way. Issues of power are profoundly important in culture-centered counseling, and racism is usually defined as prejudice plus the power to enforce that prejudice on others. Socioeconomic status has emerged as an important cultural identity in part because it represents access to power, for as long as the dominant cultural group perceives itself to be under attack by minorities in a competition for power, harmony is unlikely. And as long as minority groups perceive themselves as victims of the dominant culture, harmony is unlikely. An appropriate role for dominant-culture groups relative to minority groups needs to be defined in ways that are mutually beneficial to prevent fragmentation of minority groups and provide common ground for win-win outcomes through culture-centered counseling. Win-win outcomes occur when majority and minority groups realize they can maintain their unique identity while working toward shared common-ground positive values and expectations.

CULTURE-GENERAL MODELS

The culture-general model is a more recent phenomenon for preparing counselors to work in a variety of multicultural settings by examining themes and issues that cut across the various specific cultures. A key element of this model is training counselors to become more self-aware of their own cultural identity and how that identity has shaped counseling interventions. Culture-general models emphasize the cultural skills and perspectives that apply to all psychological interventions, as noted in the previously cited literature. For example, there is a presumption that counselors who are able to manage a higher degree of complexity might make more effective counseling interventions in multicultural settings. There is a presumption that counselors who are more aware of and in control of their own culturally learned assumptions will be better able to

compensate for those assumptions in a variety of culturally difficult counseling interventions. There is a presumption that awareness, knowledge,
and skill can be taught independent of any particular cultural context and
so prepare counselors to be more effective in their culture-centered interventions. Culture-general models raise key issues, such as the following,
that need to be addressed:

- *Whether multiculturalism is a method for working with specific cultural
  groups or a generic theory of counseling for all groups.* Previous sections of
  this book have attempted to build a case that culture-centered counseling
  is more than a method for working with different groups. According to the
  broad definition of culture, all counseling relationships are cross-cultural
  to a greater or lesser extent. Differences of ethnographic, demographic,
  status, and affiliation variables may become salient in the counseling
  intervention. The counselor must follow that rapidly changing salience to
  interpret the client's behavior appropriately in the client's cultural context.
  If failure of a counseling intervention is the result of failing to interpret the
  client's behavior in the cultural context that gave that behavior meaning,
  then the culture-centered approach may be able to explain failure and
  predict success as a generic theory in its own right. Multiculturalism as a
  "fourth force" theory is different from other theories in that it is not the
  top-down product of any particular theorist but the bottom-up response
  by culturally different consumers of counseling. Culture-centeredness also
  does not compete with psychodynamic, humanistic, or behavioral theories
  but, rather, reframes these alternatives by making the cultural context
  "central" to each alternative theoretical perspective.

- *How to manage the complexity of both cultural similarities and differences
  at the same time.* The individual's or group's identity is defined by emphasizing differences that are unique or special. Without those unique and
  special aspects the individual or group's cultural identity is minimized.
  The working relationship necessary for cooperation requires identifying
  similarities of "common ground" across cultural groups or individual
  identities. If either similarities or differences are minimized, the counseling intervention is unlikely to succeed. The Cultural Grid described earlier
  suggests that the same positive expectations for trust, respect, caring, and
  success provide important aspects of similarity, even though the behaviors
  by which those expectations are expressed might be very different across
  cultures. Differences of behavior might enhance a relationship where
  similar positive expectations exist. Approaches to counseling that overemphasize differences are likely to result in stereotyping, just as approaches that overemphasize similarities are likely to result in domination
  by the most powerful group. Teaching counselors to simultaneously emphasize both similarities and differences is a difficult task in need of more
  research.

CULTURE-FREE OR
CULTURE-FAIR MODELS

Culture-free models have attempted to develop measures that are not dependent on any particular cultural context and are free of cultural bias. Culture-fair models have recognized the pervasiveness of culture but attempt to compensate for cultural differences in ways that are equitable and fair to different cultural groups. As demonstrated in previous discussion, both of these approaches to the theory and practice of counseling have failed. Counseling has attempted to manage cultural differences within the traditional framework by adapting the tools and theories of counseling. As long as cultural differences are perceived as exotic and tangential to the theory and practice of counseling, then counselors might presume to accommodate culturally different clients with minor modifications of the counseling process. If, however, culture is described as central to the counseling process, then the fundamental understanding of counseling as a process needs to be reconsidered. The problem is not in the tools of counseling but in the counselors themselves. Previously cited research suggests that all measures are to some extent culturally biased but that a skilled counselor should be able to interpret data from culturally biased measures in ways that are helpful to culturally different clients. These models raise key issues, such as the following, that need to be addressed:

■ *How to deal with cultural bias in the measures and theories of counseling generally.* We may presume that any theory or measure that fits precisely for one cultural context will not fit as well in a radically different cultural context. In the past, attempts to modify the measures themselves have been unsuccessful because culture is so complex and dynamic. More recent attempts to train skilled counselors to compensate for cultural bias in the theories and measures of counseling have been more promising. A skilled counselor can help clients understand the meaning of their score or behavior relative to others without judging or evaluating that client according to the counselor's own self-reference criteria. Previously discussed research suggests how an increased awareness of culturally learned assumptions, knowledge about cultural information, and skill in appropriate interventions prepare culture-centered counselors to work with culturally different clients.

■ *Becoming aware of culturally learned assumptions and their effect on counseling interventions.* The "self-reference criterion," discussed previously, imposes the counselor's own more familiar cultural expectations on culturally different clients. A sympathetic counselor might inappropriately project one's own feelings if in the client's place. An empathic counselor more appropriately understands the client's situation from the client's own independent viewpoint. Ridley (1995) discusses the problems of unintentional racism among counselors as a problem to be overcome. Culturally learned assumptions control our behavior with or without our permission. The culture-centered counselor identifies assumptions that are inappropriate and changes them to fit the client's cultural context.

CULTURE-DEFICIT MODELS

Culture-deficit models blame the failure of psychological interventions on the "unfavorable" cultural climate. This form of scapegoating has pressured clients to abandon their cultural identity for alternative identities more closely matched to the counselor's. Counseling and counselors have a bad reputation in many minority groups for protecting the system against the individual even when the client is clearly right and the system is wrong. Counseling has often become a vehicle of "adjustment" for culturally different clients to accommodate the more powerful profile of the dominant culture and abandon their indigenous identity. In some multicultural settings, discussed earlier, counseling involves a process of resocialization that is unacceptable to some traditional cultural groups and leads to underusing counseling services. The culture-deficit model suggests key issues, such as the following, for future discussion:

- *How to distinguish cultural differences from individual differences.* By defining culture broadly as complex and dynamic, are we reducing culture to the level of individual differences? Skin color at birth is an individual difference, but what that skin color has come to mean over time is cultural. A drawing of culture might take the form of a Venn diagram with 1,000 overlapping circles, each circle representing a separate teacher or potentially salient cultural influence in the person's life. The complexity of cultural differences is so overwhelming that counselors and counselor educators are reluctant to deal with the full range of cultural identities a client depends on in each cultural context. The difficulties in defining culture broadly without destroying the traditional constructs of culture have already been discussed.
- *Understanding how cultures change.* Counselors who are intimidated by sociocultural systems must understand that cultures change and adapt in small increments rather than grand sweeping and instantaneous revolutions. When everything seems to be changing for a culture it is important

to identify those fundamental elements that do not change. Culture is like a door that swings open or closed because the hinges remain permanently in place. The fundamental and unchanging "hinges" of a particular culture make change possible. Cultural systems change and adapt to fit the requirements of each cultural context. Rather than blame the culture in a "deficit" judgment, the counselor may want to understand the changing and unchanging elements of a client's culture more completely.

RELATIVISM AND ABSOLUTISM
AS POLARIZED MODELS

Historically, there has been a tendency to polarize choices between absolutist, universal, and unchanging alternatives, on the one hand, and relativist, particularized, and constantly changing elements, on the other. Anthropology has tended to emphasize cultural relativism, whereas psychology has tended to emphasize a more absolute and universal measure of culture-related behavior. The interdisciplinary synthesis that characterizes more recent approaches to culture combines the strengths of both a relativist and an absolutist perspective in the theory and practice of counseling. The literature on this area related to counseling theory, practice, and ethics has been cited earlier. Developing a third alternative to relativism and absolutism is a difficult task that needs to be accomplished if counseling interventions are to be successful in culturally different contexts. Combining absolutism and relativism raises key issues, such as the following, for discussion.

- *Definition of ethical guidelines in multicultural settings.* We need to distinguish those fundamental but abstract principles necessary for ethical counseling from other discretionary approaches or context-sensitive methods of achieving the fundamental principles that differ in each time and place. Ethical guidelines have demonstrated cultural bias wherever the same standards have been applied in the same way for all settings in a one-size-fits-all perspective. A more situational and relational alternative is necessary to guide culture-centered counselors adequately.

- *Finding common ground across cultures without sacrificing cultural integrity.* Culture-centered counseling relationships recognize the client's need to be different and yet be connected with others. Culture provides a metaphor for finding common ground, in that two culturally different persons may disagree without one necessarily being wrong and the other right. Culture-centered counseling is an attempt to develop relationships across cultures by emphasizing the common ground of shared values and expectations among and between people who might otherwise judge others' behavior as hostile and threatening.

Culture-centered counseling is guided more by adapting to culturally different clients than by theoretical structures, which need to be extrapolated from examples of success with culturally different clients. It is important to remember that the counseling audience of the future is a globally defined population. Solutions to problems of culture-centered counseling will rely on both Western and non-Western cultures. By making culture central to the counseling process, this book has demonstrated ways that culture can facilitate the quality of counseling and the effectiveness of counselors, for disregarding the cultural context leads counselors toward abstract projections of their own self-referenced criteria and the illusion of a monocultural future. Culture-centered counseling skills are based on a high level of counselor self-awareness.

FUNDAMENTAL CHANGES AND TRENDS

The field of counseling is experiencing a revolution that is much more apparent to those counselors working in multicultural settings than it is to counselors who continue to minimalize the role of culture. Whereas the revolutionary impact of psychodynamic, behavioral, and even humanistic approaches to counseling were top-down models, driven by a small centralized core group of leaders, the revolutionary change in the contemporary field of culture-centered counseling is bottom up and in response to decentralized consumer pressures by client populations from different cultures. This revolution is most obvious with regard to ethnic and nationality groups but is also apparent for cultures defined by gender, age, lifestyle, socioeconomic status, and physiological abilities. These special interest groups are challenging the criteria by which counseling interventions are evaluated. This change is even more pronounced as counseling interventions are adapted to meet the needs of other countries and cultures outside the Euro-American context.

With the evolution of internal dynamics for change in mental health professions, external circumstances in the changing world around us, and advances in scientific knowledge, we are at a crucial point in history. As Kleinman (1988) sees it,

We will look backward toward this period either as a continuation of powerful professional resistance to the coming crisis in our priorities or as the beginning of the transition toward a global psychiatry whose science and practices accommodate an international mental health agenda, cross-cultural differences, the social context, and, not least of all, the social sciences. (p. 185)

Although the direction of change in the future is still ambiguous, the need for change is apparent. The domination of the counseling profession by narrowly defined, White, male, Euro-American, middle-class values is evident in the demographic background of providers, the historical origins of the counseling profession, the financial prerequisites for participation as a client, the sociopolitical usefulness of advocating "adjustment" by deviant clients, and the philosophical foundations of individualism. The traditional rules of counseling are being changed in fundamental ways that cannot be satisfied by the cosmetic modifications of eclecticism.

Waldrop (1992) describes six of the fundamental social transitions that will take place within the next few decades in a global context:

- Demographic transition to a roughly stable world population
- Technological transition to a minimal environmental impact per person
- Economic transition to a world in which serious attempts are made to charge the real costs of goods and services—including environmental costs—so that there are incentives for the world economy to live off nature's income rather than depleting its capital
- Social transition to a broader sharing of that income along with increased opportunities for nondestructive employment for the poor families of the world
- Institutional transition to a set of supranational alliances that facilitates a global attack on global problems and allows various aspects of policy to be integrated with one another
- Informational transition to a world in which scientific research, education, and global monitoring allow large numbers of people to understand the nature of the challenges they face

There are at least three obvious future directions toward which counseling might change in response to pressure from culturally different client groups. If the past is indeed the best predictor of the future, then counseling might move toward an authoritarian defensive stance to protect one set of narrowly defined traditional standards to preserve counseling as a profession or guild. This mode opposes change. The second possibility is a multidirectional complexity where the functions of counseling are broadly defined and professional boundaries are minimalized. In this mode, change is accepted as constant and essential. The third possibility is some sort of harmony of traditional and nontraditional factors. In this mode, good changes are differentiated from bad ones in a purposeful, intentional, and dynamic balance.

There are several changes likely to occur in the profession of counseling irrespective of which future direction is taken. Some of these predictable changes are the following:

- Increased awareness of the revolutionary changes taking place in counseling as a result of cultural similarities and differences
- Culture defined more as a generic aspect in each context and less as an exotic condition of far-from-home groups
- Increased pressure by culturally different consumers of counseling to reduce cultural bias in counseling
- Each special interest group defining its own identity as a culture with an articulate membership
- Counseling theories modified to fit the requirements of culturally different contexts
- Counseling methods modified to fit the requirements of culturally different relationships
- Counseling becoming more popular globally as cultures become more industrialized, urbanized, and modernized
- Non-Western cultures having a greater impact on defining the theory and practice of counseling
- Culturally encapsulated dominant culture's control of counseling being challenged
- Counseling becoming more interdisciplinary in practice to appropriately address clients' cultural context
- Counseling becoming more readily available to consumers seeking help in their own culturally defined terms
- Counselors who oppose these changes becoming defensive and self-protective but ultimately adapting or being left behind

AUTHORITARIAN INDIVIDUALISM AS A CENTRALIZED ALTERNATIVE

The counseling profession has protected itself against change through defending implicit or sometimes explicit assumptions in an authoritarian definition of appropriate counseling interventions. This authoritarian theme is most obvious in an individualistic perspective. Working with individual persons has always been a central theme of counseling. The individual is presumed to be a separate independent and autonomous entity guided by traits, abilities, values, and motives that distinguish individuals from one another. Berry et al. (1992) describe individualistic cultures as more "idiocentric," emphasizing competition, self-confidence, and freedom as contrasted with collectivistic cultures that emphasize communal responsibility, social usefulness, and acceptance of authority. Taylor (1989) describes the role of individualism in psychological well-being from a Westernized perspective as a "disguised ideology" that has shaped the social sciences. Psychology has described behavior using the same natural scientific approaches developed during the Enlightenment, but Christopher (1992) counters that "naturalism not only involves an attempt to understand human beings as part of nature but also demands that we abstain entirely from the use of subjective or anthropocentric categories in our account of the human" (p. 13). This pretention to psychological objectivity has sought to imitate the physical sciences in sharing the same assumptions for human behavior that apply to physical objects.

Authoritarian individualism is designed to protect the dignity of the person, the priority of autonomy, the healthfulness of self-direction, the goals of self-development, and the legal right to privacy. Individualism became a religious belief in dignity that extended to "natural rights" regardless of social commitments or obligation. Lukes (1973) describes five different varieties of individualism:

- *Methodological* explains social behavior through facts and empirical data about individuals.
- *Political* bases authority on the purpose and use of power by individuals.
- *Economic* justifies the deregulation of self-serving economic behaviors.
- *Religious* connects the person directly to God without intermediaries.
- *Ethical* defines morality according to individual actions or consequences.
- *Epistemological* presumes that all knowledge is the property of individuals.

Triandis (1993) suggests that both collectivism and individualism constructs are cultural syndromes. Kagitcibasi (1990) describes how "home based" intervention contributes to both human and socioeconomic development in developing countries just as individualistic approaches have worked toward development in more industrialized countries: "For example, if competition, individual achievement, and separation from the in-group are encouraged without regard for family welfare, there might be resistance to such an intervention. What needs to be done is to work through the closely knit family system to introduce autonomy into it" (p. 131).

Individualism is not the opposite of collectivism, for even collectivistic cultures may treat "outsiders" in individualistic ways. The same person may follow individualism and collectivism, depending on the situation, suggesting that they are not opposites but independent variables. Individualists might consider the good of the individual best achieved by doing what is good for society, whereas collectivists may behave in "ideocentric" ways as representatives of the group (Triandis, Brislin, & Hui, 1988). Sampson (1988) divides individualism into two categories: "self-contained" individualism as exclusionary, with well-defined and differentiated self-nonself boundaries, and "ensembled" individualism that is more fluid than rigid, more inclusive of person and/or self, and more field focused on the same core cultural values of freedom, responsibility, and achievement but in a cultural context. Most of the problems result from from "self-contained" individualism.

To the extent that a Westernized lifestyle has come to represent an authoritarian individualism, measures of health and illness have been grounded in objectively verifiable behaviors rather than relativistic subjectivism. Individualism has been presumed necessary for modernization. Segall et al. (1990) conclude that "psychological research on modernization will focus on individual behavioral variables—treating them either as independent, mediating or dependent—that need to be measured" (p. 303).

As a consequence, in part, of individualistic thinking, Heilbronner (1975) suggests we are being threatened by overpopulation, the spread of nuclear weapons and engines of mass destruction, and the demands for technical advancement at the expense of environmental resources. Individualistic patterns of Western thinking that may have been adaptive at one point in history require modification toward a more ecological balance for postindustrial societies. As Third World cultures seek to overcome their own social and human problems resulting from modernization, the need for counseling services is likely to increase. Although modern science, technology, and industrialization have provided material comforts, they have not enhanced psychological well-being: "The same individualistic cultural patterns that may have been adaptive at one stage of social development may require modification toward a more ecological perspective of preindustrial societies of our past and perhaps postindustrial societies of our future as well" (Pedersen, 1994, p. 58).

Although domination by narrowly defined assumptions of authoritarian individualism is one alternative for the future, it would require that counseling ignore the diverse needs of an increasingly articulate client population representing a variety of special interest groups. The functions of counseling would probably be taken over by other professional or paraprofessional groups, encapsulating "counselors" in an institutionalized role as a narrowly defined specialty. The alternative future of authoritarian individualism could result in predictable consequences, some of which are the following:

- The best interest of counselors as a "professional guild" will determine good practice as that which promotes professional self-interest.
- Data challenging traditional assumptions of counseling will be disregarded or dismissed without serious consideration.
- A single standard of "normal" behavior will prevail in the measures and outcome goals of counseling, irrespective of the client's cultural context.
- Individualism will be the criterion of healthy behavior, and dependencies will become signs of neurosis.
- Counseling will be defined narrowly as a professional activity discouraging communication with other disciplines.
- The gap between counseling theory and practice of counseling will widen, with counselors specializing in one or the other direction.
- Linear thinking will prevail as the only cognitive style judged to be rational.
- Counseling will become a tool of social institutions seeking to encourage the adaptation and accommodation of the system by deviant individuals.
- Cultural biases by professional counselors will go unexamined and not be taken seriously.
- Westernized interpretations of science will predominate over non-Western alternatives.
- Counseling psychology will seek to imitate the physical "hard" sciences of the medical model and distance itself from the "soft" social sciences and the psychoeducational model.
- Alternative approaches to the functions of counseling will continue and flourish outside the discipline.

COMPLEX DIVERSITY AND DECENTRALIZED ALTERNATIVES

If the boundaries of counseling are expanded to include all formal and informal methods in all formal and informal contexts, then counseling as a professional activity becomes extremely complicated. In many cultures, the client might go inside oneself to remembered teachings or Confucian proverbs as the first line of defense in dealing with personal problems. In other cultures, problems are best ignored, and any attention to personal problems by the self or an outsider such as a counselor is thought to exacerbate the problem. Teaching people to mobilize their endorphin production to cure diseases through self-medication may become a future form of counseling, for example. Other methods of orthodox and unorthodox healing may also qualify. The variety and styles of dealing with personal problems already describe a great diversity of contrasting or contradictory approaches. The professional identity crisis of counseling is reflected in the terminology being introduced to describe counseling functions such as helping, human services, and co-relational therapies. Corsini (1981) has described hundreds of different innovative therapies with each approach defining counseling in a distinctly different manner. As indigenous counseling modes from non-Western cultures become better known, the range of nontraditional counseling approaches will expand still more.

The radical alternative of extreme diversity would create serious problems of credentialing the profession and safeguarding clients as well as otherwise regulating the process of help giving. Culture's complexity, as illustrated by the thousands of culturally learned roles and identities that compete for salience in our lives, has led many counselors and counseling researchers to disregard this apparent chaos for more simplistic alternatives. There is considerable interest in teaching counselors to manage complexity in the developmental counseling literature (Stoltenberg & Delworth, 1987), in the social cognitive perspective (Abramson, 1988), and in developing multicultural counseling skills (Pedersen, 1994). Because counselors cannot ignore the extreme diversity of culture-centered clients they can easily be overwhelmed by the chaotic interaction of the client's thousands of potentially salient cultures with an equally complex counseling repertoire.

Historically, we have been moving toward increased complexity. Maruyama (1992) describes the process of contextual understanding of human behavior as having gone through four historical phases of "mindscapes": The first, the "H" (hierarchical) type, attempted to deal with complexity by broadening the categories being considered through interdisciplinary, cross-field, interdepartmental, and problem-centered approaches to the social sciences. By the 1960s, rebellion against mainstream perspectives produced an "I" (isolationist) mindscape that became popular in special interest groups, ethnic groups, and other inward-looking perspectives that shut themselves off from the outside world. The H type and the I type are related in a dialectical opposition to one another throughout history. The third mindscape is the "S" (pattern stabilizing) type that focuses on understanding heterogenistic and interactive sociocultural contexts. The fourth mindscape is the "G" (pattern generating) type that focuses on managing complexity without reductionism or theoretical simplification by generating new patterns of contextual understanding. Epistemologically different mindscapes exist. They differ from one person to another, and these complex differences have been obscured by a dominant mainstream culture. The real problem is not the overwhelming complexity but the inadequacy of traditional ways of thinking to deal with it. Diversity requires a more subjective and less objective approach to counseling.

The second alternative to chaotic diversity presumes that we do not have direct access to a singular, stable, and fully knowable external reality but that our thinking is culturally embedded, interpersonally forged, and necessarily limited (Neimeyer, 1993). This constructivist perspective emphasizes personal meaning and subjective knowledge beginning with the study of "self." The self is described in "diological" terms (Hermans, Kemper, & Van Loon, 1992). The diological view is based on stories and dialogues people use to understand themselves and their role. The self is constructed in a cultural context through a plurality of relationships. Personal construct theory (Kelly, 1955) demonstrates how constructs become the criteria by which things are both alike and different in ways that challenge objective reality. Steenbarger (1991) applies the contextualist theme to counseling as an alternative to linear, stage-based, convergent hierarchies. The linear models are inadequate because they cannot account for the complexity of human development, the complexity of situational influences in the developmental process, and problematical value premises required for uniform sequences in multicultural settings.

Claiborn and Lichtenberg (1989) deal with cultural complexity through interactional counseling where change is reciprocal through multidirectional rather than unidirectional processes. Each event is both cause and effect, roles are negotiated, and new roles are created through dialogue. Hoshmand and Polkinghorne (1992) approach the science-practice relationship of culture-centered counseling through postmodern perspectives of knowledge that redefine psychological sciences. Science and practice are combined in a productive complementary rather than competitive mode. These patterns are more obvious in the practice of counseling where appropriate counseling responses to each cultural context are constructed.

McNamee and Gergen (1992) describe the spectrum of discontent that is giving rise to chaotic diversity:

1. Counseling practices are not politically, morally, or valuationally neutral but favor certain cultural perspectives, as we have already documented.
2. Individuals are not the centers of malfunction but are responding appropriately or inappropriately to a context.
3. Individual pathology cannot be separated from the community cultural context.
4. Current mental health standards are oppressive and debilitating to women and other specified groups.
5. Preconceptions about individual dysfunction may get in the way of accurate diagnosis.
6. The traditional separation between the knower and the known is challenged by constructivism.
7. Hermeneutics challenges the traditional view of the therapist as an objective analyst.
8. The current system for classifying pathology is oppressive, objectifying, demeaning, and self-serving for the mental health profession.

Will the second alternative future of chaotic diversity take control of counseling in an attempt to meet the many divergent populations and problems? Is that diversity essential to an accurate and appropriate practice of culture-centered counseling to protect us from ourselves? These are important questions that must be addressed as we take seriously the cultural context in which counseling occurs. In its extreme form, complex diversity will also bring about a series of radical changes for counseling, such as the following:

- Counseling will not be defined as a particular approach or profession.
- Counseling will become more of a social movement resembling religion or philosophy in their popular forms.
- Structures of referral networks will break down for all but the most seriously psychotic clients.
- Authenticity and validity of counseling approaches will be determined by their popularity.

- Credentialing and certification processes will be minimalized.
- Clients will be on their own to find reputable counselors and will develop cultlike loyalties to those counselors.
- Relativist measures of ethical and professional behavior will be defined by the popularity of usage.
- Counseling will become more subjective and mystical as a process.
- Existing theories and tools of counseling will be minimalized.
- A search for patterns of complex and dynamic behavior across cultures will be made.
- Developmental theories will be replaced by constructivist and postmodernist subjectivity.
- Counseling theory will become less important than practice in the polarization of theory from practice.

THE PLURALIST ALTERNATIVE

The third alternative future relies more on non-Western models of helping as a "restoration of balance." Balance in cognitive theory means changing, ignoring, differentiating, resolving, or transcending inconsistencies to avoid dissonance. In non-Western cultures, balance is often described as "asymmetrical," defined by tolerating inconsistency and dissonance rather than resolving differences to achieve apparent consistency. Western therapies have idealized restoring and maintaining a steady-state balance. Balance is an important construct in social, religious, philosophical, political, and economic "health" around the world. Asymmetrical balance is two-directional—recognizing the necessary presence of both pleasure and pain to provide meaning—rather than a one-directional search for pleasure to avoid pain, just as both light and darkness combine in the Yin and Yang symbol of Taoism.

Wittkower and Warnes (1974) explain how cultural preferences for therapy in achieving this balance are expressed differently in different cultures. This is why they claim that psychoanalysis succeeds in the U.S. individualistic setting, whereas work therapy succeeds in the Marxist Soviet Union and Morita therapy succeeds in Japan's context of rigid self-discipline. Tseng and Hsu (1980) describe the function of therapy as compensation for social deficiencies. Thus, highly controlled and overregulated cultures might encourage therapies that provide a safety valve release for feelings or emotions, whereas underregulated or anomic cultures might prefer externalized social control. Lin and Lin (1978) attribute mental illness to harmful emanations affecting the Yin and Yang when they are disturbed or out of balance. Watts (1961) compares counseling to a social game where the therapist involves clients in a "countergame" to restore a meaningful balance between ego and environment. In some cultures, mediators or brokers (Bolman, 1968; Weidman, 1986) are brought in to help counselors negotiate a balance. Benesch and Ponterotto (1989) suggest that Asian clients rely more on intuition than reason in achieving balance, assuming that ordinary consciousness is not the optimal state, higher states of "multiple consciousness" exist, people can attain higher states of consciousness through training, and verbal communication about these higher states of consciousness is necessarily limited.

Non-Western approaches to counseling are less likely than Westernized approaches to separate the person from the problem and cultural context. In non-Western cultures, the problem is usually defined by relationships between people and the environment or even the larger cosmos. Balance describes a dynamic order and design where all elements, pain as well as pleasure, serve a necessary function in a more holistic perspective than is typical for Western societies (Pedersen, 1993b).

The assumptions underlying Asian psychological interventions relate to collective or corporate philosophical assumptions about the self in a cultural context. Asian cultures usually put less emphasis on individualism and more on a corporate identity, a more positive interpretation of dependencies within the sociocultural context, and a stronger support role for the unit (family, clan, class, and state) that define each cultural context. The development of psychological interventions in India emphasizes inner harmony through Buddhism. Good and evil are synthesized through a dynamic balance in the cosmic context. Buddhism seeks to protect that balance by following the four noble truths and the eightfold path.

When Buddhism was adopted in China it was modified to emphasize the social responsibility of ethical teachings combined with Confucian "characterological theory" guided by face, filial piety, and proper conduct. The ultimate synthesis of Buddhism, Taoism, and Confucianism results in a balance of "sageliness within and kingliness without." Hsu (1985) describes this dynamic balance as a "psychosocial homeostasis," which defines the essence of personhood through psychic and interpersonal equilibrium with the cosmos. Psychological, somatic, and situational factors all contribute to the cultural context in a systems model.

The Japanese have adapted and expanded these models of balance and harmony in the uniquely Japanese notion of Zen. Zen Buddhists believe that persons are emancipated from the dualistic bondage of subjectivity and objectivity of mind and body by being awakened to their own true nature through the condition of Satori or enlightenment. In that state, the person is finely tuned to the reality both inside and outside. Reynolds (1980) describes this process as "phenomenological operationalism," where uneasy minds are refocused and regulated. Carefully prescribed role relationships create social stability. DeVoss (1973) credits "internalized sanctions" in Japanese culture for encouraging a sense of social responsibility for maintaining the balanced perspective. Each individual reconciles tension by living according to prescribed roles defined by the family and society. Mental health requires balancing individual ambition and role responsibility without either tendency taking control or being weakened by the other.

The third alternative of asymmetrical balance combines elements of a complicated constructivist perspective with orderly guidelines of a more authoritarian perspective. Just as counseling has historically depended on Westernized social models, counseling in the future might meaningfully depend on non-Westernized alternative social models where tolerance of complexity rather than the resolution of ambiguity is the more frequently defined end goal. Putting counseling in the larger cosmic context and substituting relational for absolute values in a collectivist rather than individualist perspective provides new rules for culture-centered counseling.

The third alternative of asymmetrical balance combines elements of both authoritarian-individualism and complex-diversity in a synthesis of each. If the alternative future defined by an asymmetrical balance is realized, some of the changes for counseling may include the following:

- Tolerance of ambiguity will become an important outcome goal of counseling.
- A balance of pain and pleasure leading to increased "meaning" in life will replace the search for pleasure through counseling.
- Non-Western models of counseling will become important resources and models to supplement traditional Western models.
- The function of counseling will be to restore a sense of balance and meaning to individuals.
- The individual will not be seen as separate from the collective cultural context of the environment.

- Intuition will become as important as abstract reasoning to the counseling process.
- Higher states of consciousness will become important goals in counseling.
- Problems will be viewed in a larger "cosmic" context of time and space rather than as isolated behaviors.
- Social responsibility will become important in each cultural context.
- Both similarities of shared values across cultural groups and differences in how each cultural group expresses those values will become important in counseling.
- There will be more emphasis on the historical context of relationships in the counseling process.
- Counselors will become more aware of their own cultural biases and work actively to reduce the dysfunctional effect of those biases on counseling.

EXERCISE

AGING IS A CULTURAL PROCESS OF UNPACKING ONE'S LIFE

Objective

The one culture we can all expect to enter, if we are fortunate, is that of "old age." This exercise, developed anonymously, is used by the staff of residential agencies to help them perceive the choices of residents and protect the quality of life that these residents deserve.

Instructions

Identify just the top 10 factors from the following list that you consider most essential to contributing to quality in YOUR life. Mark those items with an "x" or a check mark.

1. _____ Helping others/community involvement
2. _____ Exercise
3. _____ Self-respect
4. _____ Health
5. _____ Happiness/inner peace
6. _____ Mobility
7. _____ Pet(s)
8. _____ Independence
9. _____ Hobbies
10. _____ Sports
11. _____ Safety/security
12. _____ Music and the arts
13. _____ Faith/religion/spiritual development
14. _____ Love/opportunity to love
15. _____ Family/relationships with relatives
16. _____ Sex/intimate relationships
17. _____ Friends/relationships with friends
18. _____ Work/gainful activity
19. _____ Humor
20. _____ Travel
21. _____ Creativity/self-expression
22. _____ Finances/financial security

23. _____Freedom/choices
24. _____Wisdom/intellectual development
25. _____Shopping

When everyone has identified these 10 factors, read the following instructions:

"It is now 10 years later and you must give up three of those factors. Please indicate on your sheet those three factors you choose to give up."
(Allow time for participants to identify the three factors they will give up.)
   "It is now 20 years later and you must give up another three of those factors. Please indicate on your sheet those three factors you choose to give up."
      (Allow time for participants to identify the three factors they will give up.)
      "It is now 30 years later and you must give up another three of those factors. Please indicate on your sheet those three factors you choose to give up."
         (Allow time for participants to identify the three factors they will give up.)
         "Break into small groups to discuss the one remaining factor you have not yet given up and compare similarities and differences as well as consequences of your choices."

Debriefing

Discuss the experience of having to "give up" important parts of your life as an authentic experience of aging or any adaptation from one cultural context to a cultural context that offers less opportunity.

- What were the similarities and differences among persons in the 10 factors selected first and the single factor left at the end?
- How would you explain to yourself and others why you maintained the one enduring factor after having eliminated 9 of the 10 alternatives?
- Can you think of other factors not on this list that would be more important than the one you finally selected?
- What are the emotional consequences of having these factors taken away from you by outsiders?
- If you were to do the exercise again, would you make the same choices? In 10 years? In 20 years? In 30 years?

References

Abraham, F. D., Abraham, R. H., & Shaw, C. D. (1990). *A visual introduction to dynamical systems theory for psychology.* Santa Cruz, CA: Aerial Press.

Abramson, L. Y. (Ed.). (1988). *Social cognition and clinical psychology: A synthesis.* New York: Guilford.

Adler, P. S. (1975). The transitional experience: An alternative view of culture shock. *Journal of Humanistic Psychology, 15*(4), 23-40.

Adler, J., Starr, M., Chideya, F., Wright, L., Wingert, P., & Haac, L. (1990, December 24). Taking offense: Is this the new enlightenment on campus or the new McCarthyism? *Newsweek,* pp. 48-54.

Albee, G. W. (1994). The sins of the fathers: Sexism, racism and ethnocentrism in psychology. *International Psychologist, 35*(1), 22.

Alexander, A. A., Klein, M. H., Workneh, F., & Miller, M. H. (1981). Psychotherapy and the foreign student. In P. Pedersen, J. Draguns, W. Lonner, & J. Trimble (Eds.), *Counseling across cultures* (2nd ed., pp. 227-243). Honolulu: University of Hawaii Press.

Allen, F. C. L., & Cole, J. B. (1987). Foreign students syndrome: Fact or fable. *Journal of American College Health, 35,* 182-186.

Althen, G. (1983). *The handbook of foreign student advising.* Vershire, VT: Intercultural Press.

Althen, G., & Stott, F. W. (1983). Advising and counseling students who have unrealistic academic objectives. *Personal and Guidance Journal, 61,* 608-611.

Ambrowitz, D., & Dokecki, P. (1977). The politics of clinical judgment: Early empirical returns. *Psychological Bulletin, 84,* 460-476.

American Counseling Association. (1993). Code of ethics and standards of practice. *Guidepost,* October 15-22.

American Psychological Association. (1987). *Casebook on ethical principles of psychologists.* Washington, DC: Author.

American Psychological Association. (1992). Ethical principles of psychologists and code of conduct. *American Psychologist, 47*(12), 1597-1611.

American Psychological Association. (1993). Guidelines for providers of psychological services to ethnic linguistic and culturally diverse populations. *American Psychologist,* 48(1), 45-48.

Amir, Y. (1969). Contact hypothesis in ethnic relations. *Psychological Bulletin, 71,* 319-342.

Amir, Y. (1992). Social assimilation or cultural mosaic. In J. Lynch, C. Modgil, & S. Modgil (Eds.), *Cultural diversity and the schools: Volume 1.* Washington, DC: Falmer.

Anastasi, A. (1988). *Psychological testing* (6th ed.). New York: Macmillan.

Arce, C. A. (1981). A reconsideration of Chicano culture and identity. *Daedalus, 110,* 77-192.

Atkinson, D. R., Morten, G., & Sue, D. W. (1993). *Counseling American minorities: A cross-cultural perspective* (4th ed.). Dubuque, IA: William C. Brown & Benchmark.

Atkinson, D. R., Staso, D., & Hosford, R. (1978). Selecting counselor trainees with multicultural strengths: A solution to the Bakke decision crisis. *Personal & Guidance Journal. 5b,* 546-549.

Axelson, J. A. (1993). *Counseling and development in a multicultural society.* Pacific Grove, CA: Brooks/Cole.

Bailey, F. M. (1981). *Cross-cultural counselor education: The impact of microcounseling paradigms and traditional classroom methods on counselor trainee effectiveness.* Unpublished doctoral dissertation, University of Hawaii, Honolulu.

Bamford, K. W. (1991). Bilingual issues in mental health assessment and treatment. *Hispanic Journal of Behavioral Sciences, 13,* 377-390.

Banks, J. A. (1991). *Teaching strategies for ethnic studies.* Needham Heights, MA: Allyn & Bacon.

Barna, L. M. (1983). The stress factor in intercultural relations. In D. Landis & R. W. Brislin (Eds.), *Handbook of intercultural training: Volume 2. Issues in training methodology* (pp. 19-49). New York: Pergamon.

Barton, S. (1994). Chaos, self-organization and psychology. *American Psychologist, 49*(1), 5-14.

Bateson, G. (1979). *Mind and nature: A necessary unity.* New York: Dutton.

Beardsley, L., & Pedersen, P. (1997). Health and culture-centered intervention. In J. W. Berry, M. H. Segall, & C. Kagitcbasi (Eds.), *Social behavioral applications.* Boston: Allyn & Bacon.

Bellah, R. N. (1965). *Religion and progress in modern Asia.* New York: Free Press.

Bemak, F., Cheung, R. C., & Bornemann, T. H. (1996). Counseling and psychology with refugees. In P. Pedersen, J. Draguns, W. Lonner, & J. Trimble (Eds.), *Counseling across cultures* (4th ed., pp. 243-265). Thousand Oaks, CA: Sage.

Benedict, R. (1946). *The chrysanthemum and the sword.* Boston: Houghton Mifflin.

Benesch, K. F., & Ponterotto, J. G. (1989). East and West: Transpersonal psychology and cross-cultural counseling. *Counseling and Values, 33*(2), 121-131.

Bergin, A. (1991). Values and religious issues in psychotherapy and mental health. *American Psychologist, 46*(4), 394-403.

Berry, J. W. (1980). Ecological analysis for cross-cultural psychology. In N. Warren (Ed.), *Studies in cross-cultural psychology* (pp. 000-000). New York: Academic Press.

Berry, J. W., Poortinga, Y. H., Segall, M. H., & Dasen, P. J. (1992). *Cross-cultural psychology: Research and applications.* Cambridge, England: Cambridge University Press.

Bitter, J. R., & Corey, G. (1996). Family systems therapy. In G. Corey (Ed.), *Theory and practice of counseling and psychotherapy* (pp. 365-441). Pacific Grove, CA: Brooks/Cole.

Blowers, G. H., & Turtle, A. M. (1987). *Psychology moving East: The status of Western psychology in Asia and Oceania.* Boulder, CO: Westview.

Bochner, S. (1972). Problems in culture learning. In S. Bochner & P. Wicks (Eds.), *Overseas students in Australia.* Auburn: New South Wales University Press.

Bochner, S., & Meredith, G. (1968). *Role and attitude modification in multinational living.* Paper presented at the Conference Workshop on Psychological Problems in Changing Societies, East-West Center, University of Hawaii.

Bolman, W. (1968). Cross-cultural psychotherapy. *American Journal of Psychiatry, 124,* 1237-1244.

Bond, M. (1994). Into the heart of collectivism: A personal and scientific journey. In U. Kim, H. Triandis, C. Kagitcibasi, S. Choi, & G. Yoon (Eds.), *Individualism and collectivism* (pp. 66-76). Thousand Oaks, CA: Sage.

Bond, M. H. (1986). *The psychology of the Chinese people.* New York: Oxford University Press.

Brammer, L. M. (1988). *The helping relationship: Process and skills* (4th ed.). Englewood Cliffs, NJ: Prentice Hall.

Brewer, M. B. (1991). The social self: On being the same and different at the same time. *Personality and Social Psychology Bulletin, 17,* 475-482.

Brislin, R., Landis, D., & Brandt, M. E. (1983). Conceptualization of intercultural behavior and training. In D. Landis & R. Brislin (Eds.), *Handbook of intercultural training: Volume 1. Issues in theory and design* (pp. 1-35). New York: Pergamon.

Brislin, R. W. (1993). *Understanding culture's influence on behavior.* Orlando, FL: Harcourt Brace Jovanovich.

Bruner, J. S. (1986). *Actual minds, possible worlds.* Cambridge, MA: Harvard University Press.

Bulthuis, J. D. (1986). The foreign student today: A profile. In K. R. Pyle (Ed.), *Guiding the development of foreign students* (pp. 19-28). San Francisco: Jossey-Bass.

Butz, M. R. (1992a). Chaos: An omen of transcendence in the psychotherapeutic process. *Psychological Reports, 71,* 827-843.

Butz, M. R. (1992b). The factual nature of the development of the self. *Psychological Reports, 71,* 1043-1063.

Butz, M. R. (1993). Systemic family therapy and symbolic chaos. *Humanity and Society, 17*(2), 200-223.

Cadieux, R. A. J., & Wehrly, B. (1986). Advising and counseling the international student. In K. R. Pyle (Ed.), *Guiding the development of foreign students* (pp. 51-64). San Francisco: Jossey-Bass.

Caplan, G. (1976). The family as support system. In G. Caplan & M. Killilea (Eds.), *Support systems and mutual help: Multidisciplinary explorations* (pp. 50-64). New York: Grune & Stratton.

Carter, R. (1991). Cultural values: A review of empirical research and implications for counseling. *Journal of Counseling and Development, 70*(1), 164-173.

Casas, J. J. (1984). Policy training and research in counseling psychology: The racial/ethnic minority perspective. In S. Brown & R. Lent (Eds.), *Handbook of counseling psychology* (pp. 785-831). New York: John Wiley.

Casas, J. M., & Thompson, C. E. (1991). Ethical principles and standards: The racial ethnic minority perspective. *Counseling and Values, 35,* 186-195.

Chambers, J. C. (1992). *Triad training: A method for teaching basic counseling skills to chemical dependency counselors.* Unpublished doctoral dissertation, University of South Dakota, Department of Educational Psychology and Counseling.

Chaubey, N. (1972). Indian family structure and risk-taking behavior. *Indian Journal of Psychology, 47,* 213-221.

Cheatham, H. E., & Stewart, J. B. (1990). *Black families: Interdisciplinary perspectives.* New Brunswick, NJ: Transaction.

Chiu, L. H. (1972). A cross-cultural comparison of cognitive styles in Chinese and American children. *International Journal of Psychology, 109,* 235-242.

Chodorow, N. (1978). *The reproduction of mothering: Psychoanalysis and the sociology of gender.* Berkeley: University of California Press.

Christopher, J. C. (1992). *The role of individualism in psychological well-being: Exploring the interplay of ideology, culture and social science.* Unpublished doctoral dissertation, University of Texas at Austin.

Church, A. T. (1982). Sojourner adjustment. *Psychological Bulletin, 91,* 540-572.

Claiborn, C. D., & Lichtenberg, J. W. (1989). Interactional counseling. *The Counseling Psychologist, 17,* 355-453.

Cobb, S. (1976). Social support as a moderator of life stress. *Psychosomatic Medicine, 38,* 300-314.

Coffman, T. L. (1978). *Application for a postdoctoral research training fellowship.* Submitted to the Duke University Center for the Study of Aging and Adult Development.

Coffman, T. L., & Harris, M. C. (1984, August). *The U-curve of adjustment to adult life transitions.* Paper presented at the annual meeting of the American Psychological Association, Toronto, Canada.

Cohen, M. (1990, July 29). Schools grappling with new diversity. *Boston Sunday Globe,* p. 75.

Corey, G., Corey, M. S., & Callahan, P. (1993). *Issues and ethics in the helping professions* (4th ed.). Pacific Grove, CA: Brooks/Cole.

Corsini, R. (1981). *Innovative psychotherapies.* New York: Wiley Interscience.

Crano, S. L., & Crano, W. D. (1990). *Development of a measure of international student adjustment.* Unpublished manuscript, Department of Psychology, Texas A&M University, College Station.

Cross, W. (1971). The negro-to-Black conversion experience. *Black Worlds, 20,* 13-17.

Cross, W. (1991). *Shades of black.* Philadelphia: Temple University Press.

Cross, W. E. (1995). The psychology of Nigrescence: Revisiting the Cross model. In J. Ponterotto, J. M. Casas, L. A. Suzuki, & C. M. Alexander (Eds.), *Handbook of multicultural counseling* (pp. 93-122). Thousand Oaks, CA: Sage.

Dadfar, S., & Friedlander, M. L. (1982). Differential attitudes of international students toward seeking professional psychological help. *Journal of Counseling Psychology, 29,* 335-338.

Dana, R. H. (1993). *Multicultural assessment perspectives for professional psychology.* Boston: Allyn & Bacon.

Dana, R. H. (1994). Testing and assessment ethics for all persons: Beginning an agenda. *Professional Psychology: Research and Practice, 25*(4), 349-354.

Davenport, D. S., & Yurich, J. M. (1991). Multicultural gender issues. *Journal of Counseling and Development, 70*(1), 64-71.

Day, R. C., & Haij, F. M. (1986). Developing counseling services to international students: The experience of the American University in Beirut. *Journal of College Student Personnel, 27,* 353-357.

De Anda, D. (1994). Bicultural socialization: Factors affecting the minority experience. *Social Work, 29,* 101-107.

Delworth, U. (1989). Identity in the college years: Issues of gender and ethnicity. *Journal of the National Association of Student Personnel Administrators, 26,* 162-166.

DeVos, G. (1973). *Socialization for achievement: Essays on the cultural psychology of the Japanese.* Berkeley: University of California Press.

Dillard, J. M., & Chisolm, G. B. (1983). Counseling the international student in a multicultural context. *Journal of College Student Personnel, 24*(2), 101-105.

Doi, L. (1969). Japanese psychology, dependency need and mental health. In W. Caudill & T. Lin (Eds.), *Mental health research in Asia and the Pacific*. Honolulu: East-West Center Press.

Draguns, J. G. (1981). Cross-cultural counseling and psychotherapy: History, issues, current status. In A. J. Marsella & P. Pedersen (Eds.), *Cross-cultural counseling and therapy*. Elmsford, NY: Pergamon.

Draguns, J. G. (1989). Dilemmas and choices in cross-cultural counseling: The universal versus the culturally distinctive. In P. Pedersen, J. Draguns, W. Lonner, & J. Trimble (Eds.), *Counseling across cultures*. Honolulu: University of Hawaii Press.

D'Souza, D. (1991). *Illiberal education: The politics of race and sex on campus*. New York: Free Press.

Du Bois, W. E. B. (1990). The Negro American family. In H. Cheatham & J. Stewart (Eds.), *Black families* (pp. 44-60). New Brunswick, NJ: Transaction. (Original work published 1908)

Ebbin, A. J., & Blankinship, E. S. (1986). A longitudinal health care study: International versus domestic students. *Journal of American College Health, 34*, 177-182.

Eenwyk, J. R. (1991). Archtypes: The strange attractors of the psyche. *Journal of Analytical Psychology, 36*, 1-25.

Elkaim, M. (1981). Non-equilibrium, chance and change in family therapy. *Journal of Marital and Family Therapy, 7*, 291-297.

Encyclopedia Britannica (15th ed.). (1990). Chicago: Author.

Erickson, F., & Schultz, J. (1982). *The counselor as gatekeeper: Social interaction in interviews*. New York: Academic Press.

Escobar, J. E. (1993). Psychiatric epidemiology. In A. C. Gaw (Ed.), *Culture, ethnicity and mental illness* (pp. 43-73). Washington, DC: American Psychiatric Press.

Exum, H. A., & Lau, E. Y. (1988). Counseling style preference of Chinese college students. *Journal of Multicultural Counseling and Development, 16*, 84-94.

Fernandez, M. S. (1988). Issues in counseling Southeast Asian students. *Journal of Multicultural Counseling and Development, 16*, 157-166.

Flaherty, J. H., Gaviria, F. M., & Pathak, D. (1988). Developing instruments for cross-cultural psychiatric research. *Journal of Nervous and Mental Disease, 176*, 257-263.

Foley, V. (1987). Family therapy. In R. Goisen (Ed.), *Encyclopedia of psychology*. New York: John Wiley.

Fukuyama, M. A. (1990). Taking a universal approach to multicultural counseling. *Counselor Education and Supervision, 30*, 6-17.

Furnham, A., & Bochner, S. (1986). *Culture shock: Psychological reactions to unfamiliar environments*. London: Methuen.

Furnham, A., & Trezise, L. (1983). The mental health of foreign students. *Social Science and Medicine, 17*(6), 365-370.

Garrett, M. T., & Meyers, J. E. (1996). The rule of opposites: A paradigm for counseling Native Americans. *Journal of Multicultural Counseling and Development, 24*(2), 89-104.

Geleick, J. (1987). *Chaos making a new science*. New York: Viking-Penguin.

Gielen, U. P. (1994). American mainstream psychology and its relationship to international and cross-cultural psychology. In A. L. Comunian & U. P. Gielen (Eds.), *Advancing psychology and its applications: International perspectives* (pp. 26-40). Milan, Italy: Franco Angeli.

Gielen, U. P., & Markoulis, D. C. (1994). Preference for principled moral reasoning: A developmental and cross-cultural perspective. In L. L. Adler & U. P. Gielen (Eds.), Cross-cultural topics in psychology. Westport, CT: Greenwood.

Gilligan, C. (1982). In a different voice. Cambridge, MA: Harvard University Press.

Gilligan, C. (1987). Moral orientation and moral development. In E. F. Kittay & D. T. Meyers (Eds.), Women and moral theory (pp. 19-33). Totowa, NJ: Rowman & Littlefield.

Glover, S. H. (1992). The influence of individual values on ethnical decision making. Dissertation Abstracts International, 53(3A), 877.

Goldenberg, H., & Goldenberg, I. (1995). Family therapy. In R. J. Corsini & D. Wedding (Eds.), Current psychotherapies (pp. 356-385). Itasca, IL: F. E. Peacock.

Goldstein, A. (1981). Psychological skill training: The structural learning technique. New York: Basic Books.

Goldstein, A. (1994). Teaching prosocial behavior to low-income youth. In P. Pedersen & J. Carey (Eds.), Multicultural counseling in schools (pp. 157-176). Boston: Allyn & Bacon.

Goldstein, A., & Michaels, G. (1985). Empathy: Development, training and consequences. Hillsdale, NJ: Lawrence Erlbaum.

Goodyear, R. K., & Sinnett, E. R. (1984). Empathy: Development, training and consequences. Hillsdale, NJ: Lawrence Erlbaum.

Govinda, L. A. (1961). The psychological attitude of early Buddhist philosophy. London: Rider.

Griffith, R. S. (1992). New APA ethics code: Long on legalism, short on spirit. National Psychologist, 1(6), 1-5.

Gudykunst, W. B., & Hammer, M. R. (1983). Basic training design: Approaches to intercultural training. In D. Landis & R. Brislin (Eds.), Handbook of intercultural training (pp. 118-154). New York: Pergamon.

Gudykunst, W. B., & Ting-Toomey, S. (1988). Culture and interpersonal communication. Newbury Park, CA: Sage.

Guidano, V. F. (1991). The self in process. New York: Guilford.

Gushue, G. V., & Sciarra, D. T. (1995). Culture and families: A multidimensional approach. In J. G. Ponterotto, J. M. Casas, L. A. Suzuki, & C. M. Alexander (Eds.), Handbook of multicultural counseling (pp. 586-606). Thousand Oaks, CA: Sage.

Guthrie, G. M. (1966). Cultural preparation for the Philippines. In R. B. Textor (Ed.), Cultural frontiers of the Peace Corps (pp. 16-34). Cambridge: MIT Press.

Guthrie, G. M. (1975). A behavioral analysis of culture learning. In R. Brislin, S. Bochner, & W. Lonner (Eds.), Cross-cultural perspectives on learning (pp. 95-115). New York: John Wiley.

Guthrie, G. M., & Zektick, I. N. (1967). Predicting performance in the Peace Corps. Journal of Social Psychology, 71, 11-21.

Hackney, H., & Cormier, L. (1988). Counseling strategies and interventions (3rd ed.). Englewood Cliffs, NJ: Prentice Hall.

Hall, E. T. (1976). Beyond culture. Garden City, NY: Anchor.

Hall, E. T. (1983). The dance of life: The other dimension of time. New York: Anchor.

Hall, E. T. (1991). Context and meaning. In L. Samovar & R. Porter (Eds.), Intercultural communications (pp. 45-55). Belmont, CA: Wadsworth.

Hall, E. T. (1994). Context and meaning. In L. A. Samovar & K. E. Porter (Eds.), Intercultural communications: A reader (pp. 60-70). Belmont, CA: Wadsworth.

Hardiman, R. (1982). *White identity development: A process-oriented model for describing the racial consciousness of White Americans.* Unpublished doctoral dissertation, University of Massachusetts, Amherst.

Heider, F. (1958). *The psychology of interpersonal relations.* New York: John Wiley.

Heilbronner, R. L. (1975). *An inquiry into the human prospect.* New York: Norton.

Helms, J. E. (1985). Cultural identity in the treatment process. In P. Pedersen (Ed.), *Handbook of cross-cultural counseling and therapy* (pp. 239-245). Westport, CT: Greenwood.

Helms, J. E. (1990). *Black and white racial identity: Theory, research and practice.* Westport, CT: Greenwood.

Helms, J. E. (1994). How multiculturalism obscures racial factors in the therapy process. *Journal of Counseling Psychology, 41*(2), 162-165.

Herlihy, B., & Corey, G. (1996). *ACA ethical standards casebook* (5th ed.). Alexandria, VA: American Counseling Association.

Hermans, H. J. M., Kemper, H. J. G., & Van Loon, R. J. P. (1992). The dialogical self: Beyond individualism and rationalism. *American Psychologist, 47*(1), 23-33.

Hernandez, A. G., & Kerr, B. A. (1985, August). *Evaluating the Triad Model and transitional cross-cultural counselor training.* Paper presented at the annual meeting of the American Psychological Association, Los Angeles.

Hernstein, R. J. (1994). *The bell curve: Intelligence and class structure in American life.* New York: Free Press.

Hilliard, A. (1986, March). *Keynote address.* Presented at the 1st National Symposium on Multicultural Counseling, Atlanta, GA.

Hines, A. B., & Pedersen, P. (1980). The cultural grid: Matching social system variables and cultural perspectives. *Asian Pacific Training Development Journal, 1*, 5-11.

Hiroke, S. (1982). *An outline of moralogy: A new approach to moral science* (pp. 2-11). Hikarigaoka, Japan: Institute of Moralogy.

Ho, M. K. (1987). *Family therapy with ethnic minorities.* Newbury Park, CA: Sage.

Hofstede, G. (1991). *Cultures and organizations: Software of the mind.* London: McGraw-Hill.

Hosford, R., & Mills, M. (1983). Video in social skills training. In P. Dowrick & S. Biggs (Eds.), *Using video: Psychological and social applications* (pp. 125-166). New York: John Wiley.

Hoshmand, L. T., & Polkinghorne, D. E. (1992). Education and training in psychology: Redefining the science-practice relationship and professional training. *American Psychologist, 47*(1), 55-66.

Howard, G. S. (1991). Culture tales: A narrative approach to thinking, cross-cultural psychology and psychotherapy. *American Psychologist, 46*, 187-197.

Hsu, F. L. K. (1971). Psychosocial homeostasis and *Jen*: Conceptual tools for advancing psychological anthropology. *American Anthropologist, 73*, 23-44.

Hsu, F. L. K. (1985). The self in cross-cultural perspective. In A. J. Marsella & F. L. K. Hsu (Eds.), *Culture and self: Asian and Western perspectives* (pp. 25-55). New York: Tavistock.

Hsu, L. R., Hailey, B. J., & Range, L. M. (1987). Cultural and emotional components of loneliness and depression. *Journal of Psychology, 12*, 61-70.

Ibrahim, F. A. (1991). Contributions of cultural worldview to generic counseling and development. *Journal of Counseling and Development, 70*(1), 6-12.

Ibrahim, F. A., & Arrendondo. (1990). Ethnical issues in multicultural counseling. In B. Herlihy & L. B. Golden (Eds.), *AACD ethnical standards casebook* (4th ed., pp. 37-145). Alexandria, VA: American Counseling Associations.

Ibrahim, F. A., & Kahn, H. (1985, August). *Assessment of world views*. Paper presented at the annual meeting of the American Psychological Association, Los Angeles.

Irvin, R., & Pedersen, P. (1993). *The internal dialogue of culturally different clients: An application of the Triad Training Model*. Unpublished manuscript.

Irvine, S. H., & Berry, J. W. (1993). *Human assessment and cultural factors*. New York: Plenum.

Ivey, A. E. (1987). The multicultural practice of therapy: Ethics, empathy and dialectics. *Journal of Social and Clinical Psychology, 5,* 195-204.

Ivey, A. E. (1988). *Intentional interviewing and counseling: Facilitating client development*. Pacific Grove, CA: Brooks/Cole.

Ivey, A. E. (1990). Training as treatment and directions for the future. *The Counseling Psychologist, 18*(3), 428-443.

Ivey, A. E., (1993). *Intentional interviewing and counseling* (3rd ed.). Monterey, CA: Brooks/Cole.

Ivey, A. E., Ivey, M., & Simek, D. (1987). *Counseling and psychotherapy*. Englewood Cliffs, NJ: Prentice Hall.

Ivey, A. E., Ivey, M. B., & Simek-Morgan, L. (1993). *Counseling and psychotherapy: A multicultural perspective*. Boston: Allyn & Bacon.

Jackson, B. (1975). Black identity development. In L. Golubschick & B. Persky (Eds.), *Urban social and educational issues* (pp. 158-164). Dubuque, IA: Kendall-Hall.

Jandt, F. E., & Pedersen, P. B. (Eds.). (1996). *Constructive conflict management: Asia-Pacific cases*. Thousand Oaks, CA: Sage.

Janis, I. (1982). *Counseling on personal decisions: Theory and research on short-term helping relationships*. New Haven, CT: Yale University Press.

Jensen, A. R. (1969). How much can we boost IQ and scholastic achievement? *Harvard Educational Review, 39,* 1-123.

Jensen, A. R. (1992). Understanding in terms of information processing. *Educational Psychology Review, 4*(3), 271-308.

Jordan, A. E., & Meara, N. M. (1990). Ethics and the professional practice of psychologists: The rule of virtues and principles. *Professional Psychology: Research and Practice, 21,* 107-114.

Kagan, N., Krathwohl, D., & Farquhar, W. (1965). *Interpersonal process recall*. East Lansing: Michigan State University Press.

Kagitcibasi, C. (1988). Diversity of socialization and social change. In P. Dasen, J. Berry, & N. Sartorius (Eds.), *Health and cross-cultural psychology: Towards applications* (pp. 25-47). Newbury Park, CA: Sage.

Kagitcibasi, C. (1990). Family and home-based intervention. In R. W. Brislin (Ed.), *Applied cross-cultural psychology* (pp. 121-141). Newbury Park, CA: Sage.

Kagitcibasi, C. (1996). *Family and human development across cultures*. Mahwah, NJ: Lawrence Erlbaum.

Kakar, S. (1971). The theme of authority in social relations in India. *Journal of Social Psychology, 84,* 93-101.

Katz, J. H. (1978). *White awareness: Handbook for anti-racism training*. Norman: University of Oklahoma Press.

Katz, R. (1993). *The straight path: A story of healing and transformation in Fiji*. Reading, MA: Addison-Wesley.

Kealey, D. J. (1988). *Explaining and predicting cross-cultural adjustment and effectiveness: A study of Canadian technical advisors overseas*. Unpublished doctoral dissertation, Queens University, Kingston, Ontario, Canada.

Keith-Spiegel, P., & Koocher, G. P. (1985). *Ethics in psychology: Professional standards and cases*. Hillsdale, NJ: Lawrence Erlbaum.

Kelly, E. W. (1995). *Spirituality and religion in counseling and psychotherapy: Diversity in theory and practice*. Alexandria, VA: American Association for Counseling and Development.

Kelly, G. (1955). *The psychology of personal constructs*. New York: Norton.

Kendler, H. H. (1993). Psychology and the ethics of social policy. *American Psychologist*, 48(10), 1046-1053.

Kierstead, F. D., & Wagner, P. A. (1993). *The ethical, legal and multicultural foundations of teaching*. Dubuque, IA: Brown & Benchmark.

Kim, B. C. (1981). *New urban immigrants: The Korean community in New York*. Princeton, NJ: Princeton University Press.

Kim, U., & Berry, J. W. (Eds.). (1993). *Indigenous psychologies: Research and experience in cultural context*. Newbury Park, CA: Sage.

Kim, Y. Y. (1994). Intercultural personhood: An integration of Eastern and Western perspectives. In L. A. Samovar & R. E. Porter (Eds.), *Intercultural communication: A reader* (pp. 415-424). Belmont, CA: Wadsworth.

Kinloch, G. (1979). *The sociology of minority group relations*. Englewood Cliffs, NJ: Prentice Hall.

Kleinman, A. (1988). *Rethinking psychiatry*. New York: Free Press.

Klineberg, O. (1982). Contact between ethnic groups: A historical perspective of some aspects of theory and research. In S. Bochner (Ed.), *Cultures in contact: Studies in cross-cultural interaction* (pp. 320-335). Oxford: Pergamon.

Klineberg, O., & Hull, W. F. (1979). *At a foreign university: An international study of adaptation and coping*. New York: Praeger.

Kohlberg, L. (1984). *The psychology of moral development: The nature and validity of moral stages*. San Francisco: Harper & Row.

Koss-Chioino, J. D., & Vargas, L. A. (1992). Improving the prospects for ethnic minority children in therapy. In L. A. Vargas & J. D. Koss-Chioino (Eds.), *Working with culture: Psychotherapeutic interventions with ethnic minority children and adolescents* (pp. 300-309). San Francisco: Jossey-Bass.

Kraemer, H. (1958). *From mission field to independent church*. London: SCM Press, Ltd.

LaFromboise, T. D., Coleman, H. L. K., & Hernandez, A. (1991). Development and factor structure of the Cross-Culture Counseling Inventory—revisited. *Professional Psychology*, 22(5), 1-9.

LaFromboise, T. D., & Foster, S. L. (1989). Ethics in multicultural counseling. In P. Pedersen, J. Draguns, W. Lonner, & J. Trimble (Eds.), *Counseling across cultures* (3rd ed., pp. 115-136). Honolulu: University of Hawaii Press.

Lambert, M. J. (1981). Evaluating outcome variables in cross-cultural counseling and psychotherapy. In A. Marsella & P. Pedersen (Eds.), *Cross-cultural counseling and psychotherapy* (pp. 136-158). Elmsford, NY: Pergamon.

Langs, R. (1992). Towards building psychoanalytically based mathematical models of psychotherapeutic paradigms. In R. L. Levine & H. E. Fitzgerald (Eds.), *Analysis of dynamic psychological systems* (Vol. 2, pp. 371-393). New York: Plenum.

Larson, D. L. (1984). *Counseling approach preference of Latin American international undergraduate students and U.S. American undergraduate students*. Unpublished doctoral dissertation, University of Kansas, Lawrence.

Lee, C. C. (1991). Promise and pitfalls of multicultural counseling. In C. C. Lee & B. L. Richardson (Eds.), *Multicultural issues in counseling: New approaches to diversity* (pp. 1-13). Alexandria, VA: American Association for Counseling and Development.

Lee, C. C., & Armstrong, K. L. (1995). Indigenous models of mental health interventions: Lessons from traditional healers. In J. G. Ponterotto, J. M. Casas, L. A. Suzuki, & C.

M. Alexander (Eds.), *Handbook of multicultural counseling* (pp. 441-456). Thousand Oaks, CA: Sage.

Lee, C. C., & Richardson, B. L. (Eds.). (1991). *Multicultural issues in counseling: New approaches to diversity.* Alexandria, VA: American Association for Counseling and Development.

Leong, F. T. L. (1984). *Counseling international students* (Information analysis paper). Ann Arbor, MI: ERIC.

Leong, F. T. L., & Sedlacek, W. E. (1985). *A comparison of international and U.S. student preferences for help sources* (Research Rep. No. 1-85). College Park: University of Maryland, Counseling Center.

Leong, F. T. L., & Sedlacek, W. E. (1986). A comparison of international and U.S. student preferences for help sources. *Journal of College Student Personnel, 27,* 426-430.

LeVine, R., & Padilla, A. (1980). *Crossing cultures in therapy: Pluralistic counseling for the Hispanic.* Monterey, CA: Brooks/Cole.

Lin, T. Y., & Lin, M. C. (1978). Service delivery issues in Asian-North American communities. *American Journal of Psychiatry, 135*(4), 454-456.

Liu, Z. V. (1985). *A cross-cultural study of depression among foreign graduate students from six selected areas.* Unpublished doctoral dissertation, George Peabody College for Teachers, Vanderbilt University, Nashville, TN.

Locke, D. C. (1990). A not so provincial view of multicultural counseling. *Counselor Education and Supervision, 30*(1), 18-25.

Locke, D. C. (1992). *Increasing multicultural understanding: A comprehensive model.* Newbury Park, CA: Sage.

Lomak, P. P. (1984). *An investigation of foreign students' awareness, utilization and satisfaction with selected student personnel services and programs at Ohio University, Athens, 1983/1984.* Unpublished doctoral dissertation, Ohio University, Athens.

Lomov, B. F., Budilova, E. A., Koltsova, V. A., & Medvedev, A. M. (1993). Psychological thought within the system of Russian culture. In U. Kim & J. W. Berry (Eds.), *Indigenous psychologies: Research and experience in cultural context* (pp. 104-117). Newbury Park, CA: Sage.

Lonner, W. (1990). An overview of cross-cultural testing and assessment. In R. W. Brislin (Ed.), *Applied cross-cultural psychology* (pp. 56-76). Newbury Park, CA: Sage.

Lonner, W. J., & Ibrahim, F. A. (1989). Assessment in cross-cultural counseling. In P. Pedersen, J. Draguns, W. Lonner, & J. Trimble (Eds.), *Counseling across cultures* (3rd ed., pp. 229-334). Honolulu: University of Hawaii Press.

Lopez, S. R. (1989). Patient variable biases in clinical judgment: Conceptual overview and methodological considerations. *Psychological Bulletin, 106,* 3-29.

Lopez, S. R., & Lopez, A. A. (1993). Mexican Americans' initial preferences for counselors: Research methodologies or researchers' values? Reply to Atkinson and Wampold. *Journal of Counseling Psychology, 40*(2), 249-251.

Lorion, R. P. (1974). Patient and therapist variables in the treatment of low-income patients. *Psychological Bulletin, 81,* 344-354.

Lorion, R. P., & Parron, D. L. (1985). Counter in the countertransference: A strategy for treating the untreatable. In P. Pedersen (Ed.), *Handbook of cross-cultural counseling and therapy* (pp. 79-86). Westport, CT: Greenwood.

Lukes, S. (1973). *Individualism: Key concepts in the social sciences.* Oxford: Basil Blackwell.

Lumbantobing, P. (1956). *The structure of the Toba Batak belief in the High God.* Amsterdam: Jacob van Campen.

Marcia, J. E. (1980). Identity in adolescence. In J. Adelson (Ed.), *Handbook of adolescent psychology* (pp. 159-187). New York: John Wiley.

Maruyama, M. (1992). *Context and complexity: Cultivating contextual understanding.* New York: Springer-Verlag.

McFadden J., & Wilson, I. (1977). *Non-white academic training with counselor education, rehabilitation and student personnel program.* Unpublished manuscript.

McGuire. (1966). The current status of cognitive consistency theories. In S. Fieldman (Ed.), *Cognitive consistency* (pp. 57-94). New York: Academic Press.

McNamee, S., & Gergen, K. J. (1992). *Therapy as social construction.* Newbury Park, CA: Sage.

Melis, A. I. (1982). Arab students in Western universities: Social properties and dilemmas. *Journal of Higher Education, 53*(4), 439-447.

Mestenhauser, J. A. (1983). Learning from sojourners. In D. Landis & R. W. Brislin (Eds.), *Handbook of intercultural training* (Vol. 2, pp. 153-185). New York: Pergamon.

Midgette, T. E., & Meggert, S. S. (1991). Multicultural counseling instruction: A challenge for faculties in the 21st century. *Journal of Counseling and Development, 70*(1), 38-46.

Miles, R. (1989). *Racism.* New York: Routledge.

Miller, D. F., & Harwell, D. J. (1983). International students at an American university: Health problems and status. *Journal of School Health, 53,* 45-49.

Miller, J. G. (1994). Cultural diversity in the morality of caring: Individually oriented versus duty-based interpersonal moral codes. *Cross-Cultural Research, 28*(1), 3-39.

Miller, N., & Brewer, M. (1984). *Groups in contact: The psychology of desegregation.* New York: Academic Press.

Moghaddam, F. M., & Taylor, D. M. (1986).

Molnar, S. (1992). *Human variation* (3rd ed.). Englewood Cliffs, NJ: Prentice Hall.

Mossman, M. (1976). *Kulia i ka lokahi i ke ola* [Strive for harmony in life]. Unpublished manuscript, Pikake Wahilani, Honolulu.

Murgatroyd, W. (1995). *Application of the Triad Model in teaching counseling skills and multicultural sensitivity.* Unpublished monograph, Department of Counseling, University of New Orleans, New Orleans, LA.

Murphy, G., & Murphy, L. (1968). *Asian psychology.* New York: Basic Books.

Murray, T. H. (1993). Moral reasoning in social context. *Journal of Social Issues, 49*(2), 185-200.

Mwaba, K., & Pedersen, P. (1994). The relative importance of intercultural, interpersonal and pathological attributions in judging critical incidents of multicultural counselors. *Journal of Multicultural Counseling and Development, 18*(3), 106-117.

Nakakuki, M. (1973, September). *Japanese cultural and mental health: Psychodynamic investigation.* Paper presented at the 9th International Congress of Anthropological and Ethnological Sciences, Chicago.

Nakamura, H. (1964). *Ways of thinking of Eastern peoples: India, China, Tibet, Japan* (P. P. Weiner, Ed.). Honolulu: University of Hawaii Press.

Nakane, C. (1972). *Human relations in Japan.* Tokyo: Ministry of Foreign Affairs.

Narvaez, D. (1993). *Moral perception.* Paper for the preliminary oral examination, Department of Educational Psychology, University of Minnesota.

Neimeyer, G. J. (1993). *Constructivist assessment: A casebook.* Newbury Park, CA: Sage.

Neimeyer, G. J., & Fukuyama, M. (1984). Exploring the content and structure of cross-cultural attitudes. *Counselor Education and Supervision, 23*(3), 214-224.

Neimeyer, G. J., Fukuyama, M. A., Bingham, R. P., Hall, L. E., & Mussenden, M. E. (1986). Training cross-cultural counselors: A comparison of the pro- and anticounselor Triad Models. *Journal of Counseling and Development, 64,* 437-439.

Newcomb, T. M. (1953). An approach to the study of communicative acts. *Psychological Review, 60,* 393-404.

Nichols, K. R., & McAndrew, F. T. (1984). Stereotyping and autostereotyping in Spanish, Malaysian and American college students. *Journal of Social Psychology, 124,* 179-189.

Norbeck, E., & DeVos, G. (1961). Japan. In F. L. K. Hsu (Ed.), *Psychological anthropology* (pp. 19-47). Homewood, IL: Dorsey.

Nwachuku, U. T., & Ivey, A. E. (1991). Culture-specific counseling: An alternative training model. *Journal of Counseling and Development, 70*(1), 106-111.

Oberg, M. K. (1958). *Culture shock and the problem of adjustment to new cultural environments.* Washington, DC: U.S. Department of State.

Oetting, E. R., & Beauvais, F. (1991). Orthogonol cultural identification theory: The cultural identification of minority adolescents. *International Journal of the Addictions, 25,* 655-685.

Opotow, W. (1990). Moral exclusion and injustice: An introduction. *Journal of Social Issues, 46*(1), 1-20.

Othman, A. H., & Awang, A. (1993). *Counseling in the Asia-Pacific region.* Westport, CT: Greenwood.

Owan, T. C. (1985). *Southeast Asian mental health: Treatment, prevention, services, training and research.* Washington, DC: U.S. Department of Health and Human Services.

Panglinawan, L. (1972). *Ho'oponopono Project II.* Honolulu: Cultural Committee, Queen Liliuokaloni Children's Center.

Paniagua, F. A. (1994). *Assessing and treating culturally different clients: A practical guide.* Thousand Oaks, CA: Sage.

Parham, W., & Moreland, J. R. (1981). Non-white students in counseling psychology: A closer look. *Professional Psychology, 12,* 499-507.

Pate, R. H., & Bondi, A. M. (1992). Religious beliefs and practice: An integral aspect of multicultural awareness. *Counselor Education and Supervision, 32,* 108-115.

Patterson, C. H. (1978). Cross-cultural or intercultural psychotherapy. *Hacettepe University Bulletin of Social Sciences, 1,* 119-134.

Patterson, C. H. (1986). Culture and counseling in Hong Kong. *Chinese University Education Journal, 14*(2), 77-81.

Payton, C. R. (1994). Implications of the 1992 Ethics Code for diverse groups. *Professional Psychology: Research and Practice, 25*(4), 317-320.

Pearson, R. (1985). The recognition and use of natural support systems in cross-cultural counseling. In P. Pedersen (Ed.), *Handbook of cross-cultural counseling and therapy.* Westport, CT: Greenwood.

Pearson, R. E. (1990). *Counseling and social support: Perspectives and practice.* Newbury Park, CA: Sage.

Pedersen, A., & Pedersen, P. (1985). The cultural grid: A personal cultural orientation. In L. Samovar & R. Porter (Eds.), *Intercultural communication: A reader* (pp. 50-62). Belmont, CA: Wadsworth.

Pedersen, A., & Pedersen, P. (1989). The cultural grid: A complicated and dynamic approach to multicultural counseling. *Counseling Psychology Quarterly, 2,* 133-141.

Pedersen, P. (1968). *Religion as the basis of social change among the Bataks of North Sumatra.* Unpublished doctoral dissertation, Claremont Graduate School, Claremont, CA.

Pedersen, P. (1975). Personal problem-solving resources used by University of Minnesota foreign students. In R. Brislin (Ed.), *Topics in cultural learning* (Vol. 3, pp. 55-65). Honolulu: East-West Center Press.

Pedersen, P. (1980). Role learning as a coping strategy for uprooted foreign students. In G. V. Coelho & P. I. Ahmed (Eds.), *Uprooting and development* (pp. 295-320). New York: Plenum.

References

Pedersen, P. (1981). Triad counseling. In R. Corsini (Ed.), *Innovative psychotherapies* (pp. 840-854). New York: Wiley Interscience.

Pedersen, P. (1983a). Asian theories of personality. In R. Corsini & A. Marsella (Eds.), *Contemporary theories of personality* (rev. ed., pp. 537-582). Itasca, IL: Peacock.

Pedersen, P. (1983b). The effect of group differences among church-related youth in Indonesia, Malaysia and Singapore. *Counseling and Values, 27*(3), 130-141.

Pedersen, P. (1984). Cross-cultural training of mental health professionals. In R. Brislin & D. Landis (Eds.), *Handbook of cross-cultural training: Volume 2. Methodology* (pp. 325-352). Elmsford, NY: Pergamon.

Pedersen, P. (1985). A procedure for testing an American test in an Indonesian context. *International School Psychology, 6*(3), 151-158.

Pedersen, P. (1986a). Attitudes of church-related youth in Indonesia, Malaysia and Singapore. In A. A. Sitompul & A. Sovik (Eds.), *Horas HKBP* (pp. 173-185). Pematangsiantar, North Sumatra: Sekolah Tinggi Telogia HKBP.

Pedersen, P. (1986b). Developing interculturally skilled counselors: A prototype for training. In H. Lefley & P. Pedersen (Eds.), *Cross-cultural training for mental health professionals* (pp. 73-88). Springfield, IL: Charles C Thomas.

Pedersen, P. (1988). *A handbook for developing multicultural awareness*. Alexandria, VA: American Counseling Association.

Pedersen, P. (1990). Complexity and balance as criteria of effective multicultural counseling. *Journal of Counseling and Development, 5,* 550-554.

Pedersen, P. (1991a). Multiculturalism as a fourth force in counseling. *Journal of Counseling and Development, 70*(1), 5-25.

Pedersen, P. (1991b). Counseling international students. *The Counseling Psychologist, 19*(1), 10-58.

Pedersen, P. (1993a). Primal alternatives to talk therapy: The Batak "Tondi" of North Sumatra. *Counseling and Values, 37*(2), 52-60.

Pedersen, P. (1993b). Mediating multicultural conflict by separating behaviors from expectations in a Cultural Grid. *International Journal of Intercultural Relations, 17,* 343-353.

Pedersen, P. (Ed.). (1994). *Handbook for developing multicultural awareness* (2nd ed.). Alexandria, VA: American Association for Counseling and Development.

Pedersen, P. (1995a). Culture-centered ethical guidelines for counselors. In J. Ponterotto & M. Casas (Eds.), *Handbook of multicultural counseling and therapy* (pp. 34-49). Thousand Oaks, CA: Sage.

Pedersen, P. (1995b). *Five stages of culture shock: Critical incidents around the world*. Westport, CT: Greenwood/Praeger.

Pedersen, P., Fukuyama, M. A., & Heath, A. (1989). Client, counselor and contextual variables in multicultural counseling. In P. Pedersen, J. Draguns, W. Lonner, & J. Trimble (Eds.), *Counseling across cultures* (3rd ed., pp. 23-53). Honolulu: University of Hawaii Press.

Pedersen, P., Holwill, C. F., & Shapiro, J. L. (1978). A cross-cultural training procedure for classes in counselor education. *Journal of Counselor Education and Supervision, 17,* 233-237.

Pedersen, P., & Ivey, A. E. (1993). *Culture-centered counseling and interviewing skills*. Westport, CT: Greenwood/Praeger.

Pedersen, P., & Marsella, A. C. (1982). The ethical crisis for cross-cultural counseling and therapy. *Professional Psychology, 13,* 492-500.

Phinney, J. S. (1989). Stages of ethnic identity in older adolescents from four ethnic groups. *Journal of Adolescence, 13,* 1971-1983.

Phinney, J. S. (1990). Ethnic identity in adolescents and adults. *Psychological Bulletin, 108,* 499-514.

Pike, R. (1966). *Language in relation to a united theory of the structure of human behavior.* The Hague: Mouton.

Pinderhughes, E. (1984). Teaching empathy: Ethnicity, race and power at the cross-cultural treatment intervention. *American Journal of Social Psychiatry, 4*(1), 5-12.

Ponterotto, J. G. (1988). Racial/ethnic minority research: A content analysis and methodo-logical critique. *Journal of Counseling Psychology, 3,* 410-418.

Ponterotto, J. G., & Casas, J. M. (Eds.). (1991). *Handbook of racial/ethnic minority counseling research.* Springfield, IL: Charles C Thomas.

Ponterotto, J. G., Casas, J. M., Suzuki, L. A., & Alexander, C. M. (Eds.). (1995). *Handbook of multicultural counseling.* Thousand Oaks, CA: Sage.

Ponterotto, J. G., & Pedersen, P. (1993). *Preventing prejudice: A guide for counselors and educators.* Newbury Park, CA: Sage.

Ponterotto, J. G., Reiger, B. P., Barrett, A., & Sparks, R. (1994). Assessing multicultural counseling competence: A review of instrumentation. *Journal of Counseling and Development, 72*(3), 316-322.

Poortinga, Y. H. (1990). Towards a conceptualization of culture for psychology. *Cross-Cultural Psychology Bulletin, 24*(3), 2-10.

Prince, R. (1984). Shamans and endorphins: Exogenous and endogenous factors in psycho-therapy. In P. Pedersen, N. Sartorius, & A. J. Marsella (Eds.), *Mental health services: The cross-cultural context* (pp. 59-78). Beverly Hills, CA: Sage.

Pukui, M. K., Hartig, E. W., & Lee, C. A. (1972). *Nana i ke kumu.* Honolulu: Hui Hana.

Putnam, F. (1988). The switch process in multiple personality disorder and other state-change disorders. *Dissociation, 1,* 24-32.

Putnam, F. (1989). *Diagnosis and treatment of multiple personality disorder.* New York: Guilford.

Ramirez, M. (1991). *Psychotherapy and counseling with minorities: A cognitive approach to individual and cultural differences.* New York: Pergamon.

Ravitch, D. (1990, October 24). Multiculturalism yes, particularism no. *Chronicle of Higher Education,* p. A44.

Rest, J. R. (1995). Background: Theory and research. In J. R. Rest & D. F. Narvaez (Eds.), *Moral development in the professions: Psychology and applied ethics.* Hillsdale, NJ: Lawrence Erlbaum.

Revitch, R., & Geertsma, R. (1969). Observations media and psychotherapy training. *Journal of Nervous and Mental Disorders, 148,* 310-327.

Reynolds, D. K. (1980). *The quiet therapies: Japanese pathways to personal growth.* Honolulu: University of Hawaii Press.

Ridley, C. (1989). Racism in counseling as an aversive behavorial process. In P. Pedersen, J. Draguns, W. Lonner, & J. Trimble (Eds.), *Counseling across cultures* (3rd ed., pp. 55-79). Honolulu: University of Hawaii Press.

Ridley, C. (1995). *Overcoming unintentional racism in counseling and therapy.* Thousand Oaks, CA: Sage.

Ridley, C. R., Mendoza, D. W., & Kanitz, B. E. (1994). Multicultural training: Reexami-nation, operationalization and integration. *The Counseling Psychologist, 22*(2), 227-289.

Ridley, C. R., Mendoza, D. W., Kanitz, B. E., Angermeier, L., & Zenk, R. (1994). Cultural sensitivity in multicultural counseling: A perceptual schema model. *Journal of Coun-seling Psychology, 41*(2), 125-136.

References

Roland, A. (1988). *In search of self in India and Japan: Toward a cross-cultural psychology.* Princeton, NJ: Princeton University Press.

Ruben, B. D., & Kealey, D. J. (1979). *Behavioral assessment of communication competency and the prediction of cross-cultural adaptation.* Ottawa, Canada: International.

Rubin, J. Z., Kim, S. H., & Peretz, N. M. (1990). Expectancy effects and negotiation. *Journal of Social Issues, 46*(2), 125-139.

Rushton, J. P. (1988). Race differences in behavior: A review and evolutionary analysis. *Journal of Personality and Individual Differences, 22,* 1009-1040.

Sabelli, H. C., Carlson-Sabelli, L., & Javaid, J. I. (1990). The thermodynamics of bipolarity: A bifurcation model of bipolar illness and bipolar character and its psychotherapeutic publications. *Psychiatry, 53,* 346-368.

Sampson, E. (1977). Psychology and the American ideal. *Journal of Personality and Social Psychology, 11,* 767-782.

Sampson, E. E. (1988). The debate on individualism: Indigenous psychologies of the individual and their role in personal and societal functioning. *American Psychologist, 43*(1), 15-22.

Sampson, E. E. (1993). Identity politics: Challenges to psychology's understanding. *American Psychologist, 48*(12), 1219-1230.

Sarbin, T. R. (1986). The narrative as a root metaphor for psychology. In T. R. Sarbin (Ed.), *Narrative psychology: The storied nature of human conduct* (pp. 3-21). New York: Praeger.

Sartorius, N., Pedersen, P., & Marsella, A. (1984). Mental health services across cultures: Some concluding thoughts. In P. Pedersen, N. Sartorius, & A. Marsella (Eds.), *Mental health services: The cross-cultural context* (pp. 13-27). Beverly Hills, CA: Sage.

Satir, V. (1969). *Conjoint family therapy.* Palo Alto, CA: Science & Behavior Books.

Schmid, G. B. (1991). Chaos theory and schizophrenia: Elementary aspects. *Psychopathology, 24,* 185-198.

Segall, M. H., Dasen, P. R., Berry, J. W., & Poortinga, Y. H. (1990). *Human behavior in global perspective: An introduction to cross-cultural psychology.* New York: Pergamon.

Selye, H. (1974). *Stress without distress.* New York: Lippincott.

Serpell, R. (1994). The cultural construction of intelligence. In W. J. Lonner & R. Malpass (Eds.), *Psychology and culture* (pp. 157-164). Boston: Allyn & Bacon.

Sheikh, A., & Sheikh, K. S. (Eds.). (1989). *Eastern and Western approaches to healing: Ancient wisdom and modern knowledge.* New York: John Wiley.

Shook, E. V. (1985). *Ho'oponopono.* Honolulu: University of Hawaii Press.

Shweder, R. A. (1990). Cultural psychology—What is it? In J. W. Stigler, R. A. Shweder, & G. Herdt (Eds.), *Cultural psychology: Essays on comparative human development* (pp. 73-112). New York: Cambridge University Press.

Shweder, R. A., Mahapatra, M., & Miller, J. A. (1990). Culture and moral development. In J. Stigler, R. A. Shweder, & G. Herdt (Eds.), *Cultural psychology: Essays in comparative human development* (pp. 130-204). New York: Cambridge University Press.

Simon, G. (1914). *The progress and arrest of Islam in Sumatra.* London: Marshall Brothers.

Slack, C. W., & Slack, E. N. (1976, February). It takes three to break a habit. *Psychology Today,* pp. 46-50.

Sleek, S. (1996). Ensuring accuracy in clinical decisions. *APA Monitor, 26*(4), 30.

Sloan, T. S. (1990). Psychology for the Third World? *Journal of Social Issues, 46*(3), 1-20.

Smith, H. (1991). *The world's religions.* San Francisco: Harper.

Smith, P. S. Z., & Smith, H. (1989, June). *Asian students in North American universities: Implications for faculty and staff.* Paper presented at the World Congress of Comparative Education, Montreal, Canada.

Snarey, J. R. (1985). Cross-cultural universality of social-moral development: A critical review of Kohlbergian research. *Psychological Bulletin, 97,* 202-232.

Solomon, G., & McDonald, F. J. (1970). Pretest and posttest reactions to self-viewing one's teaching performance on videotape. *Journal of Educational Psychology, 61,* 280-286.

Solomon, R. (1971). *Mao's revolution and the Chinese political culture.* Berkeley: University of California Press.

Spaulding, S., & Flack, M. (1976). *The world's students in the United States: A review and evaluation of research on foreign students.* New York: Praeger.

Spengler, P. M., & Strohmer, D. C. (1994). Clinical judgmental biases: The moderating roles of counselor complexity and counselor client preferences. *Journal of Counseling Psychology, 41,* 1-10.

Spengler, P. M., Strohmer, D. C., Dixon, D. N., & Shivy, V. A. (1995). A scientist-practitioner model of psychological assessment: Implications for training practice and research. *The Counseling Psychologist, 23*(3), 506-537.

Steenbarger, B. N. (1991). All the world is not a stage: Emerging contextualist themes in counseling and development. *Journal of Counseling and Development, 70*(2), 288-296.

Stewart, G. M., & Hartt, J. (1987). Multiculturalism: A community among differences. *Bulletin of the Association of College Unions-International, 55,* 4-8.

Still, R. (1961). *Mental health in overseas students.* Proceedings of the British Health Association.

Stoltenberg, C., & Delworth, U. (1987). *Supervising counselors and therapists: A developmental approach.* San Francisco: Jossey-Bass.

Stonequist, F. V. (1937). *The marginal man: A study in personality and cultural conflict.* New York: Russell & Russell.

Storey, K. E. (1982). The student development professional and the foreign student: A conflict of values. *Journal of College Student Personnel, 23*(1), 66-70.

Strike K., & Soltis, J. (1985). *The ethics of teaching.* New York: Teachers College Press.

Strong, S. (1978). Social psychological foundations of psychotherapy and behavior change. In S. Garfield & A. Bergin (Eds.), *Handbook of psychotherapy and behavior change: An empirical analysis* (pp. 101-136). New York: John Wiley.

Strous, M., Skuy, M., & Hickson, J. (1993). Perceptions of the Triad Model's efficacy in training family counselors for diverse South African groups. *International Journal for the Advancement of Counseling, 16,* 307-318.

Sue, D. W. (1978). Eliminating cultural oppression in counseling: Toward a general theory. *Journal of Counseling Psychology, 25,* 419-428.

Sue, D. W. (1980). *Evaluation report from DISC 1978-1979.* Honolulu: East-West Center Press.

Sue, D. W. (1990). Culture specific strategies in counseling: A conceptual framework. *Professional Psychology, 21*(6), 424-433.

Sue, D. W., Arredondo, P., & McDavis, R. J. (1992). Multicultural counseling competencies and standards: A call to the profession. *Journal of Counseling and Development, 70,* 477-486.

Sue, D. W., Bernier, J. E., Durran, A., Feinberg, L., Pedersen, P., Smith, C. J., & Vasquez Nuttall, G. (1982). Cross-cultural counseling competencies. *The Counseling Psychologist, 19*(2), 45-52.

References

Sue, D. W., Ivey, A. E., & Pedersen, P. B. (1996). *Multicultural counseling theory.* Pacific Grove, CA: Brooks/Cole.

Sue, D. W., & Sue, D. (1990). *Counseling the culturally different: Theory and practice.* New York: Wiley Interscience.

Sundahl-Hansen, L. (1985). Sex-role issues in counseling men and women. In P. Pedersen (Ed.), *Handbook of cross-cultural counseling and therapy* (pp. 213-222). Westport, CT: Greenwood.

Sundberg, N., Rohila, P., & Tyler, L. (1970). Values of Indian and American adolescents. *Journal of Personality and Social Psychology, 16,* 374-397.

Surya, N. C. (1969). Ego structure in the Hindu joint family: Some considerations. In W. Caudill & T. Y. Lin (Eds.), *Mental health research in Asia and the Pacific.* Honolulu: East-West Center Press.

Szapocznik, J., & Kurtines, W. M. (1993). Family psychology and cultural diversity: Opportunities for theory, research and application. *American Psychologist, 48,* 400-407.

Taft. R. (1976). *The personality of the mediating person.* Paper presented for the East-West Center project "The Mediating Person," Honolulu.

Taft, R. (1977a). Coping with unfamiliar cultures. In N. Warren (Ed.), *Studies in cross-cultural psychology* (pp. 120-135). London: Academic Press.

Taft, R. (1977b). Comments on the 1974 Tapp Report on the ethics of cross-cultural research. *IACCP Cross-Cultural Psychology Newsletter, 11*(4), 2-8.

Tanaka-Matsumi, J., & Higginbotham, H. (1989). Behavioral approaches to counseling across cultures. In P. Pedersen, J. Draguns, W. Lonner, & J. Trimble (Eds.), *Counseling across cultures* (3rd ed., pp. 269-299). Honolulu: University of Hawaii Press.

Tapp, J. L. (1986, August). *Cross-cultural ethics revisited: Foster children in our parents' house or the alien in the U.S.!* Paper presented at the annual meeting of the American Psychological Association.

Tapp, J. L., Kelman, H., Triandis, H., Wrightsman, L., & Coelho, G. (1974). Continuing concerns in cross-cultural ethics: A report. *International Journal of Psychology, 9,* 231-349.

Tart, C. (1975). *Transpersonal psychologies.* New York: Harper & Row.

Taylor, C. (1989). *Sources of the self: The making of the modern identity.* Cambridge, MA: Harvard University Press.

Thomas, C. (1971). *Boys no more.* Beverly Hills, CA: Glencoe Press.

Thomas, K. A. (1985). *A comparison of counseling strategies reflective of cultural value orientations on perceptions of counselors in cross-national dyads.* Unpublished doctoral dissertation, University of Minnesota, Minneapolis.

Thomas, K. A., & Althen, G. (1989). Counseling foreign students. In P. Pedersen, J. Draguns, W. Lonner, & J. Trimble (Eds.), *Counseling across cultures* (3rd ed., pp. 205-241). Honolulu: University of Hawaii Press.

Thompson, M., Ellis, R., & Wildavsky, A. (1990). *Cultural theory.* San Francisco: Westview.

Tompkins, L. D., & Mehring, T. (1989). Competency testing and the international student: A common sense approach to detecting cultural bias in testing instruments. *Journal of Multicultural Counseling and Development, 17,* 72-78.

Torrey, E. F. (1986). *Witchdoctors and psychiatrists: The common roots of psychotherapy and its future.* New York: Harper & Row.

Triandis, H. C. (1972). *The analysis of subjective culture.* New York: John Wiley.

Triandis, H. C. (1977). *Interpersonal behavior.* Monterey, CA: Brooks/Cole.

Triandis, H. C. (1993). Collectivism and individualism as cultural syndromes. *Cross-Cultural Research, 27*(3-4), 155-180.

Triandis, H. C., Bontempo, R., Leung, K., & Hui, C. H. (1990). A method for determining cultural, demographic, and personal constructs. *Journal of Cross-Cultural Psychology, 21,* 302-318.

Triandis, H. C., Brislin, R., & Hui, C. H. (1988). Cross-cultural training across the individualism-collectivism divide. *International Journal of Intercultural Relations, 12,* 302-318.

Trimble, J. (1981). Value differentials and their importance in counseling American Indians. In P. Pedersen, J. Draguns, W. Lonner, & J. Trimble (Eds.), *Counseling across cultures* (2nd ed., pp. 203-226). Honolulu: University of Hawaii Press.

Tseng, W. S., & Hsu, J. (1972). The Chinese attitude toward parental authority as expressed in Chinese children's stories. *Archives of General Psychiatry, 26,* 28-34.

Tseng, W. S., & Hsu, J. (1980). Minor psychological disturbances of everyday life. In H. Triandis & J. Draguns (Eds.), *Handbook of cross-cultural psychology: Volume 6. Psychopathology* (pp. 61-98). Boston: Allyn & Bacon.

Tseng, W. S., & Wu, D. Y. H. (1985). *Chinese culture and mental health.* Orlando, FL: Academic Press.

Turtle, A. M. (1987). A silk road for psychology. In G. H. Blowers & A. M. Turtle (Eds.), *Psychology moving East: The status of Western psychology in Asia and Oceania* (pp. 1-23). London: Westview.

United Nations Educational Scientific and Cultural Organization. (1979). *Declaration on race and racial prejudice.* Paris: Author.

Valla, J. P., & Prince, R. H. (1989). Religious experiences as self-healing mechanisms. In C. Ward (Ed.), *Altered states of consciousness and mental health* (pp. 149-166). Newbury Park, CA: Sage.

Vargas, L. A., & Koss-Chioino, J. D. (Eds.). (1992). *Working with culture: Psychotherapeutic interventions with ethnic minority children and adolescents.* San Francisco: Jossey-Bass.

Vergouwen, J. D. (1964). *The social organization and customary law of the Toba Batak of Northern Sumatra.* The Hague: Martinus Nijhoff.

Vogel, E. F. (1969). A preliminary view of family and mental health in urban Communist China. In W. Caudill & T. Y. Lin (Eds.), *Mental health research in Asia and the Pacific.* Honolulu: East-West Center Press.

Wade, P., & Bernstein, B. L. (1991). Culture sensitivity training and counselor's race: Effects on Black female client's perceptions and attrition. *Journal of Counseling Psychology, 38*(1), 9-15.

Waldrop, M. M. (1992). *Complexity: The emerging science at the edge of order and chaos.* New York: Touchstone.

Walsh, R. (1989). Toward a synthesis of Eastern and Western psychologies. In A. A. Sheikh & K. S. Sheikh (Eds.), *Eastern and Western approaches to healing: Ancient wisdom and modern knowledge* (pp. 542-555). New York: John Wiley.

Walz, G. R., & Johnson, J. A. (1963). Counselors look at themselves on videotape. *Journal of Counseling Psychology, 10,* 232-236.

Ward, C. (1967). Some observations on the underlying dynamics of conflict in a foreign student. *Journal of the American College Health Association, 10,* 430-440.

Ward, C. (1989). *Altered stages of consciousness and mental health.* Newbury Park, CA: Sage.

Warheit, G. J., Holzer, C. E., & Areye, S. A. (1975). Race and mental illness: An epidemiological update. *Journal of Health and Social Behavior, 16,* 243-256.

Warneck, J. (1909). *The living Christ and dying heathenism.* London: Fleming H. Revell Co.

References

Watts, A. W. (1961). *Psychotherapy East and West*. New York: Mentor Press.

Wehrly, B. (1986). Counseling international students: Issues, concerns, and programs. *International Journal for the Advancement of Counseling, 9*(1), 11-12.

Wehrly, B. (1988). Cultural diversity from an international perspective: Part 2. *Journal of Multicultural Counseling and Development, 16*(1), 3-15.

Wehrly, B. (1995). *Pathways to multicultural counseling competence*. Pacific Grove, CA: Brooks/Cole.

Weidman, H. (1975). Concepts as strategies for change. *Psychiatric Annals, 5*, 312-313.

Weidman, H. H. (1986). Attaining the transcultural perspective in health care: Implications for clinical training. In H. P. Lefley & P. B. Pedersen (Eds.), *Cross-cultural training for mental health professionals* (pp. 311-330). Springfield, IL: Charles C Thomas.

Weiss, A. S. (1995). Can religion be used as a science in psychotherapy? *American Psychologist, 50*(7), 543-544.

Whiteley, J. M., & Jakubowski, P. A. (1969). The coached clients as a research and training resource in counseling. *Counselor Education and Supervision, 2*, 19-29.

Williams, C. L. (1987). *An annotated bibliography on refugee mental health*. Rockville, MD: U.S. Department of Health and Human Services.

Williams, C. L., & Berry, J. W. (1991). Primary prevention of acculturative stress among refugees. *American Psychologist, 46*(6), 632-641.

Wilson, K. M. (1986). *The relationship of GRE General Test scores to first-year grades for foreign students: Report of a cooperative study* (GRE Board Research Rep. No. 82, pp. 86-94). Princeton, NJ: ETS Research Reports.

Wittkower, E. D., & Warnes, H. (1974). Cultural aspects of psychotherapy. *American Journal of Psychotherapy, 28*, 566-673.

Wong-Rieger, D. (1984). Testing a model of emotional and coping responses to problems in adaptation: Foreign students at a Canadian university. *International Journal of Intercultural Relations, 8*(2), 153-184.

Worchel, S., & Goethals, G. R. (1989). *Adjustment: Pathways to personal growth* (2nd ed.). Englewood Cliffs, NJ: Prentice Hall.

Worthington, E. L. (1989). Religious faith across the life span. *The Counseling Psychologist, 17*(4), 555-612.

Wrenn, G. (1962). The culturally encapsulated counselor. *Harvard Educational Review, 32*, 444-449.

Wrenn, G. (1985). Afterword: The culturally encapsulated counselor revisited. In P. Pedersen (Ed.), *Handbook of cross-cultural counseling and therapy* (pp. 323-329). Westport, CT: Greenwood.

Wrightsman, L. S. (1992). *Assumptions about human nature: Implications for researchers and practitioners*. Newbury Park, CA: Sage.

Wurtzburg, C. E. (1954). *Raffles of the Eastern Isles*. London: Hodder & Stoughton.

Yee, A. H., Fairchild, H. H., Weizmann, F., & Wyatt, G. E. (1993). Addressing psychology's problems with race. *American Psychologist, 48*(11), 1132-1140.

Yum, J. O. (1994). The impact of Confucianism on interpersonal relationships and communication patterns in East Asia. In L. A. Samovar & R. E. Porter (Eds.), *Intercultural communication: A reader* (pp. 75-86). Belmont, CA: Wadsworth.

Zuk, G. (1971). *Family therapy: A triadic-based approach*. New York: Behavioral Publications.

Zwingman, C. A. D., & Gunn, A. D. G. (1983). *Uprooting and health: Psycho-social problems of students from abroad*. Geneva, Switzerland: World Health Organization.

Index

Abraham, F. D., 60
Abraham, R. H., 60
Abramson, L. Y., 13, 177, 284
Adler, J., 11
Adler, P. S., 54
Ageism, 8
Albee, G. W., 250
Alexander, A. A., 129
Alexander, C. M., 249
Allen, F. C. L., 124
Allport, G. W., 104
Althen, G., 123, 124, 136, 138
Ambrowitz, D., 257
American Association of Physical
    Anthropologists, 49
American Counseling Association, 203,
    243, 245
American Psychological Association, 203,
    228, 229, 240, 241, 242, 245, 250,
    265, 267
    approved counselor training programs,
    207
    Committee on International Relations in
    Psychology, 231
Amir, Y., 50, 51
Anastasi, A., 253
Angermeier, L., 202, 252

Anti-semitism, 250
Appropriate psychologies, 75
Arce, C. A., 261
Areye, S. A., 257
Armstrong, K. L., 102, 103
Arredondo, P., 203, 207, 213, 243
Asian-American identity development
    model, Kim's, 261
Asian counseling assertions:
    construct of personality in, 78-94
    corporate identity and, 288
    dependencies on sociocultural context
    and, 288
    strong support role for family and,
    288
    versus Western counseling assertions,
    78, 94-95
Asian cultural context:
    versus Euro-American cultural context,
    71, 76-77, 94-95
Atkinson, D. R., 160, 219, 261, 263
Atman, 79-80
Authoritarian individualism:
    as centralized alternative, 280-283
    predictable consequences of, 283
Awang, A., 264
Axelson, J. A., 156, 268

About the Author

Paul B. Pedersen is Professor in the Department of Human Studies at the University of Alabama-Birmingham. He has been a university faculty member at the University of Minnesota, the University of Hawaii, and Syracuse University and for six years in Indonesia, Malaysia, and Taiwan. He is a Fellow in Divisions 9, 17, and 45 of the American Psychological Association and an active member of AMCD and ACES in the American Counseling Association. He has published 26 books, 44 chapters, and 76 articles on various aspects of multicultural counseling and communication.